A Guide
to Canadian
Children's
Books

A Guide to Canadian Children's Books

in English

DEIRDRE BAKER AND KEN SETTERINGTON

Illustrations by Kady MacDonald Denton

National Library of Canada Cataloguing in Publication

Baker, Deirdre F. (Deirdre Frances), 1955–
A guide to Canadian children's books in English /
Deirdre Baker and Ken Setterington.

Includes bibliographical references.
ISBN 0-7710-1064-8

1. Children–Books and reading–Canada. 2. Children's literature,
Canadian (English)–Bibliography. 3. Best books. I. Setterington, Ken II. Title.

Z1378.B35 2003   015.71'062   C2002-905762-0

Published simultaneously in the United States of America by
McClelland & Stewart Ltd., P.O. Box 1030, Plattsburgh, New York 12901

Library of Congress Control Number: 2002116592

We acknowledge the financial support of the Government of Canada through the Book Publishing Industry Development Program and that of the Government of Ontario through the Ontario Media Development Corporation's Ontario Book Initiative. We further acknowledge the support of the Canada Council for the Arts and the Ontario Arts Council for our publishing program.

Typeset in Times by M&S, Toronto
Printed and bound in Canada

McClelland & Stewart Ltd.
The Canadian Publishers
481 University Avenue
Toronto, Ontario
M5G 2E9
www.mcclelland.com

1   2   3   4   5   07   06   05   04   03

For Donna and in memory of Bob Baker, who started me off.
                                              – D.F.B.

In memory of Jack and for Mildred Setterington, who showed me the way to the library, and for Martin Fichman, who has patiently listened to me talk about children's books for years.
                                              – K.S.

Contents

Acknowledgements

Many thanks from both of us to the staff at the Canadian Children's Book Centre, for the benefit of their expertise and the use of their extensive library.

From Deirdre: Thank you, too, to the staff at the Hornby Island branch of the Vancouver Island Public Library, and to the publicists who were so helpful (particularly those who never had to be contacted twice) in getting books to me – and to Heather and Peter Berrang, who lent me their trailer for a workspace. And deepest thanks to Bob, Ariel, Robin, and Mum, who gave me time and much more.

From Ken: Thanks to Lyn Cook, the first Canadian author I ever met, Eva Martin, who impressed upon me the need to support Canadian children's books, and the helpful staff at my local library, the Pape-Danforth branch of the Toronto Public Library. Thanks to Emily, Julian, and Maddy, who read and discussed many of these books with me.

Introduction

WHY DID WE WRITE THIS BOOK?

Three abiding passions inspired us to write this guide.

The first is our passion and love for language, rooted in a firm belief that in words lies the preservation of the world. "The world stands on the breath of school children," one sage comments, speaking of children reciting text. Particularly in our current climate, when the globe seems so small and every action so consequential, this statement rings frighteningly true. What children learn determines the future. It is all the more important, then, that they learn, through the imaginative experience of reading, how to see the world and its joys and woes in diverse ways. In stories lie understanding, information, and wisdom; in language lies the possibility of new perception, alternate vision, and life-saving, critical analysis.

The second is our passion for sharing Canadian children's books. While there are various annotated bibliographies, Web sites, and guides to children's books in general, most of them don't include works by Canadian authors and illustrators, nor those set in Canadian places or about Canadian events. But in the last twenty-five years or so, Canadian publishers – and foreign publishers, with Canadian authors and illustrators – have produced a rich and commanding array of accomplished works by Canadians. Now Canadian children can read works set in places familiar to them; now they have access to stories written from uniquely Canadian perspectives, in uniquely Canadian voices – voices which, among other things, reflect Canada's historic "mosaic" approach to multiculturalism, its concern for the common good, or its preservation of its British literary roots. Most importantly, many of these stories by Canadians – of Indian, African, British, Cree, Salish, or some other origin – are powerful, moving, life-changing, or absolutely hilarious. We want to share them with children in Canada, and we want to introduce them to readers in other parts of the English-speaking world.

Finally, the third passion that brought us to write this guide is the passion to bring together children and the stories that might really touch, inspire, and excite them. Anyone who has worked in the field of children's books knows how often a parent, a teacher, or a children's librarian wants to find the perfect book for a child – one that will meet the needs of that child at that time, accommodating her or his interests, capacities, and aversions. Often there's no one around who has the breadth or depth of knowledge to make an informed suggestion, and the child goes unsatisfied, perhaps even uncomforted. This book aims to help adults find the right books for children at the right time, in a guide that's informative and easy to use.

HOW DID WE CHOOSE THE BOOKS?

We have used a number of criteria in choosing the books for this guide. First of all, we asked ourselves how we would define a "Canadian" children's book. We interpreted Canadian to mean by a Canadian writer or illustrator, living in Canada or elsewhere, or by a non-Canadian writer living in Canada. Many of the books in this guide are published by Canadian publishers; a few are published by British or American publishers. Many of the stories deal with distinctly Canadian regions, historical events, or culture. Some of them could be about any child in urban or suburban North America; some are set in Europe, India, China, and elsewhere – and some are set out of this world altogether. But every one of them is influenced by a Canadian perspective, a view that has been shaped by, or responds to, Canadian culture in one of its many guises.

We do not include here Canadian stories that exist only in French, although we do bring forward a number that were originally written in French, and are now available in English translation.

We have included only works that are now, or were recently, available. It can be extremely frustrating to learn about a story that seems the perfect fit for a certain child, only to discover that it has to be ordered through a lengthy interlibrary-loan process or else is unavailable. You should be able to buy or borrow all of these books from bookstores and libraries in the foreseeable future.

High literary quality has been the determining feature in our first round of selection. What do we mean by high literary quality? Usually, we experience stories through four elements – style, character, plot, and setting. For style, we have looked for vigorous, innovative writing, words used in such a way that they make our scalps prickle, our hearts jump with new perception or satisfying recognition. Here we find distinctive voices – from writers such as Martha Brooks, Brian Doyle, and Julie Johnston – taking us, through the magic of their words, to understandings that we might not be able to arrive at on our own.

All of us, especially children, participate in story through its characters. In this area we have looked for depth, for complexity, for characters that show a fully rounded and often unpredictable (because they're truly human!) approach to the world. Noticing the characters' distinctive qualities and troubles, children can begin to recognize and articulate their own feelings and perceptions. Or they can identify these qualities in others and sympathize with them. Like style, complex characters can take us beyond our own experience, beyond our current limits. Characters such as Kit Pearson's Norah, Teddy Jam's Charlotte, or Diana Wieler's Ran Van are at once recognizable and mind-expanding.

A plot that surprises, at least in some way, is also part of what we've looked for. Some things about a plot should be predictable; children love to be correct in their suggestions about what happens next or how the story will end. But particularly with novels for older readers, a degree of unpredictability and cleverness is stimulating. A plot may turn on external events or inner growth; often it's not so much where the story goes as how it gets there that reveals a writer's originality of vision. A sudden revelation in Monica Hughes's *The Keeper of the Isis Light* makes us understand the story in a whole new way. The inversion of fairy-tale elements makes kids shout with laughter at Robert Munsch's *The Paper Bag Princess*. Gruesome characters and stormy seas together keep us turning the pages in Iain Lawrence's *High Seas* novels.

Sometimes the setting (time or place) of a story seems unimportant. At other times, the setting is so vivid, it's like a character itself. "It's the taste and touch and feel of a place that make it part of you," one character remarks in a novel by Katherine Holubitsky. We've looked for the precise, sensual, and accurate evocation of atmosphere, region, and time. Writers such as Tim Wynne-Jones, Tomson Highway, and Mary Sheppard make us feel we can smell the air of Northern Ontario, northern Manitoba, or outport Newfoundland. Reading Kenneth Oppel's *Silverwing*, we feel we've seen the world from a bat's-eye view – aerially, and in black-and-white.

In excellent picture books, illustrations don't just support the text, they extend it, deepening and expanding the meaning of the words on the page, pointing out some of language's many-layered qualities. "Chair. Telephone. Door. Cheese. Bath. Bed," reads Pierre Pratt's *Home*, mundane words that become a story of loneliness, companionship, and great fun when combined with Pratt's quirky illustrations. In Marie-Louise Gay's *On My Island*, a boy's droning complaints about boredom are deliciously ironic in the light of the dramatic, fantastical events we see happening all around him.

Character, mood, and logic can all be conveyed through illustration, an essential part of a child's experience of the book. In Barbara Reid's *The Golden Goose*, a string of characters latch onto a hapless hero. And although each has only a bit part in the story, the character's dress (a tweed suit, a frilly apron) and features show that he or she is a fully developed person: the final celebration in the story is fraught with emotional undercurrents – about which the text says nothing. The immense solitude and vast, subtle beauty of the uninhabited north shine through in Brian Deines's paintings for Tomson Highway's *Caribou Song* and *Dragonfly Kites*, giving children a chance to experience some of the exhilaration of the boys in the story. In Heather Collins's drawings for Barbara Greenwood's *A Pioneer Story*, children can see clearly how the tools and technologies of the 1840s functioned.

Most importantly, though, the best picture-book artists expand and stimulate a child's aesthetic experience. Picture books may be the only exposure that many children ever have to fine visual arts, so it's all the more important that they see the works of accomplished artists with distinctive, developed visions. Texture, colour, composition, line, movement – not to mention the varieties of media such as collage, watercolour, oil, ink, and so on – all contribute to a child's visual perceptions of the world. Indeed, many a child finds not only uproarious fun, information, or drama in a book's illustration, but also the pleasure and solace of beauty.

We have also included many stories that have some, but not all, of the outstanding literary and artistic qualities outlined above. These are works that seem to be particularly useful and successful in exploring certain issues or in meeting the needs of certain kinds of readers – such as readers who might at first need to be wooed by fast-paced action and conventional plot and language. Or perhaps these are stories that are set in Canadian places or deal with distinctively Canadian experiences, or describe historical events that no one else has written about for children. Although these books might not have the same strength of invention and originality of language that we find in the works of the finest writers, they are certainly enriching and can often lead a child into reading stories of greater depth and intellectual nourishment.

HOW TO USE THIS BOOK

We've organized this guide by age and genre. The board books discussed in the first chapter are excellent for babies and toddlers; in the second two chapters, we deal with concept books – those that involve the alphabet, counting, or linguistic concepts such as opposites – and with picture books. Since picture books can appeal to an enormous age range – from babies to teenagers – we've pointed out those whose appeal will be limited to younger listeners, and those which might be enjoyed by older children, more able to comprehend complex ideas and longer texts. Chapters on traditional tales and poetry and rhyming stories follow those on picture books; although most of our suggestions in these categories are for a younger audience, some are directed towards the intermediate grades and adolescents. "Beginning readers," and first novels or "chapter books," covered in the next chapter, are designed to be accessible to emerging readers in the primary grades, although many can be enjoyed as picture books by younger children. In the next five chapters, novels, short story collections and anthologies, and series books are listed for the 7-to-12 group and the 12-and-ups. We've cross-listed works that span the 10-to-14 age group in order to help those who might overlook stories relegated to a section "too young" for them. The final chapter is a limited list of non-fiction books (a category which deserves a guide book in its own right), focusing on works in which the vivacious writing or intriguing subject matter might entice readers who find fiction unappealing.

A note about ages: we can only suggest the approximate age of child for whom any given book might strike a chord. You know your child and your students, and once you look at the book you will be better able to assess if it's comfortably within an individual child's reading ability, too much of a challenge, or won't meet her or his intellectual and emotional demands. Once your child is reading novels with pleasure, your choice will be less directed by reading level and more focused on subject matter, style, or genre. Your child may read a book in the 12-and-up category easily, but it might deal with matters that he or she isn't yet ready to handle.

Books are listed within each chapter alphabetically by author or editor, last name first. The name of the illustrator follows (if there is one); if author and illustrator are one and the same, there is no entry for illustrator. Title, date of original copyright, number of pages, and age range follow in that order. The publishing industry is in a constant state of flux, so we do not include information on publishers, realizing that this information quickly becomes outdated. Please note that number of pages does not indicate the sophistication of a novel – a very short novel may be an energizing challenge in language or content – but it will help those who are looking for texts that might suit readers daunted by very thick volumes. Since most picture books are 24 or 32 pages, we haven't included number of pages within that category, unless the work deviates from this norm. Except in the chapter on "series" books, we've listed any entries from a publisher's series by the title of the first volume, followed by the series' name. Books that feature the same character in volume after volume, but do not have a series name, are treated as regular titles.

"Highly recommended" indicates what we consider to be the very best of Canadian writing and illustration for children, the *crème de la crème*. These may not be the books that have won the most popularity or prizes, but they are the works that we believe will enrich readers most deeply. Asterisks also mark these books.

Generally, we give an idea of plot, main characters, and setting for each story, so that you, as an adult looking for a book that will interest a particular child, may judge by subject matter whether the story will be of interest. We also try to convey a sense of the writer's style (the "flavour" of the book), point out general themes, and in many cases indicate the sort of audience to which the story might appeal. We've pointed out both strengths and weaknesses where we see them, so that you will have some sense of what to address when discussing these stories with children.

In the back of the book, we have provided a subject index that will help you find books on particular themes (bereavement, single parents, racism, siblings, various cultural and ethnic groups) and within particular genres (history, adventure, fantasy, mystery, etc.). Other indexes group authors by their region and, where appropriate, mention the regions in which stories take place.

❧

Here you'll find books exciting, gorgeous, and sad; stories that are startling, terrifying, or deeply heart-warming. Comic drawings, lavish colours, and sombre shadows are all available through these pages, and so too are cowards, magicians, sly tricksters, and brave girls and boys. They're all here to inspire and move a young audience, from the infant who likes to devour its literature – literally – to the "almost-adult" about to step into the world of adult responsibility.

Board Books

The books in this section belong in the hands of a baby or toddler. The sturdy construction of the board pages, the bright colours, and minimal – or non-existent – text will endure through hundreds of readings, re-readings, and chewing sessions. And while babies and toddlers love sharing "regular" picture books with adults, they can "read" these nearly indestructible books all by themselves. The sequence of images, the conversation prompted by pictures or text, the movement from one page to the next, are all elements that help introduce very young children to the experience of reading.

Bailey, Debbie. Photogr. Susan Huszar. *Talk-About-Books*. **2000–2002. Infant to 5.**
The name of this series and the sixteen titles in it (*Toys*, *Hats*, *Shoes*, *Clothes*, *My Mom*, *My Dad*, etc.) give parents an idea of what this collection is all about. These 14-page books have full-colour photo illustrations that show children, from babies to toddlers to five-year-olds, in everyday situations. A themed text, rather than a story, makes them good for child-adult discussion. Children of all races, ages, and cultural backgrounds will see themselves reflected in the photos, so the books are an excellent choice not only for families, but also for libraries and daycares with diverse clienteles. Bold, colourful borders and excellent durability make these inexpensive books popular with children and parents alike.

Collins, Heather. *This Little Piggy, Wee Willie Winkie,* **and others. 1997–2000. Infant to 2.**
A caring community of stuffed animal friends makes up the cast in Collins's interpretation of familiar nursery rhymes. With their repetition, rhythm, and rhyme, nursery rhymes are ideal for infants, and Collins turns some of these enigmatic verses into charming visual narratives. *Wee Willie Winkie* ends in a pillow fight; *This Little Piggy* is about a shopping venture to fill the fridge. Animals help each other out in Collins's idyllic fairy-tale countryside. Also available: *Eensy Weensy Spider; Hickory Dickory Dock; One, Two, Buckle My Shoe; Rock-A-Bye Baby; Row, Row, Row Your Boat;* and *Twinkle, Twinkle, Little Star.*

Pratt, Pierre. *Hippo Beach.* **Trans. from French. 1997. 2 to 4.**
The text of this book consists of two sentences: "Today is Sunday" and, as a conclusion, "And already, Jeff is dreaming about next Sunday." In between, Jeff the hippo yawns in his deep blue pond; his yawn becomes a shoe; his shoe becomes a car; the car drives away into the blue sky. Pratt shows the many possibilities of shape under the influence of imagination – the hippo's basking head provokes a series of visual associations and jokes. With the texture of deep oil pastels and heavy outlines, and the surreal nature of the changing images, this represents a fantastical, dream-like Sunday-afternoon reverie. Quirky and clever as a board book, this would also be a good aid in an art lesson.

* **Pratt, Pierre.** *The Very Busy Life of Olaf and Venus* **series.** *Home* **and others. Trans. from French. 2000. Infant to 3.**
"Chair. Telephone. Door. Cheese. Bath. Bed," may not seem like much of a story, but Pratt's incomparable Olaf and Venus (elephant and mouse respectively) show the narrative possibilities that exist in simple nouns – a lonely look, a phone call, a welcome friend, a feast, a lively bath, and a sleepover. Each of four titles – *Home, Park, Shops, Car* – tells a similar visual tale, and each ends in a good splash and a nap. Lanky, purply-blue Olaf and ruby-nosed Venus live an elegant, vigorous life; Pratt's stylish oil-pastel illustrations offer toddlers the chance to identify objects, but even better, invite them to make up the words of the story themselves. Witty, energetic, and fun. Highly recommended.

Pratt, Pierre. *I See . . . My Cat / I See . . . My Sister.* **Trans. from French. 2001. Infant to 3.**
This volume – "two books in one!" – shows a baby's-eye view of family pets and members. The text is simple: "My sister's knees. / My sister's hands. / My sister's belly button." The close-up view of a sister's scabby knees, stuck-out tongue, and bravely bulging biceps communicates not just the names of body parts, but personality. Pratt's heavy outlines and solid colours make the books visually bold and direct. The kooky family he presents and his offbeat approach to the subject are amusing and allow lots of scope for discussion. Also available *I See . . . My Mom / I See . . . My Dad.*

Reid, Barbara. *Zoe's Snowy Day* **and others. 2001. Infant to 3.**
Toddler Zoe, with a sturdy, clomping gait, goes out in all weathers to swing in the breeze, swish through the leaves, and taste the snowflakes. The genius of these books is in Reid's precise visual observation: all the paraphernalia of toddlerhood is here for children to recognize. Outdoors, nothing escapes notice: a prudish neighbour rakes leaves; an intent art student hurries through the park. Reid's attention to physical detail conveys worlds about her characters and offers much scope for adult-child discussion. The illustrations are scenes made of Plasticine. Titles include *Zoe's Windy Day*, *Zoe's Rainy Day*, and *Zoe's Sunny Day*.

Concept Books

Most Canadian alphabet and counting books are not designed to teach letters or numbers to small children; rather, they're celebrations of a particular region or theme, structured around ABCs or counting from, say, one to ten. Often, elaborate art accompanies these productions and, much of the time, the pictures present a puzzle to the reader even as they illustrate a short text: what else can you find in here that starts with the letter? In this way, the books reinforce a child's knowledge of the alphabet, invite her or him to look a little more closely, and also give a glimpse of particular aspects of Canadian culture and geography. Some of those listed below (such as Kevin Major's *Eh? to Zed*) will provide great fun for older readers too, even adults.

ALPHABET BOOKS

Bannatyne-Cugnet, Jo. Illustr. Yvette Moore. *A Prairie Alphabet*. 1992. 4 and up.
Moore's detailed illustrations are like a series of windows opening onto the sights and expanses of the Canadian prairie. Some are etched and dark; others glow with the hard luminosity of relentless sun. All show sights and activities typical of prairie life – grain elevators, a livestock auction, and so on. A simple sentence accompanies each picture (e.g., "The engine pulls empty cars up to the elevators"). Readers can identify more objects in the picture beginning with the letter (a list is included at the end), and a commentary on each picture can be found at the back of the book.

Grassby, Donna. Illustr. Susan Tooke. *A Seaside Alphabet*. 2000. 5 and up.
Tooke depicts a different place on the Atlantic coast in each of her paintings, while Grassby points out, in her text and in her commentary at the back of the book, how what's shown in each illustration relates to the letter of the alphabet. "Sailors salute Cape Spear's salient shores" is one example. The knowledge here is specialized, but the book does work to give children a view of the coast of the northern United States as well as of the Canadian Atlantic provinces. Tooke's thick, heavy colours may not appeal to some children.

Harrison, Ted. *A Northern Alphabet*. 1982. 3 to 7.
Harrison's stylized, almost primitive, drawings in vivid, solid colours have come to be symbolic of the Yukon for many Canadians; their simplicity of line and colour make them ideal for a children's book. For each letter, Harrison provides a half-page drawing; the text appears on the adjacent half-page, visually isolated so it's reader-friendly. Despite the odd situations brought about by the alphabet theme ("The owl can see the oilrig from the outhouse"), kids can sense the vast expanse and extraordinary colours of northern Canada. At the same time they learn some of the objects and features of northern life. Each page is bordered by northern place names that begin with that letter of the alphabet (Nome, Nunalla, Nesketahin, Naknek), revealing the abundance of linguistic traditions in the region. The book is full of pleasures and possibilities for storytelling and spot-the-other-objects games.

Major, Kevin. Illustr. Alan Daniel. *Eh? to Zed: A Canadian ABeCedarium*. 2000. All ages.
Using words that refer to "things" – place names, objects, brand names, qualities – that are either typically or uniquely Canadian, Major moves through the alphabet in a series of tightly rhythmic, rhyming couplets: "Arctic, apple, aurora, Anik . . . Bonhomme, Bluenose, beaver, bannock . . ." The rhythm is irresistibly bouncy, chantable even for those who don't know the meaning of the words. This silly rhyming alphabet is a great way to expand general knowledge, and Major's entertaining, informative notes at the back are written with an ironic,

irreverent humour consonant with the text. Daniel illustrates the "Trivial Pursuit"–like verse with stylized images of Canadian icons: the maple leaf is shown in a carved maple-sugar mould; a Tlingit hat refers to the word "potlatch." An eccentric, energetic abecedarium.

McLean, Dirk. Illustr. Ras Stone. *Play Mas'! A Carnival ABC*. 2000. 5 to 8.
McLean describes the Caribbean Carnival season, then goes on to provide texts that function alphabetically on the vocabulary of Carnival traditions – Crop Over, Dimanche Gras, J'ouvert. Many of these terms are explained at the end of the book. Stone's illustrations, of uneven quality, emphasize the colour of the event.

Milich, Zoran. *The City ABC Book*. 2001. 3 and up.
This book of ingenious black-and-white photographs is excellent for children who are starting to master their letters, for it invites them to look for letter-shapes in unusual places. Milich has found and photographed the shape of each letter as it may be seen in the patterns of city architecture. An external staircase makes a K; a venting system makes an L; the round arch and pilaster of a doorway make an R. In each photo, Milich has highlighted the shape of the letter by painting it red. The book is clever, fun, and easy to use; it's a great example of how children may be nudged to see things differently.

Moak, Allan. *A Big City ABC*. 1984/2002. 3 and up.
These twenty-six illustrations of important aspects of city life will appeal to children anywhere, although it's clear that Moak is depicting a particular city, Toronto. Simple text, from *A is for art* to *Z is for zoo*, accompanies each picture. A further explanation of the location and the concept of each illustration is given at the back of the book. Moak shows the current multicultural makeup of the city, at the same time reflecting the Toronto of an earlier day. First published in 1984, it came out in a 2002 edition that includes five new pictures and a revised text. The art is exuberant and full of details that will intrigue children. A perfect introduction to Canada's largest city.

Nichol, Barbara. Illustr. Cornelius Van Horne. *Trunks All Aboard.*
2001. 4 and up.
Van Horne, who oversaw the building of the CPR in the late nineteenth
century, amused his grandson by sending him postcards of ink and
watercolour drawings of elephants. Nichol takes some of these and, by
assigning names to the elephants, organizes them to represent the
letters of the alphabet.

"For A let us meet Ahmed, on a boat. When it set sail, / He went on
deck. He knew he would look handsome at the rail," begins the litany.
Nichol turns this into a witty parade of affluence and peculiarity. With
their stylish haberdashery, cigars, and canes, the elephants exude
Victorian complacency; Nichol slyly suggests funny and sometimes
wicked undercurrents to their genteel appearance. Particularly appealing to imaginative children.

Owens, Mary Beth. *A Caribou Alphabet.* **1998. 3 to 7.**
Each letter in this austerely beautiful work illustrates a feature of
caribou life. Rhyming couplets describe the letter-specific activity or
thing ("*Migrating* bulls follow trails old and worn; While *newborns*
arrive where their mothers were born"); each letter is illustrated with
caribou entwined with or framed by the appropriate letter, as a capital
and in lower case. Owens's stencil-like illustrations have clean edges;
subtle blues and browns, stippled with white and surrounded by the
white expanse of the page, give this the feel of a northern landscape in
which caribou provide the only colour. The book has quiet atmosphere;
at the same time, it's very informative. A compendium in the back
gives more information on caribou habits.

Ruurs, Margriet. Illustr. Andrew Kiss. *A Mountain Alphabet.* **1996.**
4 to 7.
A series of Kiss's paintings of mountain scenes from British Columbia
and Alberta show the land- and skyscapes of the area. Ruurs's short
text points out some of the wildlife, plant life, and human activity characteristic of the region. At the back of the book is a brief commentary
on what's portrayed in each painting, as well as a list of "extra" objects
children can look for. Kiss's paintings open out the world, with their
towering, massive mountains and expansive river valleys.

COUNTING

Burton, Katherine. Illustr. Kim Fernandes. *One Grey Mouse.* **1995. 2 to 4.**

Cheerful three-dimensional illustrations combined with an uncomplicated rhyming text make this a charming book for children who are learning to count to ten. With its clear pictures and large numbers, this is accessible even to the very young. Fernandes's Fimo illustrations are bright and uncluttered, and the simple rhyme will stand up to repeated readings. A grey mouse is hidden on each page spread, providing additional interest. A simple and effective work.

Crysler, Ian. *The Big City Big Country Counting Book.* **1998. 2 to 4.**

If you open the book from one direction, you see photographs from the country – *one* shiny red truck (a pickup), *two* mailboxes (end of the drive), *three* big horses (farm-wagon horses); flip the book over, and you see *one* shiny red truck (whizzing fire truck), *two* mailboxes (Canada Post boxes), *three* big horses (mounted urban police) from the city. This proceeds all the way through to ten, and then both sides meet in a double-page celebration of ten friends in the middle of the book. Aside from the counting possibilities this story is full of potential for child-adult discussion; the photographs in either direction show busy, lively worlds.

* Kusugak, Michael Arvaarluk. Illustr. Vladyana Krykorka. *My Arctic 1, 2, 3.* **1996. 2 to 6.**

Kusugak counts up to ten, then leaps to 20, 100, and 1,000,000 in a counting book that features Arctic animals, such as a polar bear, ringed seals, and siksiks (Arctic ground squirrels). Krykorka's illustrations don't just show the animals, but also reveal something of the way of life in Kusugak's community in Rankin Inlet, and in his childhood home, Repulse Bay, Nunavut. In an afterword to the counting text, Kusugak gives more information and tells personal anecdotes about his family's interaction with Arctic creatures. Inuktitut names and script further enrich this text. Krykorka's luminous illustrations bloom with soft purples, blues, and greens; her tiny brush strokes make the creatures' fur look soft as air. Highly recommended.

McFarlane, Sheryl. Illustr. Kirsti Anne Wakelin. *A Pod of Orcas.* **2002. 2 to 5.**
Creatures and features of British Columbia's south coast and Gulf Islands figure in this rhyming counting book. A "lonely lighthouse," two freighters, harbour seals, trawlers, and more, add up past 16 to the "super pod of orcas," then count down to one "lonely lighthouse" again. Wakelin shows the flora and fauna of the region accurately, and depicts beautifully the blue of the coastal mountains and the special quality of light reflected from Georgia Strait.

OTHER

* Harris, Pamela. *Hot Cold Shy Bold: Looking at Opposites.* **1995. Infant to 7.**
Harris pairs photographs of faces with a few well-chosen rhyming words in this effective book for babies and toddlers. "A hot face / a cold face / a shy face / a bold face" – each attribute is illustrated with a photo of a child's face, with a few "old people" thrown in to represent the words mom, dad, old, and bearded.

Harris's photos are delightfully evocative: not only will babies love this encounter with the human face, but older viewers will find in these children's expressions much more than just a simple attribute. They suggest a whole story, complex characters, and intense feeling. Harris's rhythm and rhyme is impeccable; Canada's multiracial population is lovingly celebrated. One of Canada's very best books for babies. Highly recommended.

Ladner, Cobi. Illustr. Lisa Smith. *Why Is an Orange Called an Orange?* **2002. 3 to 6.**
See Picture Books.

Milich, Zoran. *City Signs.* **2002. 2 to 8.**
In this series of colour photographs, Milich focuses on everyday urban sights that involve print – using different kinds of vehicles, people in uniform, and road signs – to show not only that we're surrounded by words, but that reading may not be very difficult after all. It's hard for a child not to recognize the word "POLICE" on the back of a police car; or the word "LIFEGUARD" on the back of a lifeguard. The physical object

clues the emerging reader in; the print reinforces the reading. This is an excellent reading strategy, whether in real life or in a book, and Milich's photos will encourage children to go out into the world and read signs with confidence. With its focus on transportation and people in uniform, this book will appeal particularly to toddlers fascinated by fire trucks, trains, and so on.

Most people associate picture books, with their 32-page format and full-colour pictures, with children between infancy and 7 years. While most of the books listed here are suitable for this age group, there are some that have a certain appeal and usefulness to older readers. Reviews of these works with broader appeal are included in the main body of this chapter; for ease of reference, they're also listed at the end of the chapter.

Alderson, Sue Ann. Illustr. Ann Blades. *A Ride for Martha*. 1993. 4 to 7.
Walking to a picnic on Saltspring Island in British Columbia, Ida and her friends take turns giving baby Martha a ride – "a quickly ride, a jiggly ride, a tricky ride, a giggly ride." When the girls stop to explore the beach, they deposit Martha in a nearby dugout canoe. The tide rises and the wind blows: Martha gets the "tricky ride" of the poem and, after a rescue, Ida decides she'll never complain about carrying her sister again. The story ends with a clam supper with local Cowichan families.

The pale watercolour illustrations, in Gulf Island greens and blues, have the clean simplicity of a child's drawings. Blades depicts visually the multi-ethnic nature of Saltspring's early population, a mixture of European, Cowichan (local First Nations), and the descendants of freed African-American slaves. Another episode involving Ida on Saltspring can be found in ***Ida and the Wool Smugglers***, a story about Gulf Island sheep-farming.

Aldis, Dorothy. Illustr. Heather Collins. *Hiding*. 1993. 3 to 5.
A toddler hides and waits for his parents to find him. A simple rhyming text tells how the parents look for him: "And I just heard my father say to my mother – 'But darling, he must be somewhere or other.'" The fun in this book is that the boy is hiding in many impossible places – he appears in miniature in a picture above his bed, then riding a plastic duck in the goldfish bowl. Collins's imaginative illustrations invite the audience to find the little boy in his red sleeper pyjamas. In a satisfying conclusion his parents find him hiding under the covers in his bed. Aldis's poem first appeared in 1927; it's still delightful.

Allinson, Beverley. Illustr. Barbara Reid. *Effie*. 1990. 3 to 5.
Effie is like all ants – except she has a thunderous voice that scares away all the other ants, insects, and spiders, leaving her with no one to talk to. When it looks like an unwitting elephant is going to step on Effie and the others, however, Effie's booming voice is the only one that can stop him. Effie not only saves the ants, she also gains a friend and ensures that the rest of the elephants will tiptoe through the grass.

Reid's trademark Plasticine illustrations tell the story from many different visual angles, and bring additional delightful humour to this story of an ant "from a long line of ants." The reader gets an ant's-eye view of the huge foot of the elephant about to descend; on the next page we look down Effie's throat and see a huge set of teeth and a close-up of her tongue. An excellent read-aloud book that points out that even seemingly unfortunate attributes can be useful.

* Andrews, Jan. Illustr. Ian Wallace. *Very Last First Time*. 1985. 4 to 8.
Andrews celebrates a moment of utter magic in this story of an Inuit girl's "very last first time for walking alone on the bottom of the sea." Every winter, when the tide is out, Eva and the people of her village on Ungava Bay climb under the thick sea-ice and gather mussels from the seabed. Today, Eva drops through the ice hole and harvests mussels alone. Her pan full, she explores tide pools, hums, sings, and rejoices in her independence. When she hears the whoosh of the incoming sea and her candle sputters out, she has a moment of panic before she emerges safely, back into the moonlight.

The very concept of walking on the seabed is startling and magical; Andrews's restrained, elegant prose conveys the otherworldliness of the dark seabed with its cavernous roof of ice, an invisible sea in the distance. Wallace's illustrations, almost pointillist in their purples and blues and golds, reinforce the hushed, haunting atmosphere of the moment. Even the expression "very last first time" resonates with the power of a joyous rite of passage. Highly recommended.

Badoe, Adwoa. Illustr. Belinda Ageda. *Crabs for Dinner.* **1995. 4 to 7.** Crab, fufu, and palm-nut soup are adult foods that the two children in the story avoid. They eat hamburgers, pizza, and hot dogs instead, until their grandmother arrives from Ghana and the children hear the adults talk about the exquisite taste, the authentic flavour – of Grandmother's delicious soup.

Badoe captures the finicky eating habits of childhood and the careful way children approach new tastes: "If Emily doesn't die I'll have some." This story shows the difficulty many children have trying to fit into Canadian culture while being drawn to the culture of their parents' origins. Badoe and Ageda depict the children's trepidation at receiving gifts of clothing from Africa, and their delight when they hear their grandmother tell them stories. There's a great deal of authenticity here for picky eaters, children struggling with cultural divides, and those just looking for a good story.

Bedard, Michael. Illustr. Barbara Cooney. *Emily.* **1992. 6 and up.** People say the woman who lives in the yellow house across the street is crazy; she hasn't left her house in twenty years. But to the little girl of this story, an invitation to visit the "Myth" (as Emily Dickinson was known) is a glorious treat. The girl's mother is to play the piano for Emily and "bring a little spring": the girl brings Emily lily bulbs, and Emily gives her a poem in return.

Bedard's language captures the awe and the excitement of a meeting with the famous American poet, Emily Dickinson; at the same time, he conveys in his text the clean, spare style of her poetry. The oil illustrations by Cooney, a multiple-award-winning American artist, are sheer delight, and reflect the orderliness of both period and place beautifully. The young girl in hooded coat and muff, a large house with the shadow of Emily in a window – everything here is precisely rendered, evocative of Dickinson's austere, reclusive voice.

Bianchi, John. *Snowed in at Pokeweed Public School.* **1991. 4 to 6.**
"It's time for another classic day at Pokeweed School," begins the young sheep who narrates the story. The school bus, her best friend Melody (a pig), the habits of Mr. Slugmeyer the principal (a hapless pooch), and efficient Ms. Mudwortz (a cow) make up some of the pleasures of Pokeweed School, which has the attributes of any friendly elementary school. One day a surprise snowstorm results in a school-wide sleepover; in the morning the bus arrives to take the students back home. But instead of dropping them off it whizzes on past their doors: it's already time to go back to school again.

With buoyant, reassuring humour Bianchi illustrates aspects of the school schedule and environment. Cartoon-like figures show the well-meaning, cheerful populace of Pokeweed's primary class and staff, and the idea of a school sleepover has great appeal. A useful story for acquainting young children with what to expect at school.

A compendium of four Pokeweed stories is available in *Classic Days at Pokeweed Public School.*

See also **Edwards, Frank B., and John Bianchi.** *Mortimer Mooner Stopped Taking a Bath.* **1990. 2 to 5.**

Blades, Ann. *Mary of Mile 18.* **1971. 5 to 8.**
Growing up on an isolated farm on British Columbia's Alaska Highway, Mary Bergen longs to keep a wolf pup that befriends her. Mary's father insists the family can't afford to keep an animal that won't work for its keep, but when the cub warns the family of the presence of a hen-stealing coyote, Mary's father relents.

Any child who has ever wanted a dog will identify with Mary, at the mercy of the arbitrary "No" of her parents. Her longing for the cub is palpable, and her restraint as she repeatedly returns it to the wilderness, makes the story intensely poignant. Blades's primitive watercolours contrast the austere shadings of the sparsely treed, northern winter with Mary's purple, emerald, and turquoise clothing, as though only Mary's passion can brighten the huge, monochromatic wilderness. A final image of Mary in bed with the pup looks like "madonna and wolf pup" –

a turn on the gift of life in midwinter that helps show why this tale has been so enduring. This is a quiet but potent vision of a little girl's love, and a window onto a bit of northern British Columbia.

Bogart, Jo Ellen. Illustr. Sylvie Daigneault. *Sarah Saw a Blue Macaw.* **1991. 3 to 6.**
Through interconnected verses, Bogart and Daigneault introduce children to some of the creatures of the South American rain forest. Sarah, a spider monkey, swings her way through every picture, but in each we see different animals in action. Although the creatures are given first names by Bogart (Kim, Daniel, Sam), Daigneault nevertheless depicts them as wild creatures in their wild habitat – a skink, a jaguar, a tapir, and more. Bogart's scheme of rhythm and internal rhyme will make listeners think carefully about words and sound. "Where did Daniel drink? / Daniel drank down on the bank. / And on the bank where Daniel drank, / He saw a tiny skink."

Bogart, Jo Ellen. Illustr. Barbara Reid. *Gifts.* **1994. 2 to 6.**
A grandmother makes repeated trips; before each one she asks her granddaughter: "What would you have me bring?" The granddaughter's replies are riddles; she rarely asks for anything concrete. "Just a sunrise kissed by the morning mist, and the whirr of a hummingbird's wing." Or, "the secret wish of a flying fish, and a rainbow to wear as a ring." In the final verse, the granddaughter has grown up and is off to show her own baby girl the world.

　　Bogart's verse has lilt and imagination; Reid takes that and runs. The girl's riddling replies are often resolved in Reid's Plasticine illustrations – the sunset and whirr of a wing are represented by a painting of sunrise behind a Mayan pyramid; a brisk breeze blows the curtains of a window near the painting. Great attention to detail, all around the world, makes this rewarding fare for preschoolers; both grandmother and granddaughter exude character. The possibility that the grandmother has died gently suggests the idea of continuing heritage.

Booth, David. Illustr. Karen Reczuch. *The Dust Bowl.* **1996. 4 to 8.**
"Oh, the dust clouds. How I remember them," reminisces Matthew's grandfather, and he goes on to tell Matthew of the difficulties of keeping

the family farm through the drought, dust storms, heat, locusts, and winters of "the dirty Thirties." The little boy hears of the hard work, courage, and love for the land that have kept the farm in his family: at the same time, a current drought causes his own father to think of selling.

Booth captures the difficulties and determination of prairie farmers; one can almost feel the dust and the desperation in Reczuch's realistic illustrations with their sharply individualized family and vast vistas of arid prairie. This picture book documents the hardships of the past with the hope that farmers today can once again hold on until it rains.

Bourgeois, Paulette. Illustr. Brenda Clark. *Franklin in the Dark.* 1986. 3 to 6.

Franklin the turtle has a problem: he's afraid of the dark. How can a turtle who's supposed to sleep in a shell be afraid of the dark? Franklin asks his friends if they have advice, but each knows only how to deal with her or his own fears. The duck's afraid of deep water, so uses water wings. The lion's afraid of loud noises, so uses earmuffs. The bird is afraid of heights, so uses a parachute. Thinking about all this, Franklin realizes that a night light would be the solution to his problem.

The secret to Franklin's enormous popularity can be found here. Bourgeois takes a childhood emotion and, in a safe, gentle story, shows that it's nothing to be ashamed of; many children feel this way and there may be a simple solution. Clark creates a comfortable, benign world with her soft and cheerful illustrations: mama turtle has a nice smile and rosy cheeks; the world is one of flowers, calm waters, and pretty toys.

The Franklin stories are respectful and reassuring, directed towards assuaging preschooler fears and solving socialization problems. A certain formulaic quality creeps into the numerous sequels. This can be wonderfully calming for a young audience, but at a certain point, parents will want to introduce stories that allow these issues more complexity.

Bourgeois, Paulette. Illustr. Brenda Clark. *Big Sarah's Little Boots.* 1987. 3 to 5.

Sarah loves her yellow boots that go *Squish!* in the puddles. When they don't fit her any more, she does everything she can to stretch them. And when Mom insists they buy new yellow boots with fiery red stripes,

Sarah's sure they can never be as good as the old ones. But even though the new boots don't go *Squish!* Sarah's long legs can make them go *Whoosh!* as she jumps over the puddles – so growing up does have its compensations.

Children are encouraged to look at the bright side of growing out of favourite clothes in this consoling, upbeat story. Clark's illustrations, in soft, pale colours, show Sarah as a determined, expressive little girl in a loving home in a suburban environment.

Bourgeois, Paulette. Illustr. Bill Slavin. *Too Many Chickens*. **1990. 4 to 7.**

Twenty-one days after a farmer brings eggs to Mrs. Kerr's class, the chicks break out of their shells. The farmer forgets to come and collect them, and they grow increasingly noisy and disruptive. "I can't stand this any more. . . . They are noisy and ugly and they stink," says Michael Alexander, who then gets the idea to start selling their eggs. The story develops with some rabbits and then a goat arriving for the class, and the students make enough money to buy a farm.

The story is silly, but entertaining; the classroom setting makes it useful for the early grades. Slavin's illustrations capture the absurdity of the situation as well as the annoyance and enjoyment of the students and teacher.

Brownridge, William Roy. *The Moccasin Goalie*. **1995. 4 to 8.**

Cold temperatures on the prairies mean hockey to Danny and his friends, Anita, Marcel, and Petou. They live for hockey, but when an organized team is formed, Danny isn't allowed to play because he has a crippled foot and can't wear skates – he has always played goalie wearing moccasins. Of his friends, only Marcel is chosen to be on the team: Anita can't play because "she's a girl" and Petou because "he's too small." When a player is hurt, Danny is given special permission to play goalie in his moccasins and, as a result of his work, the team wins. When he's invited to join the team for good, Danny says he'll join only if all his friends are included.

Based on Brownridge's personal experiences, this story is direct and well told. Human relations are valued over winning and achieving:

Brownridge shows the game as play more than competition, a matter of joy as much as seriousness. His thick oil illustrations are exuberantly colourful, and express the verve of the children's addiction to hockey. A subsequent title, *The Final Game*, deals with some of the same characters.

Butler, Geoff. *The Hangashore*. 1998. 5 to 8.
John Payne, a boy with Down's syndrome, has a great sense of humour, and everyone in his Newfoundland outport home appreciates it. When a self-important, rigid magistrate arrives just as World War II ends, John speaks his mind about the man's pompous ways. The magistrate threatens to send him to an institution but, when John rescues him from a runaway boat, the magistrate realizes that indeed he's been acting like a "hangashore" – a man so pathetic one can only pity him.

This lengthy, soberly related story has the air of a family or village anecdote, and shows the refreshing comeuppance of a person in authority by one who's considered incapable. Butler's heavy oil illustrations are in the style of late-nineteenth-century land- and seascapes; they give a glimpse of the features of the life of that time and that place.

In *The Killick: A Newfoundland Story*, also written and illustrated by Butler, a boy and his grandfather are marooned on an ice-pan overnight.

Carney, Margaret. Illustr. Janet Wilson. *At Grandpa's Sugar Bush*. 1997. 4 to 7.
A young child visits his grandparents during the school break and helps his grandfather make maple sugar in the traditional method – with buckets, spiles, and the large sap pan.

The slight story serves to show how maple syrup is made, from drilling and hammering in the spiles to straining the syrup through a cloth to get rid of dirt and ash. Wilson's art is what makes this book memorable. Her oil illustrations show the beauty of the sugar bush as spring arrives, and communicate the joy of a child helping his grandfather. It seems the grandmother in this story is as traditional as the method of making syrup: she is only seen at breakfast with pancakes.

* Carrier, Roch. Illustr. Sheldon Cohen. *The Hockey Sweater.* **Trans. from French. 1979. 5 and up.**

For young Roch and his pals, hockey is the purpose of life, and Maurice Richard of the Montreal Canadiens is the only hockey player in the world. Each one of the kids has a Canadiens sweater with number 9 on it – "five Maurice Richards against five other Maurice Richards." When Roch's sweater wears out, his mother orders another, but to Roch's disgust it's blue and white, the colours of the Toronto Maple Leafs. Roch suddenly finds he's not so popular on the rink and, after a fit of temper, the curate sends him in to say his prayers. "I asked God to send me right away, a hundred million moths that would eat up my Toronto Maple Leafs sweater," Roch concludes his story.

Cryptic, self-mocking, and gently ironic, Carrier delineates the childhood angst of hockey passion when it confronts a mother's relentless reasoning. Cohen's thickly painted, heavily outlined illustrations are in the style of Québecois folk art; they've come to seem an integral part of the story. This famous tale of sweater frustration has gained classic status throughout Canada. Highly recommended.

Also available by the same pair: *The Basketball Player*, *The Longest Home Run*, and *The Boxing Champion*.

Chase, Edith Newlin. Illustr. Barbara Reid. *The New Baby Calf.* **1984. Infant to 4.**

Chase's quiet poem tells of a calf's first experiences in the world: "The new baby calf took a very little walk, a teeny little walk, a tiny little walk." The gentle, rocking rhythm and occasional rhyme match the safe, nurturing relationship baby calf has with his mother, Buttercup. Reid's Plasticine illustrations, showing a placid pastoral environment, underscore the peaceful, cosy aspects of the text and, at the same time, provide scope for further discussion. An ideal quiet book for toddlers.

Chase, Edith Newlin. Illustr. Ron Broda. *Waters.* **1993. 2 to 5.**

A poem of fewer than a hundred words evokes the qualities of spring melt, a tiny brook joining a greater, the flow of a river, and finally, the "rolling, rolling, tossing, rolling" of ocean swell. Although Chase's verse here is less successful than that of *The New Baby Calf*, it has its moments: "sprinkling, wrinkling, softly tinkling" certainly gives the auditory sensation of spring melt.

But Broda's paper-sculpture illustrations are what make this book notable. The textures and shine of fresh snow, melting icicles, and splattering water are almost touchable: light reflects off water, and sunset skies offer a vista into another country. Flora and fauna are depicted with an eye for accuracy; Broda shows a different provincial flower in each scene, along with various birds and wildlife. Species are identified at the end of the book. Educational and visually pleasing.

Clement, Gary. *Just Stay Put: A Chelm Story*. 1995. 4 and up.
An inhabitant of Chelm (in traditional folk stories, a Jewish shtetl where people use hilariously faulty logic), daydreamer Mendel decides to go out and see some of the world. He sets out to walk the dusty road to Warsaw; en route he has to rest, so he takes off his boots and points them in the direction of Warsaw and goes to sleep. A shepherd passing by picks up the boots and replaces them facing in the opposite direction. Mendel awakes and returns to Chelm, but believes it to be Warsaw. Surprised at how much "Warsaw" looks like Chelm – including its identical populace – Mendel decides it's best to just stay put.

Clement retells the old story in forthright manner: he opens with a little background about Chelm, and then jumps right into Mendel's tale. His illustrations are almost surreal – Mendel is shown with his head literally in the clouds or walking with his head on backwards, and Malke, Mendel's long-suffering wife, emits sparks of anger and frustration through her eyes. The boring nature of Chelm is reflected in Clement's use of dusty tones; Warsaw, a product of Mendel's imagination, is depicted in colourful reds and greens. This book is illustrated not with traditionally pretty pictures, but rather with amusing, slightly odd, but highly effective images.

Conrad, Pam. Illustr. Eric Beddows. *The Rooster's Gift*. 1996. 3 to 6.
Young Rooster is thrilled to find that he indeed has "the Gift" – that he can call up the sun daily from his perch on the henhouse roof. But one day when Rooster is late for sunrise, he discovers that the sun comes up without him. So what is his Gift? he and Smallest Hen wonder. When

Smallest Hen tries to announce the sun and can only "bok-bok ca-bok," she and Rooster realize that his Gift lies in his clarion voice.

Grand vistas of sunrises both glorious and quiet greet the eye in full-page illustrations. Round and elegantly feathered, Smallest Hen and Rooster have tellingly expressive faces; Beddows's clean lines and delicate textures make the henyard a place of order and calm. A story of affirmation and friendship.

Crook, Connie Brummel. Illustr. Scott Cameron. *Maple Moon*. 1997. 4 to 8.
A boy of the Mississauga Nation, known by two names – one given to him by other children, "Limping Leg," and the other by his parents, "Rides the Wind" – watches a squirrel drinking sap from a maple tree and thus learns the secret of harvesting the sweet water for his people.

This story is inspired by Aboriginal legends but is a work of fiction. Crook invents a compassionate story of a disabled boy finding a way to bring a treasure to his tribe, thus earning a new name, "Wise Little Raven." Attractive illustrations by Cameron show both the firelight and the gleam in the eyes of the chief. A good story to share when the sap is running.

Dalton, Sheila. Illustr. Kim LaFave. *Doggerel*. 1996. 3 to 6.
Dalton celebrates every possible kind of pooch in vigorous, playful rhyme; a quick, strong beat and choice adjectives draw readers' attention to the pleasure and variety of dog-hood in a simple, strong vocabulary. "There are vagrant dogs, fragrant dogs (I really mean smelly) / There are flat dogs and fat dogs as jiggly as jelly / There are burly dogs, curly dogs and dogs without hair / And poodles with oodles of bows every-where . . ." A loving conclusion about "that neat dog, that sweet dog – the one that loves you" makes this a good choice for children with dogs in their homes.

LaFave takes Dalton's playfulness and runs with it in his expressive, cartoon-like illustrations. Facial expressions on humans and canines suggest volumes of emotional complexity, and just about every known breed makes its way into the dog-populated world that's presented.

Davidge, Bud. Illustr. Ian Wallace. *The Mummer's Song.* **1993.**
5 and up.

"The Mummer's Song is now a musical focal point of a marvelous tradition," writes Newfoundland writer Kevin Major in his afterword to
this book. Davidge's song celebrates the traditional Christmas mum-
mering, in which swarms of people in outlandish clothing and masks,
hiding their identity and acting like fools, go door to door bringing
Christmas cheer to the people of Newfoundland.

Wallace brings the song to life with illustrations of the adults
dressed in costume, tapping their feet and dancing up a storm. The pale
coloured-pencil illustrations at first seem too muted for the mayhem
the song suggests, but the mummers' antics are exuberant by their very
nature. A useful documentation of a regional tradition.

Denton, Kady MacDonald. *Would They Love a Lion?* **1995. 2 to 4.**

With a very special blanket and much imaginative energy, Anna spends
the morning musing over what kind of creature she'd like to be – a bird,
a bear, an elephant, a rabbit . . . But she really wants to make the world
shake. When she finally shows up for lunch as a lion, she makes the
very impression she desires. And then it's time for a nap.

Denton's text is perfectly spare and direct: Anna's transformations,
visually presented, give the story emotional drama. The animal shapes
Anna creates as she hides beneath a colourful red, blue, and yellow plaid
blanket are funny and amusing, and Anna's face – her very posture –
show her enormous self-respect and forcefulness. Anna's roar, depicted
in multicoloured swirls and jags as her mother and brother startle and
jump, is glorious. A playful tale of the possibilities of make-believe.

DeVries, John. Illustr. H. Werner Zimmermann. *In My Backyard.*
1992. 2 to 4.

"In my backyard I have a frog. My mother found him on a log." So
begins this simple rhyming story. A little boy names his frog Jim, and
then has to find a place to keep him. Turned away by his mother, father,
grandfather, and sister, his only option is to keep the frog with his dog,
Rover. Rover's doghouse is clearly the place where the little boy keeps
all his treasures, and the story ends with "Rover, you're my pal."

Zimmermann's soft watercolour illustrations greatly enhance DeVries's restrained text, showing a great deal of expressiveness in the human beings of the story and expanding on the action – the frog leaping on a computer keyboard in front of a shocked father illustrates the line "My daddy said, 'Take him away!'" The true stars of the story are the boy and Rover, both of whom show delight and curiosity with this new frog named Jim. An excellent read-aloud.

de Vries, Maggie. Illustr. Sheena Lott. *How Sleep Found Tabitha.* **2002. 2 to 5.**
Instead of looking out into the shadowy corners of her bedroom, sleepless preschooler Tabitha looks and listens with the eyes and ears of her mind. "Come sleep with me in the deep blue sea," sings the whale. "Sleep high up here, where the sky is clear," cries the eagle. "Sleep up on all fours and dream out of doors," calls the horse. Tabitha has a lively time trying to take this advice – in bed – as she acts out each creature in its sleeping quarters. It isn't until her cat, Sleep, pads into the room and snuggles down with her that she finally drops off.

This is a pleasing sleep book, true to a child's experience, gentle and lulling without being sentimental. Lott's watercolours – a shadowy orca drenched in varied water greens; a raucous eagle up in the blue, perched over a messy nest of sticks – bring the glories of the natural world right into the bedroom of the sleepless child. She points out what's behind de Vries's text: that in our imaginations we can roam throughout the elements.

Drawson, Blair. *Mary Margaret's Tree.* **1996. 4 to 7.**
Digging a hole to plant a sapling, Mary Margaret suddenly feels very small. The tree grows magically to tower above her, and Mary Margaret spends a quick season or two living in it as a very small person. Finally she descends, on a crazy ride via a leaf, spends the winter hibernating, and wakes up to discover that she herself is putting out shoots and roots. "Come in for dinner now, dear," her mother says, and Mary Margaret's fantasy tree-hood is left behind.

This journey of the imagination emphasizes the magic of growth and living things. Drawson's art underscores that magic, with its multi-hued textures and luminous greens; Mary Margaret makes a charming, strong-spirited protagonist in glasses, gumboots, and pigtails.

Edwards, Frank B., and John Bianchi. *Mortimer Mooner Stopped Taking a Bath.* **1990. 2 to 5.**
Pig Mortimer Mooner gradually gives up personal hygiene – on Monday, he stops wearing a tie; on Tuesday, he stops cleaning his room; on Wednesday, he stops washing his trotters. When Grandma comes, Mortimer realizes he's going to have to clean up before he gets the hug he desires.

Mortimer's completely authentic lack of interest in personal hygiene will strike a chord with any preschooler. Grandma puts the experiment in the realm of family love; Mortimer's a nice little pig from a good home. Edwards's and Bianchi's humorous exaggeration make this both funny and educational, a refreshing variant among humourless socialization stories for the age group. Ink and watercolour illustrations are energetic and expressive.

Sequels such as *Grandma Mooner Lost Her Voice!* are equally winning.

Ellis, Sarah. Illustr. Ruth Ohi. *Next Stop!* **2000. 3 to 6.**
On Saturday Claire rides the bus; she sits right up front and knows every stop. "Next stop, Moss Road," says the driver. "Museum," says Claire. As people climb on and off, she lets them know what's next – until a final passenger gives her and the bus driver a big kiss. "Home!" says Claire, and Mom and bus-driving Dad agree.

This story's always moving towards the little twist in its final revelation. It offers young listeners the interest of watching people board and leave the bus, while inviting them to make the final connection themselves. The repeating patterns and variations in Ellis's succinct text make it an excellent choice for emergent readers, and Ohi's illustrations, in bright, shining yellows and reds, provide enough extra detail to suggest an interesting world of human activity.

Ellis, Sarah. Illustr. Kim LaFave. *Big Ben.* **2001. 3 to 6.**
Preschooler Ben is jealous of his sister's and brother's report cards – signs of their superior capabilities – until they kindly reward him with

one of his own. His subjects are Feeding the Cat, Shoe Tying, Tooth Brushing, Whistling, and Making Us Laugh, and the comments, "Very Good, Excellent, Superb, Superior . . ." Ben goes to bed feeling very capable indeed.

Ellis doesn't waste a word, but gives a telling little glimpse into the difficulties of being the youngest child. LaFave's illustrations are cartoon-like; Ben's woebegone feelings are clear in his small stature and unruly cowlick. With its simple vocabulary and repetition, this is a good choice for an emergent reader.

Elwin, Rosamund, and Michele Paulse. Illustr. Dawn Lee. *Asha's Mums*. 1990. 4 to 7.

Asha has a problem: she is going on a class trip to the Science Centre and both her parents must sign her school form. When she comes back with the form signed by two women, the teacher tells her she can't accept it; she doesn't understand that Asha has no father, but two mothers. Eventually the misunderstanding is cleared up and Asha goes on the school trip, even though some of the other students talk about her two mums. One classmate asks, "Is it wrong to have two mummies?" but before the teacher can answer, another student yells, "It's not wrong if they're nice to you and if you like them."

This straightforward story comfortably and unthreateningly introduces the idea of same-sex parents. Lee's illustrations show Asha's mums as women of colour and the class is totally multi-cultural and multiracial. Although the production qualities of this book aren't on a par with most mainstream picture books, the story here is much better than many newer narratives dealing with same-sex parenting.

Eyvindson, Peter. Illustr. Rhian Brynjolson. *Red Parka Mary*. 1996. 4 to 6.

Mary "always wore big floppy moccasins lined with rabbit fur, thick grey wool socks, three or four sweaters heavily darned at the elbow and a Montreal Canadiens hockey toque pulled down over her straggly grey hairs. She was missing four or five front teeth and her skin was brown and wrinkled." A young boy is afraid of her until the day she offers him some chokecherries to take home to his mother. A friendship quickly develops between the two, and he saves to give Mary a red parka for Christmas.

This story is useful for its portrayal of a clearly Aboriginal grand-mother figure, and for its exploration of the possibilities of friendship across ages and racial or cultural backgrounds. Although illustrations and text are of rough quality, together they offer a look at a community that is not often reflected in picture books. The cover art, a picture of Mary standing with a bucket of berries, makes clear the intent of the story, set in an unidentified First Nations community of Canada.

Fagan, Cary. Illustr. Regolo Ricci. *The Market Wedding*. 2000. 4 to 8. Fagan's retelling of this Jewish short story by Abraham Cahan re-locates the story to Toronto's Kensington Market in the 1920s. Morris sells fish and Minnie sells hats; neither has much money. When they decide to marry, Morris figures that if they have an opulent wedding ceremony and party, the guests will bring lavish gifts. But their friends are ashamed to show up at such an elegant affair: Minnie and Morris end up dancing alone. Happily, when the two get back to their empty, unfurnished apartment, their understanding friends turn the night into a celebration more suited to their means.

Fagan tells the story with brevity and flair. Ricci's rendition of nineteenth-century Kensington, in the style of Victoriana, seems to recreate the place and period wholly. Minnie's character comes through in her stylish dress and hats; Morris's in his round, bespecta-cled face as he peddles his fish. A funny, heart-warming tale of human frailty and true affection.

Fagan, Cary. Illustr. Cybèle Young. *Daughter of the Great Zandini*. 2001. 64 pages. 7 to 10. Fanny's a whiz at magic tricks, and she adores doing them. But Papa, the Great Zandini, is sure that her brother Theo is the one who should follow him into the conjuring business. Theo has much less glorious ambitions: "I want to open a shop when I'm old enough and wear a brown suit and sell recordings," he says. When Theo fails night after night on stage, Fanny has to think up a plot to save him. She disguises herself as a boy, sets herself up as the Great Zandini's competitor, and arranges a showdown.

Fanny's a strong, intelligent protagonist, and her voice is an appealing mixture of stateliness and vivacity – perfectly suited to breaking the gender barriers of the nineteenth-century Paris setting. Her commanding account of the action, interspersed with mean-spirited newspaper reports by a conjuring reporter, keeps the story marching on, as good an evening's entertainment as a magic show. This tale is fun and clever, and has an amusing touch of melodrama. The book's many drawings and large format make it a good read-aloud for those ready to move from picture books to illustrated novels.

Fernandes, Eugenie. Illustr. Henry Fernandes. *Ordinary Amos and the Amazing Fish*. 1986. 4 to 7.
Everything about Amos's life is ordinary – his house, his pet, and his habits, which include going fishing daily. When Amos's hook is seized by a powerful fish, Amos thinks what a good trophy the catch will be when he lands it. Instead, the fish lands Amos – down in his underwater home. Little Fish keeps Amos as a pet in a bowl full of air, furnished with a comfy chair and a fireplace. Eventually, Little Fish forgets about Amos, who grows weak and bored. "He's just too little to care for a pet!" the fish mother cries when she notices neglected Amos. At last he's returned to his home, which seems absolutely wonderful after his experience of being confined as a pet.

This story, with slightly Seuss-like illustrations, is a humorous cautionary tale about pet care – but even better, it invites children to look at the world from a different perspective altogether, a non-anthropocentric one.

Froissart, Bénédicte. Illustr. Pierre Pratt. *Uncle Henry's Dinner Guests*. Trans. from French. 1990. 4 to 7.
One night Uncle Henry arrives for dinner wearing a fancy shirt with little chickens printed on it. Before the children's eyes, one of the chickens starts to move, pecks around on Uncle Henry's ample stomach, and lays an egg in his ice cream. When *all* the hundreds of shirt-chickens start flying around, Uncle Henry finally takes control. A cough and a whistle, and they're marching back onto the shirt in single file. "My parents were fed up. But my sister, my brother and I thought it was great," the narrator says candidly.

The deadpan voice of the narrator as she describes this bizarre event makes this hilarious; so too does the contrast of Uncle Henry's antics and the parents' disapproval. Pratt's stylized people and strange perspectives are perfect for the offbeat flavour; rich colours painted on black paper give the illustrations a surreal glow.

Garay, Luis. *Pedrito's Day*. 1997. 4 to 7.
Pedrito longs for the day when he can have a bicycle. His mother and father don't think he's big enough for a bike, and plan to start saving for one when he's older. Pedrito has been saving his shoeshine money to help pay for it, but one market day when he's sent to get change for a friend, he loses the money. He gives up his own savings to make up the loss, and when Pedrito's mother hears of his sacrifice, she agrees that he's now big enough for a bike – and she begins to put money aside for it.

Garay's Nicaraguan background is evident both in the moving story and the unpretentious illustrations of Pedrito and his eventful day. Bright flowers, blue sky, and colourful market scenes reflect the hope within the story, and effectively contrast with the interior scenes of crumbling walls and the sombre earthy tones used throughout much of the book. The family's strained circumstances and Pedrito's inner maturity in making up for his mistake make this a rich source for discussion.

Gay, Marie-Louise. *Rabbit Blue*. 1993. 3 to 5.
An energetic little girl with flyaway hair swings madly and sings about the amazing capabilities of her Rabbit Blue: "Rabbit Blue can catch a ball, / a planet or a star about to fall." Each half-line of hand-lettered couplet has a page of Gay's fanciful, visually active art; the ink and watercolour drawings fill out ideas barely suggested by the text. "Rabbit Blue feels the heat" is illustrated with the vision of a smiling maharajah on an elephant, heading into a windblown jungle, for example. Story and art emphasize the widely varied, often crazy, possibilities of imaginative play.

Gay's earlier works *Fat Charlie's Circus*, *Midnight Mimi*, *Angel and the Polar Bear*, and *Moonbeam on a Cat's Ear* make a similar play on reality and fantasy, celebrating both the scary and the liberating aspects of the imagination with great effectiveness.

* Gay, Marie-Louise. *Stella, Star of the Sea.* **1999. 2 to 5.**
When five-year-old Stella and little brother Sam go to the sea, it takes all Stella's exuberance to overcome Sam's timidity at meeting the open Atlantic. "It's very big and noisy," he says. "Are there sea-monsters? Is the water cold? Where do starfish come from?" "The water is lovely. Starfish are shooting stars that fell in love with the sea," she informs him. After many such exchanges, Sam finally throws caution to the wind and jumps in.

Gay treats a child's natural fears with a light, kind hand. Sam's sticking-out hair and round tummy exude anxiety; Stella's fiery mop and enormous grin show her huge personality and imaginative energy. The translucent blues and greens of the sea and of summer pervade every page, and Gay's use of collage, with dyed Japanese paper, gives her art pleasing depth and visual interest. A spare, well-chosen text allows young listeners to stretch their minds, read between the lines, and laugh with compassionate understanding. A picture book of many virtues and much originality, this is one of the best Canada has to offer. Highly recommended.

In two excellent sequels, ***Stella, Queen of the Snow***, and ***Stella, Fairy of the Forest***, Stella and Sam have similar exchanges and experiences in the natural world.

Gay, Marie-Louise. *On My Island.* **2000. 4 to 7.**
Here Gay contrasts a lonely boy's uninspired commentary with the wild events we see taking place all around him. "Alone" on his island, with a wolf, two cats, three ants, and a swooping bat, "nothing much happens," the boy drones. "We often dream of wild adventures, of mysterious happenings and odd events. But it's no use . . . nothing ever happens." Meanwhile, a fire-breathing dragon rampages. A posse of cowboys ride leaping turquoise dolphins; volcanoes erupt and parachuting elephants drift down from the heavens.

This story explores the leap between text and image – the way pictures can put an entirely different spin on words. The vibrant, surreal happenings show the viewer an ironic tension in the boy's own imagination, made clear by a final image of his round head, topped by his animal companions as he swims through shadowed sea. An excellent vehicle for discussing the nature of imagination, this is also a substantial work of art. Gay's funny, spontaneous illustrations, in handmade paper, ink, watercolour, collage, newspaper bits, and even petals, are extremely enriching, and show children the possibilities for "mixed-up media."

Gibson, Betty. Illustr. Kady MacDonald Denton. *The Story of Little Quack.* **1990. 2 to 5.**
Jackie is lonely on the farm until his mother gives him little Quack, the duck. The two become best friends, explore the farm and work and play together, until suddenly Little Quack disappears. In the end, Jackie is happily reunited with his duck when he finds her swimming at the end of the farm with her little "quacklings."

Denton's watercolour illustrations bring the barnyard to joyful life. Her animals (including little Quack) are farmyard animals and do not show emotion, but Jackie's joy, excitement, and fear are skilfully portrayed in each picture. Denton's delightful final illustration, with Jackie, Quack, and the ducklings swimming in an old tub, brings the story to a charming conclusion. Young children will enjoy pointing out all the animals to be found around the farm.

Gillmor, Don. Illustr. Marie-Louise Gay. *The Fabulous Song.* **1996. 4 to 7.**
Born into a musical family, Frederic Pipkin can't seem to take to any musical instrument. When he plays the piano, it sounds like a brick crashing through a window. When he plays the cello, it's like an argument between four snakes. But after hearing an orchestra at a concert, Frederic finds his musical gift at the very next family party – he's a fabulous conductor and composer.

This affirming story of a boy who finally finds his métier is all the more amusing because the boy's talent gives him authority over a whole family of musicians older and bigger than himself. Gay's illustrations, full of toothy, grinning relatives and abject music teachers, are characteristically wacky and laughter-inducing. Bits of cut-up sheet music fly through the air as Frederic torments the various instruments.

Additional collaborations between Gillmor and Gay are found in *Yuck, A Love Story*, *The Christmas Orange*, and *When Vegetables Go Bad*.

Gilman, Phoebe. *Jillian Jiggs*. **1985. 3 to 6.**
Jillian Jiggs is an inveterate dress-up and drama girl. Her room's so strewn with props and pieces of various costumes that it's driving her mother crazy. "Jillian Jiggs! Jillian Jiggs! It looks like your room has been lived in by pigs!" her mother cries repeatedly. But any efforts to clean up the room only result in further dress-up. Even when her mother faints, kerplop, and Jillian finally picks up the mop, she sees only its possibilities as a wig.

Gilman's verse bounces nicely and provides some charming rhymes; her illustrations show a group of highly inventive children utterly absorbed in the drama of their play. The contest of a child's fertile imagination with a mother's reasonable demands is almost universal.

Jillian has subsequent adventures in *Jillian Jiggs and the Secret Surprise*, *Jillian Jiggs to the Rescue*, *The Wonderful Pigs of Jillian Jiggs*, and *Jillian Jiggs and the Great Big Snow*.

* Gilman, Phoebe. *Something from Nothing*. **1992. 2 to 8.**
This account of a classic Jewish tale should be on every child's bookshelf. "When Joseph was a baby, his grandfather made him a wonderful blanket . . ." Gilman begins. When the blanket's worn out, Joseph claims, "Grandpa can fix it!" Grandpa turns it into a wonderful jacket. The jacket becomes a vest, the vest becomes a tie, the tie becomes a handkerchief, the handkerchief becomes a button. When the button is lost, his mother declares, "Even your grandfather can't make something from nothing." But Jacob proves her wrong in a brilliant, wise, surprise ending.

Above the text, Gilman portrays Joseph's family as they pursue their lives in the shtetl. Grandpa's a tailor; Father's a cobbler; Mama and Grandma take care of making the Sabbath, looking after the children, and shopping up and down the cobbled streets. Joseph grows from baby to school boy; his parents have a daughter; life goes on. Below the text, mice under the floorboards experience similar family expansion, making inventive use of scraps as Joseph's blanket is trimmed and tailored. Verbal patterns in the text allow children to predict what's next while still being surprised. With its rich visual interest and strong story, this is a prime candidate for repeated readings. Highly recommended.

Gilmore, Rachna. Illustr. Alice Priestley. *Lights for Gita*. **1994. 5 to 8.**
Divali, the Hindu festival of lights, is going to be a lot different for Gita
now that she lives in Canada. Gita will miss celebrating with her grandparents in New Delhi; instead she'll have five friends over to her house
in Canada, and her father has already bought the fireworks. The cold
November day turns to rain and then freezing rain, and the phone
rings: one by one her friends say that they can't come. Just after Gita
lights the *diyas* the power goes out, leaving Gita surprised and then
delighted, knowing that she has beaten the darkness.

Gilmore's story sings with authenticity and the pleasure of a child
accepting the challenges that her new country brings, and Priestley's
drawings shine with the light of Divali. Gilmore and Priestley continue
the stories of Gita's adjustment to life in Canada with *Roses for Gita*
and *A Gift for Gita*.

Graham, Georgia. *The Strongest Man This Side of Cremona*. **1998.
4 to 7.**
Even in the scope of endless prairie fields, the distant Rockies dwarfed
by sky, Matthew sees his father as the strongest man this side of the
town of Cremona. But when a freak tornado forces them to flee and
makes wreckage of the family farm, Matthew realizes there's a more
meaningful measure of strength than physical force.

A boy and his dad fix a barbed wire fence; a mom weeds the vegetables; fifty men arrive to help stricken neighbours – Graham gives a
true picture of farming in Alberta. Her photo-realistic paintings show
a field of cabbages so succulent you could pluck them, Holsteins that
look alive. But most impressive is her rendition of a land- and skyscape
so large you have to look twice to see human elements. The endless,
expansive views are a forceful commentary on the little boy's grandiose
sense of his father's power.

Gregory, Nan. Illustr. Ron Lightburn. *How Smudge Came*. **1995.
4 and up.**
Cindy knows when she finds a puppy rummaging through the trash that
it needs a home. She hides the puppy in her room and takes it with her
when she goes to work, cleaning a hospice. At work, she shows
her puppy to a young, nearly blind, dying man, and he says he can see

him as a Smudge in the dark. Cindy, an adult with Down's syndrome, knows the rules in her group home mean she won't be allowed to keep Smudge, but the hospice eventually decides to keep the puppy on her behalf.

Few picture books about adults have much impact on children, but this beautifully told tale of Cindy and Smudge packs a wallop for readers of any age. Lightburn's softly muted, coloured-pencil illustrations catch the power of the story without making it sentimental. Gregory's background as a storyteller allows her to pare the language to the bare essentials: Cindy's vulnerability and compassion – indeed, her mental capacities and incapacities – are never stated, but resonate between the lines.

* Harris, Pamela. *Hot Cold Shy Bold: Looking at Opposites.* **1995. Infant to 7.**
See Concept Books.

Harrison, Ted. *Children of the Yukon.* **1977. 5 to 8.**
Bold, bright solids, heavy outlines, and ribbons of colour across the sky illustrate this series of glimpses into activities and qualities peculiar to the Yukon. Harrison describes the remnants of the Yukon Gold Rush (an abandoned dredge and an annual Gay '90s celebration), and goes on to talk about lesser known features of Yukon life – noisy ravens that don't mind the deep cold, snowshoe racing, fishing, hunting, and the annual muskrat trapping and caribou hunt of Old Crow, inside the Arctic Circle. Drawings as well as text represent the Yukon's multi-ethnic, multiracial population. An informative work of non-fiction, this also reads well as a picture book for attentive, curious listeners.

Harrison, Troon. Illustr. Eugenie Fernandes. *Aaron's Awful Allergies.* **1996. 4 to 6.**
Aaron has a room of beloved furry pets: a dog, a cat with kittens, and multiple guinea pigs. When he starts having headaches and can't breathe properly, he learns he has to get rid of them; he's allergic to some animals. Aaron's broken-hearted, but when his parents give him a fish, he gets used to this different kind of companion, and finds that turtles, snakes, frogs, and butterflies are interesting creatures too.

This won't console a child who has to get rid of a beloved dog because of allergies, but it does show that one can find fascinating creatures as alternative pets. Fernandes's illustrations show a pleasant, unthreatening world, despite Aaron's mournful blue eyes.

Hartry, Nancy. Illustr. Linda Hendry. *Jocelyn and the Ballerina*. 2000. 4 to 7.
Any child who's had a favourite garment can sympathize with Jocelyn. She loves her "ballerina" – a bedraggled blue tutu, striped leggings attached, that she considers appropriate wear for any occasion. She won't let it be washed; she won't let it out of her sight; and she certainly won't wear a scratchy pink dress to her aunt's wedding. Well, she might. If she can fit her ballerina underneath it.

Jocelyn's stubbornness is humorously apparent in her firm jaw, ferocious eyes, and even her broad, rounded nose. Hendry's clear, pale colours and cartoonish characters suit Hartry's funny, succinct text in this tale of a strong-minded child's victory over parental conventions. With its simple vocabulary and repetition, this is a good choice for a parent to read aloud or a child to read on her own.

Heidbreder, Robert. Illustr. Kady MacDonald Denton. *I Wished for a Unicorn*. 2000. 2 to 4.
"I wished for a unicorn. I wished so hard that I found a unicorn in my backyard." Heidbreder's rhyming text and Denton's playful illustrations transform a child's backyard into a fairy kingdom complete with unicorn. The unicorn (which looks very dog-like) leads the child to a magical wood at the end of the yard – then off to a castle with a secret door, a dragon, and an evil wizard. The two storm the castle, conquer the dragon and wizard, and find a treasure map. The day ends with the two falling fast asleep, and the child awakes to discover that the unicorn is gone and the dog is asleep on the lawn.

Heidbreder's cheerful rhyme is perfectly matched by Denton's watercolour illustrations, which are more amusing than frightening even in the dramatic passages where the blue fly-away wizard raises his frightful baton. A strong beat and sound rhyming make this an excellent read-aloud book.

Hendry, Linda. *Hilda Crumm's Hats.* **1994. 4 to 6.**
Hilda Crumm loves junk, but when her neighbours complain that she must clean it up, she has to agree. Kitchen, bedroom, balcony – they're all full of it. But no sooner does Hilda start pulling at things to tidy up, than a cascade of miscellaneous items falls on her head, including a colander, several plastic flowers, and a rubber duckie with a plant pot on *its* head. "Wherever did you get that darling little hat you are wearing?" asks a passerby, and soon Hilda has a booming hat business.

This happy story of artistic resourcefulness (and possibilities for recycling) is full of lighthearted cheer. Hendry's illustrations show a world of good-humoured, multiracial people. Hilda's long nose and freckles, her carefree braids, make her seem like a big kid. Masses of detail allow viewers the chance to pore over this junk collection endlessly.

Highway, Tomson. Illustr. Brian Deines. *Caribou Song/atihko nikamon.* **2001. 4 to 8.**
Joe and Cody live a traditional migratory life with their Cree parents, following the caribou over country so far north that, although there are lakes, islands, rivers, and hills, there are few trees. One day, accordion-playing Joe and dancing Cody are swept up in a river of migrating caribou, much to the anxiety of their parents. But for the boys, being stranded in this flow of running, pounding creatures is an experience of exhilaration; they dance and sing madly, overjoyed and laughing.

Highway's prose gathers power as the caribou run – even when the flow has dwindled to a trickle, one can't forget the breathtaking force of a thousand, two thousand, ten thousand caribou. Deines's impressionistic oil illustrations, in ambers, browns, and mauves, range from aerial views of spring snow and sparse trees to almost pictographic images of the flowing, branching caribou as they race past the boys in a flood. Pictures and words work powerfully together to evoke a truly awesome experience of nature. This depiction of a traditional way of life, with its text in Cree and English, is a rewarding, valuable expression of Cree culture.

* **Highway, Tomson. Illustr. Brian Deines.** *Dragonfly Kites/pimi-hákanisa.* **2002. 4 to 8.**
Joe and Cody of *Caribou Song* (see above) reappear in this story of imaginative play in the wilderness, written in both Cree and English. "There are hundreds of lakes in northern Manitoba," Highway relates. "But no people." Joe and Cody make friends of animals – their dog, Ootsie, a baby Arctic tern, a baby loon – and even of sticks and stones, who take on rich life as John, Bobby, Mary, and Nancy. But the boys' favourite pets are the dragonflies: with a bit of thread, each boy leashes a dragonfly, a "magic kite," and lets it lead him through the wilderness. At sunset, the boys release the dragonflies; that night in their dreams, the dragonflies transport them from wave to wave, island to island, and finally, up into the glories of the northern sunset.

Deines's illustrations, almost pointillist, reflect the huge light and vast solitude of a heartbreakingly beautiful landscape. A warm glow of amber and gold, pink and mauve, suffuses the boys as they play; a final image of one of them, eyes closed in dream as he's transported by the dragonfly, radiates ecstasy. A joyous celebration of childhood freedom, this gives children a glimpse of a remarkable Canadian childhood. Highly recommended.

Hirsch, Ron. Illustr. Pierre Pratt. *No, No, Jack!* **2002. Infant to 4.**
Jack loves hiding things in the closet, then waiting for the family to find them. But the things he hides in the closet are not things a dog should have anything to do with: a wet paintbrush, a diaper, a boot. In the end, Jack finds something in the closet that surprises even him, and satisfies him, too.

This straightforward lift-the-flap book is transformed into something of urbane elegance and humour by Pratt's art. Jack looks exactly like a dog with innovative ideas about storage (tubby body, teeny legs, and insistently curly tail); the balding dad, the sinuous mom, and three kids each appear full of personality. The many portraits of Jack, which the observant child will spot on the walls, offer opportunities for a story behind this story.

Hundal, Nancy. Illustr. Laura Fernandez. *I Heard My Mother Call My Name.* **1990. 4 to 6.**
An unseen narrator hears her (or his?) mother call her name, but lingers in the summer night, noticing all the sounds and fragrances of the transitional moment between dusk and night.

The repetition of "I heard my mother call my name and I know I should go in, but . . ." gives this text its structure. The narrator observes the fireflies "playing hide and seek in the shadows," the sound of good-byes "floating in the dusky air," the "squeak, squeak, squeak" of a neighbour's rocking chair. Although sometimes rather too romantic, this is an atmospheric bedtime story. Fernandez shows the weird blues of post-sunset, the changing shadows cast by streetlight, and houses that glow in the moonlight, capturing that quiet moment.

Hundal, Nancy. Illustr. Brian Deines. *Number 21.* **2001. 4 to 7.**
Young Nancy tells of the joys she and her siblings experience getting to know their father's new commercial dump truck, with its new radio, new horn, chocolate bars in the new glove compartment. But their joy knows no bounds when their parents fill the truck's box with water and it serves double duty as a swimming pool. When Dad lets the water out, though, he washes out the driveway.

Shimmering reds and golds of summer heat fairly radiate from Deines's luxurious oil illustrations, which seem to exude not only visual sensations, but tactile ones as well. Hundal's prose is sometimes overwrought, but this truck book with a difference offers an enriching alternative to most vehicle stories, and the art itself can only expand children's minds.

Further collaborations by Hundal and Deines include *Prairie Summer* (a nostalgic and sometimes cloying reverie on summer visits to the prairies) and *Camping*. Deines's blurred, shimmering art makes both of these memorable.

Hutchins, Hazel. Illustr. Susan Hartung. *One Dark Night.* **2001. 3 to 5.**
One night when Jonathan is staying with his grandparents, he watches a summer storm approach and notices green eyes looking back at him from a tree outside his window. It's a stray cat, and it has something to bring in out of the storm: "one small kitten – soft as whispers, grey as

dawn." As the storm nears, the cat brings her whole family, one by one, to snuggle safely in Jonathan's bathrobe.

Hartung's illustrations of the dark, threatening outside and the safe, protected inside emphasize the emotions of the story: the wild world as opposed to the loving interior. This is an effective, reassuring bedtime story. Jonathan's grandparents take care of him, and he takes care of the cat family.

Jakob, Donna. Illustr. Mireille Levert. *Tiny Toes*. 1995. 3 to 6.

In simple, undemanding verse, Jakob tells what tiny toes can do: "Dirty toes squish through muddy spring puddles" or "Splashy toes paddle in the pool." Levert's delightful illustrations capture the joy of toes on the beach, in the mud, in patent shoes, or in their woolly footsie pyjamas. The audience for this book will recognize at once the joy that tiny toes can have when wriggling to Jakob's verse – verse that will withstand many readings. Levert's illustrations offer many hidden toe surprises.

Jam, Teddy. Illustr. Eric Beddows. *Night Cars*. 1988. Infant to 3.

"There was once a baby who wouldn't go to sleep," begins Jam's lullaby to a baby fascinated with the sounds, lights, and movement on the street at night. Jam's lyrical prose tells of a patient but tired father showing his baby the cars, trucks, taxis, people, and dogs on a snowy night as they gaze down from a window overlooking a city street.

Beddows's richly detailed streetscapes, with deep blues and glowing lights, show the magic of the snow falling at night and the excitement of passing fire trucks and snowploughs. This is a Canadian treasure, a beautiful match between writer and artist, resulting in a perfect book for bedtime reading.

Jam, Teddy. Illustr. Joanne Fitzgerald. *Doctor Kiss Says Yes*. 1991. 3 to 6.

After her parents read her a story and give her one million kisses, fifteen hugs, forty squeezes, and five tickles for good luck, the young Doctor Kiss (a small girl) rides off on her horse to cure the gallant Roderick of his scraped knees. Doctor Kiss has just the cure – one million kisses, fifteen hugs, forty squeezes, and five tickles, as well as her box of pineapple juice with a straw.

Jam celebrates the inventive minds of children: the attentiveness of the child to the precise details of the goodnight ritual are utterly realistic. Fitzgerald's soft, light colours and rounded lines convey an atmosphere of safety and warmth in a story that both kisses goodnight and empowers the dreamer.

Jam, Teddy. Illustr. Ange Zhang. *The Fishing Summer*. 1997. 6 to 9.
Jam celebrates an eight-year-old boy's rite of passage as an Atlantic fisherman in this tale of three uncles, a mother, and a time when "millions of cod were parked at the bottom of the ocean, waiting for lunch." Against his mother's wishes, the boy's three uncles take him out in their eccentric boat (it runs on an old car motor); in their friendly company he does his first jigging, falls into the freezing sea, and comes home full of pride. "He's a natural," one uncle pronounces. The next day, his fisherwoman mother comes too.

Deep turquoises and greens of the sea govern the illustrations, and the boy's uncles, Thomas, Rory, and Jim, have broad, beaming faces that suit their friendly humour. Zhang's bold, dramatic brush gives his art depth and intensity. Despite its nostalgic subject (now there are "lots of words, but no fish," the boy concludes), this tale celebrates family solidarity and the sweet freedom of a child's summer and first hard work.

Jam, Teddy. Illustr. Ange Zhang. *The Stone Boat*. 1999. 6 to 9.
This story is set in a Canadian farming community in the 1920s. In it, a boy recalls a significant interchange with a powerful neighbour. Fishing in the spring floods, the boy sees his neighbour Mr. Richard fall into the creek and almost drown. He manages to rescue him, but later learns that his father owes the man money. One night, the boy ventures out to ask Mr. Richard to forgive the debt; instead, unable to bring himself to speak out, he ends up working side by side with Mr. Richard to clear fieldstones by moonlight.

This tale of the very real tensions of farming debt and dependency has almost mythic overtones. Massive, taciturn Mr. Richard seems as much a force of nature as of finance as he lifts gargantuan boulders into the stone boat, or fishes with two pitchforks "like a vengeful horrible god preparing for a sacrifice." With broad brush, shadowed colour and dramatic light, Zhang makes palpable the man's monumental un-approachability. The boy's anxiety and courage, his acceptance of the mysterious, tacit ways of grown-ups, is patent in Jam's understated text. This is thought-provoking and rewarding, a good story for discussion.

In a third Jam/Zhang collaboration, *The Kid Line*, a son recollects haunting moments he shared with his father watching hockey in Maple Leaf Gardens.

Jennings, Sharon. Illustr. Mireille Levert. *When Jeremiah Found Mrs. Ming*. 1992. 3 to 5.
The friendship between preschooler Jeremiah and Mrs. Ming (seem-ingly a neighbour or perhaps a babysitter) is delightfully told by Jennings in a series of vignettes which involve bored Jeremiah looking for something to do. Each time Jeremiah declares, "I have nothing to do," Mrs. Ming – who has millions, then thousands, then hundreds of things to do – suggests reading him a story; but Jeremiah says he wants to help her work. When all the chores are done, Jeremiah finally asks, "Would you please read me a story?"

Levert emphasizes the very special bond between the small boy and Mrs. Ming in her quiet illustrations to this uncomplicated but amusing tale.

Jennings, Sharon. Illustr. Ruth Ohi. *Into My Mother's Arms*. 2000. 3 to 5.
A young girl tells of a day she shares with her mother. The day is fairly uneventful, beginning with breakfast – cereal for the girl, coffee for mother – and ending with bedtime, mother and daughter curled up together. This appears to be a single-parent family: the mother looks exhausted in the early morning and in the evening; but during their outing to the grocery store and park she is active and involved in her daughter's day. Her arms are truly welcoming.

Jennings's story is slight, but there are few beautiful picture books with single parents. Ohi's illustrations are charming, capturing many small details of childhood. This is a comforting bedtime book, espe-cially useful for single mothers.

Jocelyn, Marthe. *Hannah and the Seven Dresses*. **1999. 2 to 5.**
Collage illustrations rich with texture, pattern, and colour illustrate the story of Hannah, who loves dresses, but can't make up her mind about which dress to wear to her birthday party. Hannah has seven dresses – one for each day of the week – but since her birthday is on Tuesday, and Tuesday's dress doesn't seem like a party dress, she decides to wear them all. This causes great difficulty, and at the end of the story Hannah makes a whole new fashion statement – she appears in trousers!

Young girls will have fun with this nicely surprising, cleanly coloured wardrobe story. The limitless variants in Jocelyn's ingenious collages of fabric, buttons, and more invite close attention.

In a sequel, *Hannah's Collections*, Hannah has to decide how to share her many collections (of buttons, Popsicle sticks, shells, feathers, and more) with her class at school.

Jocelyn, Marthe. *A Day with Nellie*. **2002. 3 to 5.**
Jocelyn's bright, cheerful collage illustrations portray Nellie's day from the moment she wakes up with her blankets scattered about her bed until she jumps back into bed after storytime.

This is a perfect read-aloud book for preschoolers, who will delight in helping Nellie pick out her clothes, find her favourite breakfast foods, and count the items she has on her picnic. They will also sympathize with her pre-naptime moodiness. This is a straightforward account of the day, and Jocelyn's vibrant colours, the various textures of paper and fabric in her collages, give it visual complexity and interest. Plenty of detail encourages children to examine each page carefully. The alphabet, numbers, and different colours are seamlessly incorporated into the story, making the book a good learning tool for preschoolers.

Johnson, Gillian. *My Sister Gracie*. **2000. 3 to 6.**
Many a child longs for a sibling, only to find the real thing a disappointment, usually because the new child's too young to be any fun. Fabio, an only poodle, finds himself with a different problem: not only does he get a sister when he wants a brother, but she's too old! Large and mature, all she wants to do is lie around and cuddle with the family. Fabio tries to take her out and lose her, but when his friends

start poking fun at corpulent, good-natured Gracie, he finds he has brotherly feelings for her after all.

Johnson's illustrations render emotion humorously and expressively. The elegant curlicues of Fabio's topknot fairly quiver with feeling, and his smug, poodly smile reveals his huge complacency. Good-natured, shapeless Gracie is built like a bus or a gigantic sausage: completely amiable and guileless, she's as dear a dog as one's likely to come across. The rhythm and rhyme of this story in verse make it excellent for preschoolers; the emotional dynamics are available in the pictures, perfect for an audience that can't read.

Keens-Douglas, Richardo. Illustr. Marie Lafrance. *La Diablesse and the Baby*. 1994. 4 to 7.
The very stylish La Diablesse always wears a long gown and a wide-brimmed hat when she goes out in the moonlight looking for babies to steal. Her trademark – one human foot, one cow foot – is never revealed. One stormy night, when she arrives at a country house looking for shelter and offers to lull the baby, a clever grandmother is suspicious and doesn't let her hold the crying child. In the morning all is revealed: the footprints left behind show that the visitor was indeed La Diablesse.

This frightening character comes from the rich folk tradition of the Caribbean. Keens-Douglas tells the story as though it were his own grandmother who saved him from being carried off.

* Khalsa, Dayal Kaur. *Tales of a Gambling Grandma*. 1986. 4 and up.
In this story, the girl May remembers tales of her Russian grandma's outrageous doings, but most importantly she recalls her grandma's career as a gambler. Grandma played games with everyone, from card sharks to the Sunshine Ladies Club, in her backyard in Brooklyn. And besides taking May to Coney Island, exotic Chinese restaurants, and movies, she taught her how to play cards. The love between the grandma and granddaughter is eloquently shown in both words and pictures, and Grandma's death at the end of the story is heartbreaking.

Khalsa's bright folk-art illustrations show the delight of May and her grandma sharing each other's company. The exaggerations within the tales are also brilliantly depicted – Grandma is seen sitting in a bathtub full of orange juice while travelling on a train. The final illustration of May hugging and smelling her grandma's great big dresses lets the reader feel the reality of Grandma's death. Both funny and touching, this makes a good read for children and adults. Highly recommended.

Khalsa, Dayal Kaur. *I Want a Dog*. 1987. 3 to 7.
May has a burning desire to have a dog, but none of her tactics to convince her parents work. At last she resorts to escorting her roller skate around on a leash, taking care of it with all the tenderness and assiduity she would shower on a real dog. She walks it daily, ties it up outside when she goes into a "no dogs" place, and searches for it diligently when it's carried off. At last her parents agree that she's responsible enough to have her own dog – but this story is more about her marvellous coping than her triumph.

The lovingly detailed interiors and exteriors of May's 1960s house and neighbourhood make this a book to pore over. Khalsa's typical brilliant colours echo the depth of May's passion and imagination; her tight, concise prose doesn't waste a word. A triumphant, compassionate story for any child who has a longstanding, unfulfilled desire – especially for a dog.

Khalsa explores childhood longing and the power of the imagination with similar haunting effect in *Cowboy Dreams* and *The Snow Cat*.

* Khalsa, Dayal Kaur. *Sleepers*. 1988. 2 to 4.
A stubborn little girl's persistence about bedtime governs this amusing bedtime story – and it's resolved in a way that will satisfy both children and parents. "My father sleeps on the living room couch; my mom in a hammock that swings. / Uncle Teddy sleeps in the bathtub and he snores as loud as he sings. / But I never sleep," is the little girl's refrain. Khalsa rhymes her way through the sleeping habits of the extended family, various folk, and animals, all the while celebrating the child's independence in an area where she has control. Finally the child makes a very small amendment to her persistent declaration as she dozes off counting sheep.

Khalsa's bright paintings, framed by the margins of coloured pages (yellow, purple, blue, green), give this the look of a quilt – appropriately enough. Simple lines, solid colours, and a relatively flat perspective add to this effect. One of Canada's best bedtime books. Highly recommended.

Khalsa, Dayal Kaur. *How Pizza Came to Our Town.* **1989. 4 to 7.**
Mrs. Pelligrino arrives from Italy for a visit, but is strangely sad for much of the summer. It's only when the girls buy the ingredients for the mysterious "pizza" she is always talking about that she cheerfully unveils her rolling pin and makes a delicious pizza for everyone, stating, "Ah, pizza! Is good, no?"

Khalsa's customary naïve style of painstakingly detailed art captures the child's view of the story. The historical setting of the tale – who hasn't heard of pizza by now? – is revealed in the details of the pictures. Khalsa shows the clothing, cars, and even the kitchen appliances of the American 1950s. May and Grandma, from *Tales of a Gambling Grandma* (see above), make an appearance in this story.

Khan, Rukhsana. Illustr. Ronald Himler. *The Roses in My Carpets.* **1998. 5 to 8.**
A sponsored refugee boy tells the story of his life in the carpets he makes: "White for the shroud we wrapped my father's body in, black for the night that cloaks us from enemy eyes. Green is the colour of life. Blue is the sky. . . . Red is my favourite. Red is the colour of the blood of martyrs. But it is also the colour of roses." The difficult and tragic life of the young Muslim Afghani boy is revealed as he tells of his family's past while they struggle through life in the refugee camp. The bleakness of the story is softened by the hope symbolized in the roses he weaves in his carpets. Himler's illustrations show the horrors of bombing, the dryness of the parched earth as well as the bright roses in the carpets. The book is most useful for classroom discussions.

King, Thomas. Illustr. William Kent Monkman. *A Coyote Columbus Story.* **1992. 4 to 8.**
The traditional First Nations trickster, Coyote, stars in this bittersweet fable of how the Europeans came to exploit North America.

Coyote's the one who made rainbows, flowers, prune juice, afternoon naps, and television commercials. But she loves best to play ball, so she dances and thinks up creatures to play with her. The beavers, turtles, moose, and humans have different ideas of fun, however, so Coyote absentmindedly thinks up Christopher Columbus and his friends. They don't want to play ball; instead they decide to take and sell humans. "I'll fix this," Coyote promises; but in her next moment of absentmindedness, she dances up Jacques Cartier.

Coyote's like a bumptious, bossy kid, both winsome and dangerously distractible. King conveys vividly the atmosphere of play that surrounds the beginning of the creatures, so that the Columbus company's penchant for quantification and acquisition stands in sharp contrast. A colloquial tone and the mixture of traditional themes with modern materialism make this amusing and thought-provoking. Monkman's outlandish, woodcut-like illustrations, predominantly in hot pink, underscore the mad lunacy of both Coyote and the explorers.

For more Coyote adventures, see also King's *Coyote Sings to the Moon* (Traditional Tales).

Konzak, Burt. Illustr. Johnny Wales. *Noguchi the Samurai*. 1994. 4 to 7.
The bully Noguchi terrorizes his fellow passengers on a ferry off the coast of Japan, forcing those on board to seek help from Michihara, an elderly samurai. Michihara knows that he can't be defeated, because he will not fight. He defeats Noguchi by wit rather than physical strength, tricking the bully by inviting him to settle their quarrel on an uninhabited island. When the boat arrives at the island, Noguchi, anxious to fight, leaps from the bow; Michihara stays aboard and pushes the boat out to sea with a bamboo pole. Thus he abandons Noguchi on the island and proves that wits are the best weapons of all.

Konzak has pared this story down to its crucial elements: his prose is simple and elegant. The watercolour illustrations by Wales reflect the Japanese background of the story, but he combines this with a Western sense of humour in his depiction of Noguchi. Pale blues in water and sky are in striking contrast to Noguchi's dark temper. This story can provide an excellent entry into a discussion of bullying. It and other similar stories have been used for centuries to help students understand martial arts.

Kovalski, Maryann. *Brenda and Edward*. 1984. 3 to 5.
Brenda and Edward are urbane city dogs living in a comfortable heated cardboard box behind a French restaurant. Their life together ends when Brenda is nearly killed by a car and is rescued by its remorseful driver. Edward is left all alone. Years pass before the driver of the car takes it to the garage where Edward is employed; when he recognizes Brenda's scent he refuses to leave the car. A touching reunion results at the grand mansion where Brenda now resides.

Kovalski's art in pale shades, her rounded figures and comfortable 1950s environment, is well suited to the sweetness and warmth of this doggy love story. The images of the city, with subway cars and steaming sewer grates, evokes a place and time in which it seems possible for dogs to have jobs and live in cardboard boxes with fireplaces. The book's charm comes from the thoughtful illustrations of Brenda and Edward, sitting together sharing tea, reading the paper together, and finally dancing together beside the fire hydrant on the back cover.

Kovalski, Maryann. *The Wheels on the Bus*. 1987. 3 to 7.
Jenny, Joanna, and Grandma go shopping for winter coats; waiting for the bus they get bored, and Grandma leads them in a spirited rendition of "The Wheels on the Bus." The singers get so caught up in their singing that – guess what? They miss the bus!

Most of this story is Kovalski's lively visual interpretation of the events of the song (the wipers go swish, the people get on and off, the driver toots, etc.). An accordion player and his monkey cause a ruckus; a businessman with a bouquet of roses loses his paper; squalling babies open their mouths as wide as caverns. Most amusing is Grandma's large enthusiasm.

Kovalski pursues the adventures of Jenny, Joanna, and Grandma in ***Jingle Bells***, when Grandma takes the girls to Manhattan and they go for a carriage ride in the snow in Central Park. Singing "Jingle Bells" with gusto, they don't notice when their driver falls out of the carriage. Kovalski's illustrations show that all three "girls" have loads of personality; this is funny, interesting, and an excellent early reader. The equally imaginative sequel is the highly recommended early reader ***Rain, Rain*** (*see* Books for Beginning Readers).

Kovalski, Maryann. *Omar on Ice*. 1999. 3 to 7.
Omar the bear knows that when he grows up he wants to be an artist. Unfortunately, the teacher mistakes his picture of his mother for a picture of a rock; indeed, none of his pictures seem to be as good as those of his classmates. Disheartened, Omar decides that maybe he's not an artist after all. At recess, however, he finds his true medium: he unknowingly creates masterpieces on the ice as he skates skilfully around the rink.

Kovalski's drawings show both the humour and the pathos of Omar's situation. Her classroom scenes are full of fun – the teacher, a large bear in open-toed shoes and dangling earrings, smirks at Omar's art. Omar on ice is exuberant: his joy and delight are infectious. Kovalski's direct prose and choice of a limited vocabulary make this an excellent story for emergent readers.

Kurelek, William. *A Prairie Boy's Winter*. 1973. 5 and up.
In a series of paintings, internationally acclaimed artist William Kurelek documents the winter of a boy on a prairie farm in the 1940s, from the crows' departure before the first snowfall, through the deepest cold, and up until the return of the first crow. Looking after the animals, hauling firewood, skating on a bog ditch – all these activities are represented and more. But this collection is most remarkable for the character and atmosphere exuded by such things as the sight of the back of a milk truck heading down a ploughed road, the careless grace of a boy striding out on his skates, and, always, the expansive, multi-hued whites of the prairie's flat landscape.

In the few paragraphs that accompany each picture, Kurelek recollects, like a grandfather to his grandchild, the features of a boy's winter on the prairie. This doesn't read as a conventional story – its only structure is the turn of the season – but even a very young child will find plenty of interest in the pictures. A good book for an adult to share in a quiet moment, and a lovely preservation of a uniquely Canadian experience. A sequel, *A Prairie Boy's Summer*, is also available.

Kusugak, Michael Arvaarluk. Illustr. Vladyana Krykorka. *Baseball Bats for Christmas.* **1990. 4 to 8.**
Growing up in Repulse Bay in the 1950s, Arvaarluk and his friends are used to a land "as bald as the belly of a dog with puppies." There are no "standing-ups," otherwise known as trees, so it's hard to find a stick to play baseball when you want to. When a pilot delivers a freight of six spindly trees, the children know just what to do with them – one by one, the trees supply baseball bats throughout the summer and spring.

This has the appealing air of personal anecdote and it's full of inter-esting detail about life in Repulse Bay in the 1950s – particularly about Christmas celebrations and children's play. Krykorka's pinks and turquoises reveal a northern sky that plays with colour; her beaming children and omnipresent puppies show rollicking fun adapted to a singular landscape.

Kusugak, Michael Arvaarluk. Illustr. Vladyana Krykorka. *Northern Lights: The Soccer Trails.* **1993. 4 to 8.**
Kataujaq mourns the loss of her mother. When her grandmother explains that the northern lights, or "Soccer Trails," are the spirits of the beloved dead enjoying themselves in the heavens, Kataujaq finds some consolation. Krykorka's vision of the northern lights is hauntingly real; photographs of decorative beading from an Inuit parka ornament the pages of text.

Further collaborations of Kusugak and Krykorka can be found in *Hide and Sneak* and *A Promise Is a Promise*, the latter written in con-junction with Robert Munsch. Both of these purely fictional tales play on legendary Inuit creatures, the Ijiraq and the Qallupilluq.

* Kusugak, Michael Arvaarluk. Illustr. Vladyana Krykorka. *Arctic Stories.* **1998. 40 pages. 5 to 9.**
Three stories about fictional Agatha recall Kusugak's experiences as a child in Repulse Bay in the 1950s. Each focuses on a real incident: the day an airship full of scientists passed over the village, scaring polar bears and humans alike; the "ugly bird" raven who follows Agatha's grandmother around; and a priest's memorable skating accident at a residential school in Chesterfield Inlet. The stories are charming and

rich with detail, telling of life as Kusugak lived it as a child, from sleeping with boots in the bed, to the hundreds of birds that appeared in summer. The vision of plump Father Favard showing off his skating skills is unforgettable: "He spun like a top, his black robes puffed up all around him, his black cross, with Jesus nailed to it, swinging around him." Reference to Inuktitut is both informative and entertaining – the Inuit word for "nurses" means "pretending-to-be-nuns."

Krykorka's watercolours, with finely drawn creatures against washes of blues, greens, and white, or the duns and browns of tundra, give the feeling of a distinctive place. This collaboration, with its direct, personal voice and attractive art, is an invaluable contribution to Canadian books for children. Highly recommended.

Ladner, Cobi. Illustr. Lisa Smith. *Why Is an Orange Called an Orange?* **2002. 3 to 6.**
The English language is mysterious even to adults who have been using it for a long time. Ladner here draws attention to one of its puzzling aspects by asking the simple question of the title. No other fruit is named only for its colour – raspberries, blueberries, lemons, and more come under scrutiny. The answer to the question is nicely arbitrary, just as English itself seems: "It's simple really, there's no better word! For something sweet and round and kissed by the sun, just like I kiss you!"

Smith's watercolour illustrations have the clean, fresh sweetness of the fruit they depict; the textured, succulent glow of the orange, the perfect rounds of a handful of blueberries, and the juicy, ruby shine of a raspberry tart make this a book that's literally mouth-watering. Text pages show miniatures of mother and child engaged in activities with each fruit – pushing a grocery cart together, carrying a raspberry tart to the oven – and provide human interest for young viewers. A sweet and succinct picture book that introduces children to an important question: Why do we use the words we use?

Laurence, Margaret. Illustr. Muriel Wood. *The Olden Days Coat.* **1979/2001. 8 to 10.**
Fed up with being at Gran's house for Christmas, Sal explores an old trunk and finds there an "olden days" child's coat that takes her back in

time. In the past she meets up with friendly Sarah, who shows her a beautiful Christmas present – a finely crafted wooden butterfly. When Sal gets rid of the coat and returns to her own time, Gran gives Sal that same butterfly as an early Christmas gift.

Laurence's quiet story focuses on the moment Sal understands that inside her Gran lives a girl who once tamed birds, drove a team of horses, and was allowed to drive – alone! – in a cutter. Wood's earlier illustrations for the story are spare and haunting, with subtle colours and lines that suggest the magic of Sal's time travel. Her illustrations in the 2001 edition are more obvious: lavish with colour, they show the rich indigo of the coat, the bright reds and garish lights of Christmas. A cosy, homey story.

Lawson, Julie. Illustr. Martin Springett. *Too Many Suns*. 1996. 4 to 7.
In this boldly illustrated story, Lawson weaves together a number of sun-god myths from the Chinese tradition. There are ten suns and they each take turns shining on the world, but when they decide to shine all at once, the Immortal Archer Yi is sent to shoot them down. On the farm that is baking under the heat of the many suns, the youngest of ten brothers pleads with Yi to save one sun.

Springett's forceful illustrations show heavily outlined figures shaded in with soft, luminous colours, giving this the appearance of a power-ful and beautiful comic book. A border of suns and an illustrative ribbon about one inch wide runs beneath the text, offering glimpses into various vistas. An elegant volume.

Lawson, Julie. Illustr. Paul Mombourquette. *Emma and the Silk Train*. 1997. 4 to 7.
In the first half of the twentieth century, high speed "silkers" carried bales of silk, brought by ship from the Orient, and transported them from Vancouver to New York. Lawson's story focuses on a famous "Million-Dollar Wreck," when a silk train derailed near the Fraser Canyon, in British Columbia, and its cargo ended up in the Fraser River.

Five-year-old Emma loves watching the trains. When the derail-ment happens and the locals are salvaging silk from the river, she's intent on doing a little "silk fishing" herself. Trying to retrieve a length of the cloth, she's carried away by the current and lands up on an island. She flags passing trains, a silker among them, with her colourful banner; when her parents show up, she learns that the high-speed silker, which never stops, slowed down long enough to pass a message on to her father.

Ably told by Lawson, this is an exciting story, and Mombourquette's double-page illustrations give a vivid sense of place and drama. With its glimpse into Canada's past, this is an interesting choice for children who like train stories.

Lawson, Julie. Illustr. Sheena Lott. *Midnight in the Mountains*. 1998. 3 to 7.
Everyone is asleep except a young girl sitting by a fire in a mountain cabin. Listening to the muffled sounds of the snowy night, she remembers the glories of her first day in the mountains. The crisp cold, the feathery snow, huskies pulling the dogsled, and her mother's worries about frostbite are just a few of the memories interrupted by faraway night sounds.

Lawson's spare text conjures the unique joy that bright sun and cold, cold snow can bring; the quiet of the girl's nighttime perceptions contrasts with the quicker rhythm of her memories of the day. Lott's pale watercolours show the quiet blues of snow and shadows or the brilliant shine of sun on snow. One feels the excitement and awe of being in snowy mountains day or night. A quiet, thoughtful account of a wonderful day in the mountains.

A further collaboration between Lawson and Lott, *A Morning to Polish and Keep*, considers the beauties of a morning on the sea near British Columbia's Gulf Islands.

Lawson, Julie. Illustr. Brian Deines. *Bear on the Train*. 1999. 3 to 6.
"One fall day, deep in the mountains, Bear smelled grain." That grain is in a hopper on a westbound train, and Bear crawls in, makes a good meal, and goes to sleep. Only Jeffrey sees him. "Hey, Bear! Get off the train!" he shouts, but the train draws away, and the hibernating bear begins his winter of shuttling back and forth between Alberta and Vancouver along the railway line. Until spring comes . . .

With a nicely repetitive, succinct text and a focus on trains and bears, this is a good choice for preschoolers. It offers a quintessentially Canadian view: Deines's wide, impressionistic illustrations, stippled with blues, pinks, and gold, radiate a special, lonely train-whistle atmosphere. A western sky over the Rocky Mountain foothills, a tree-spiked valley marked by rails, even the oily mystery of the dark, powerful train evoke a uniquely Western Canadian experience.

Lee, Dennis. Illustr. Gillian Johnson. *The Cat and the Wizard*. 2001. 3 to 6.
When an indigent wizard meets up with an oh-so-stylish but lonesome cat residing in Toronto's Casa Loma, he finds his magical arts have an audience after all. He becomes a permanent guest at a feast of wine, steak, turnips, Shreddies, and beer, and both he and the cat are deeply content with the arrangement.

Lee's impeccable rhythm and linguistic energy are at work here, and Johnson brings out the fine points of his lyrical silliness. The wizard's pointed shoes tremble with eagerness, just as his pointed nose rises to conjure "sparklers and flautists and butterflies' wings"; the cat entertains with sinuous elegance, and urbane tuna fish patrol the hall. Rollicking nonsense.

Lemieux, Michèle. *What's That Noise?* Trans. from German. 1989. 3 to 7.
"A big brown bear woke from a deep sleep. I heard a noise, he thought, a funny little noise . . ." The bear wanders through the countryside, carefully listening to all the sounds he comes across. The noise is not the little birds in their nest or the woodcutters or the water wheel of the old mill. He asks the tree, the fish, and the owl for help, but they can't identify the noise. Only after he has eaten his fill of stolen tomatoes and honey and is comfortable in his den, does he realize that it is his beating heart he hears.

Lemieux's hibernation tale is beautifully told. Her watercolour landscapes reflect the passing of summer. When the bear's beating heart awakens him the following spring, his joyous dance in the forest, among shafts of sunlight that pour through the trees, evokes spring's magic.

*Lemieux, Michèle. *Stormy Night*. Trans. from German. 1999. 240 pages. 9 and up.
See Novels, 7 to 12.

Lesynski, Loris. *Boy Soup, or When Giant Caught Cold*. 1996. 4 to 7.
After consulting his *Giant's Home Medical Guide*, Giant knows that, in order to cure his illness, he needs to make Boy Soup. "One buttery boy, or better – a group! A half-dozen lads would make wonderful soup!" he cries, and he does catch five boys and, mistakenly, one girl, Kate. Kate cleverly erases his recipe (with running shoes) and announces that the recipe says the soup must be made *by* boys, not *of* boys. Together Kate and the boys make a gruesome glop for the Giant's recovery.

Lesynski's rhyming story is a pleasure to read aloud; anyone can pick up the rhythm immediately, making it ideal for storytimes. Her cartoon illustrations are just garish enough for this tale, and most effective when illustrating truly gross elements such as the horrific soup, "like skunk in a pot," that the children make.

Lesynski, Loris. *Catmagic*. 1998. 4 to 7.
"The Witches' Retirement Home has a room!" / said Arabelle Witch to the cat on her broom . . ." But Izzy the cat starts getting in the way of the witches in the Retirement Home, until they work their magic and give Izzy the upside-down run of the house. Lesynski's lively verse and comic illustrations combine to make this an entertaining, silly romp.

Further rhyming picture-book titles by Lesynski include *Ogre Fun*, *Night School*, and *Rocksy*, each of which has the same peppy rhythm and lighthearted humour. *Night School*, the tale of a boy who won't sleep, and so is sent to a bizarre all-night school, is particularly – and eccentrically – instructive for wakeful children.

Levert, Mireille. *Rose by Night*. Trans. from French. 1998. 3 to 5.
Waking in the middle of night, Rose needs to venture down the hall to the bathroom, but she imagines witches, vampires, and ogres lying in wait for her. She arms herself with her teddy bear, a wooden spoon, and a magic spell – "I am . . . Rose . . . Redberry / I am mighty . . . and tall / And I'm not scared . . . At all" – thus overcoming each of the ghouls in her way.

Levert's rhyming text suggests anxiety and suspense, but her illustrations of the common nighttime trip to the bathroom are highly stylized and take much of the fear out of the story. The trepidation on Rose's face is replaced with delight when she finally reaches the well-lit bathroom and, sitting on the toilet, says, "How wonderful, I can pee."

Lewis, Kim. *Just Like Floss*. 1998. 3 to 6.
When border collie Floss has pups, the children can't decide which one to keep – Bess or Nell, Cap, Jack, or little Sam. But when Sam wanders off on his own and finds himself surrounded by sheep with hard, black heads and horns, he shows that he's already skilled as a herder, just like his mother, Floss.

Lewis's quiet story combines the joy of the children's engagement with the pups and the practical qualities required of a working dog. Her full-page coloured-pencil illustrations depict, with soft lines and colours, the sights of a Yorkshire sheep farm, from the green Wellington boots of the children to the dry-wall fences and low hills of the moors. The downy pups make this irresistible to any dog-loving preschooler – their postures and expressions are absolutely convincing.

Other titles written and illustrated by Lewis include *First Snow*, *Friends*, *One Summer Day*, *Emma's Lamb*, and *Little Baa* (see below).

Lewis, Kim. *Little Baa*. 2001. 3 to 6.
On a Yorkshire sheep farm, Little Baa bounces and skips all over the fields, enjoying the spring air. When he's tired, he snuggles down in a hollow and sleeps soundly. But Ma is worried when she can't find her lamb: she looks among the lambs and ewes and wanders until the sun starts to set. Happily, border collie Floss finds Little Baa, and soon he and his mother are reunited.

Lewis's expansive coloured-pencil illustrations seem to open out the vistas of this Yorkshire sheep farm, soft with the colours of spring. Her sheep and lambs are so carefully observed that it's like meeting the real thing. She ascribes language to Little Baa's mother, but it's well within the realm of authentic sheep communication, so the realism of the story and pictures is maintained. The joy of mother-and-lamb reunion is universal.

Little, Jean, and Maggie de Vries. Illustr. Phoebe Gilman. *Once Upon a Golden Apple.* **1991. 4 to 7.**

A father reading a story to his children plays on their expectations by purposefully scrambling and mis-telling familiar tales. "Once upon a . . . golden apple (No! cried the girl) . . . once upon a magic pebble (No! cry the children)" goes this call-and-response tale. Does Snow White live with the Three Bears? Does a frog, once kissed, turn into a pumpkin? Finally the children steer their father successfully through to a traditional fairy-tale ending.

Children familiar with the stories to which this alludes will find the tale very amusing (all the better, because it's the children here who are empowered with superior knowledge); those who aren't familiar will learn some useful fairy-tale conventions. Gilman's frieze-like illustrations depict every mis-situation the father suggests, with the two children cast as main characters. A border of ornamental vine suggests medieval manuscript illumination.

Little, Jean. Illustr. Johnny Wales. *Gruntle Piggle Takes Off.* **1996. 4 to 7.**

Gruntle can't understand why her mother is offended by Grampa Bacon. "He won't wear clothes or read books and he's a tease," Mother says, but Gruntle has to find out for herself. She dons her rollerblades and zooms away from Pigs Digs, the family's posh apartment, to see what life's like at Grampa's farm at Swine Corners. Nude, rude animals and slops and manure turn out to be more disgusting than she'd guessed – but she figures out Grampa's secret (he can't read) and vows to return and teach him to love books.

This is enjoyable fun, with its strong-minded protagonist and corny pig jokes (Father is a professor of Pig Latin; Gruntle has a "kiddy bank"). Wales's watercolours show a highly cultured pig family in the lap of literacy; Little's jokes carry through to book titles, posters, and interior decor. Wales evokes a whole, charming piggy world – Pigopolis.

Littlechild, George. *This Land Is My Land.* **1993. 7 to 10.**

Littlechild, an acclaimed artist of the Plains Cree, brings together a series of his pictures here in order to discuss and illustrate the difficult history of his own people since the arrival of the Europeans in North America. He incorporates photographs of his own grandparents and great-grandparents (the earliest of which was born in 1858) into works of vivid collage, which display symbolically historical moments and emotions that are part of his own makeup – and by extension, that of the dispossessed First Peoples in general. Beadwork, feathers, shells, sequins, and glittering gold are embedded in paint of brilliant colour – fuchsia, turquoise, scarlet. Each work is interpreted in a short accompanying text, in which Littlechild conveys information about relevant religious or historical understanding in a candid, and even intimate, voice. An excellent, revealing accompaniment to any discussion of Aboriginal/European relations, whether of the past or the present, this book also introduces children to the playful, almost allegorical, style of Littlechild's art.

London, Jonathan. Illustr. Gilles Pelletier. *The Sugaring-Off Party*. 1995. 4 to 8.
A charming old grandmère tells "mon petit chou" the story of her childhood visits to the annual sugaring-off party at Tante Loulou's sugar bush, a sugar-maple forest. With a few words and phrases in French to give a Québecois flavour to the story, London captures the joy and delight of the girl going to the farmhouse, meeting the extended family, and participating in the ritual party to celebrate spring's arrival after a long, cold winter. London describes the process of making maple sugar; he tells too of the food, games, songs, and dances of the day. Pelletier, with lively, colourful illustrations in naïve folk-art style, shows the joy of the busy party.

Lucas, Berny. Illustr. Russ Willms. *Brewster Rooster*. 1993. 3 to 6.
Young Brewster Rooster has just learned to crow and spends his days strutting around the farm showing off his new tail feathers and practising his cock-a-doodle-doo. The farmer is pleased at first, but when Brewster practises all through the night, he's ready to turn him into soup. Brewster redeems himself the next night when he crows and warns the farmer of an impending flood.

This nicely silly and ultimately heartwarming tale of a growing rooster is illustrated with highly stylized art: Willms uses angular shapes, shifting perspectives, and rust, teal, and jade colours to show off the zaniness of the story. Willms's Brewster is enormously expressive – pride, fear, resignation, and great joy transform him by turns.

Lunn, Janet. Illustr. Kim LaFave. *Amos's Sweater.* **1988. 4 to 7.**
Amos the sheep is old and he's cold and he's tired of giving away all his wool. But Aunt Hattie goes ahead and shears him anyway, and spins and knits his wool into a sweater for Uncle Henry. Amos wants that wool back, and finally manages, after a great struggle and many mended holes, to climb into the sweater and communicate what he wants Aunt Hattie to know: he's old and he's cold and he's tired of giving away all his wool!

LaFave's wrinkly, squiggly lines show Amos's great agitation: his eyes positively bug out of his shaven head with outrage – until he finally dreams benignly in the field, comfortably warm in his colourful pullover. An amusing story of triumph through persistence.

Lunn, Janet. Illustr. Brian Deines. *Charlotte.* **1998. 7 to 10.**
In 1783, Charlotte Haines, the ten-year-old daughter of an American rebel, wants to say goodbye to her best friends and cousins who are the daughters of Loyalists fleeing their New York home. Her Patriot father forbids her to see them, and when he discovers that she has disobeyed him, she is disowned and has to flee to Canada with her uncle and his family.

Lunn's uncompromising account of this true story shows how one child suffered the effects of war over two hundred years ago. Telling historical details (Charlotte's thin kid slippers, the young slave girl carrying her lunch, and Charlotte's mother's inability to go against her husband) give readers an accurate, unromantic sense of the past. Deines's striking cover art – a picture of Charlotte running through a puddle – is perhaps the strongest of his uneven and sometimes murky illustrations. This story makes for rich classroom discussion.

Lunn, Janet. Illustr. Lindsay Grater. *One Hundred Shining Candles.* **1990. 6 to 8.**
The preparations for Christmas in 1800 are meagre, until Lucy hears the schoolmaster describe a Christmas on which a hundred candles

were lit for the celebration. In his words, "It was elegant! Most elegant!" Lucy enlists her young brother Dan to help her make the hundred candles to surprise their parents on Christmas, but the task is larger than they had imagined, and their supplies are limited. Lucy gives up the red dye that was meant for her dress, and Dan gives up his precious penny, in order to make beautiful red candles. When Christmas comes and their five – not one hundred – mottled candles are lit, their sick mother's eyes glow with delight.

This Christmas story of children planning and making something special is told with love by an expert in historical fiction. Grater's illustrations, in watercolours and pencil, capture the children's delight, frustration, and joy on Christmas morning.

Lunn, Janet. Illustr. Kady MacDonald Denton. *The Umbrella Party*. 1998. 4 to 7.

Birthday girl Christie knows her own mind, and that is that she loves umbrellas. She hopes *all* her presents will be umbrellas – and they are! – from the paper one as tiny as a matchstick, up to the beach one, as big as a party. Her guests are a bit bored with all the umbrellas, but when the beach party is suddenly deluged with rain, they realize that so many umbrellas can come in handy. They all crawl underneath and eat squashed sandwiches and cake.

Another triumph for independent-mindedness, Lunn's story is true to the certainty with which young children know their desires. The real charm in this book comes through Denton's illustrations, though. Her children offer a whole parade of sly personalities; even the adjunct people on the beach seem to be distinct, full characters. Pellucid watercolours give the feeling of a lovely summer day.

Luppens, Michel. Illustr. Philippe Béha. *What Do the Fairies Do with All Those Teeth?* Trans. from French. 1989. 4 to 7.

Losing your first tooth is an important event, and Luppens wonders what the fairies do with the teeth. He doesn't give any answers; he just offers a few ideas. Do they string them into necklaces, transform them into maracas, or perhaps use them for sets of false teeth? The possibilities are humorous and numerous and the story ends with the question: "What if they visit the animals too?"

Translated from the French, this work eschews the conventional narrative plot and instead engages in an open-ended conversation with the reader. Luppens has great fun with the idea of fairies with teeth, but it is Béha who really shines in this undertaking. His fairies, with their pointed hats and unruly long hair, look like little witches and seem to take great delight in whatever they're doing. Don't look for any answers here, just a few laughs.

MacLeod, Elizabeth. Illustr. Louise Phillips. *I Heard a Little Baa*. 1998. Infant to 3.
This bouncy, effective, lift-the-flap book invites children to connect rhyme, animal sounds, and part of a creature's body in order to predict who's hiding behind the flap. "I heard a little growl; I peeked behind a chair. First I saw a shaggy paw . . . [lift the flap] And then I saw a bear!" This deceptively simple fun is enhanced by Phillips's loose, energetic lines, bright colours (no white here), and exuberantly expressive animals.

Manson, Ainslie. Illustr. Ann Blades. *A Dog Came Too*. 1992. 6 and up.
Alexander Mackenzie was the first European to cross North America by land and reach the Pacific Ocean. The explorer wrote in his journals about his big brown dog, and inspired by this, Manson tells a captivating story of Mackenzie's travel across the country with "our dog." The dog is not a pet and doesn't even have a name; it's a working dog and accompanies the explorers, running beside the canoe and guarding their campsites at night. There's real tension in the story when the dog is left behind and almost loses the explorers.

Blades's art, in soft watercolours, shows the adventure of the story and the difficulties of the journey, in a style more sophisticated than that in some of her other works. Children get a sense of Canadian history through this intriguing and little known dog story.

Manson, Ainslie. Illustr. Karen Reczuch. *Just Like New*. 1995. 4 to 7.
Many children in England won't be receiving Christmas presents because of the Second World War, so, in Sally's church, children are asked to bring a present that is "just like new," so it can be sent across

the ocean. Sally has a dilemma: she knows that her favourite doll is the only toy she has that looks new, but she loves Ann-Marie, with her opening and closing eyes and her red plaid taffeta skirt, and hates to send her away.

Reczuch's illustrations bring out the story's warmth, and the beauty of the Canadian fall is played against Sally's apprehension and disappointment in sending away her favourite doll. The English scenes are shown in black and white until the moment Ann-Marie is unwrapped and colour comes to her new English owner on Christmas. A heartwarming, sentimental story, but one that rings true and brings a message of sharing in today's acquisitive society.

Masurel, Claire. Illustr. Kady MacDonald Denton. *Two Homes*. 2001. 3 to 7.
Masurel's text is all the more potent for being simple and clear in this reassuring book for young children who have divorced parents. "This is Daddy," reads the left-hand page; "this is Mommy," reads the right. "Daddy lives here" is followed by "Mommy lives there." The child points out her room, chair, toothbrush, kitchen, and so on, first at Daddy's place, then at Mommy's. This introduction to the two homes builds towards a final, emphatic message: "I love Daddy. I love Mommy. No matter where I am." The reassuring response: "We love you wherever *we* are. And we love you wherever *you* are."

Denton's cheerful, nursery-bright illustrations emphasize the stability of the love this child feels from both parents, despite their separation. Dad's house near the sea and Mom's apartment in the city are depicted in loving detail that shows the richness of the life that goes on in both, from the child's drawings on the walls to the wallpaper in the bathrooms. And, with her pointy nose and often sticking-out hair, this girl comes across as a real, whole person. Masurel's text is blunt and honest, making this one of the better books on the topic for this age.

McFarlane, Sheryl. Illustr. Sheena Lott. *Jessie's Island*. 1992. 4 to 7.
Jessie gets a letter in which her cousin extols the diversions of the city and pities Jessie for her boring life on one of British Columbia's Gulf Islands. Jessie writes back to give him a glimpse of all the outdoor diversions and beauties that are part of her everyday life.

McFarlane merely suggests in simple prose the long list of joys to be had in this paradisaical environment: spotting killer whales, seeing an otter family in the kelp, investigating marine life at low tide. The understatement of the prose is well matched by Lott's watercolours, which show not only the precise appearance of fauna and flora, but emanate the reflected light of sky and water, the densities and intensities of British Columbia's coastal blues. An excellent evocation of place.

The Moonsnail's Song, a further collaboration by McFarlane and Lott, also explores the natural beauties of British Columbia's Gulf Islands.

McFarlane, Sheryl. Illustr. Sheena Lott. *Going to the Fair*. 1996. 3 to 6.
Erin's trip to the fair is special, because she hopes to win first prize for her pumpkin. Her day passes quickly: she eats cotton candy with her friends, looks at antique farm machinery, and sees her friends show their livestock with the 4-H Club. Erin isn't really sure she wants to know how her pumpkin did, but is thrilled to discover she won third prize.

McFarlane's tale simply tells of a day at a country fair; Lott's pale watercolour illustrations bring the day realistically to life. The book is a quiet one, showcasing a small country fair. There are no thrills at the fair or in this book, just a pleasant outing.

McFarlane, Sheryl. Illustr. Ron Lightburn. *Waiting for the Whales*. 1993. 4 to 8.
An isolated old man living on British Columbia's southern coast waits every year to see the migrating orcas (killer whales) pass by, for "it seemed to him that there was nothing more wonderful than these great mammals of the sea." When the man's daughter and her baby girl move in with him, they join him in his annual enjoyment. The year after he dies, his granddaughter notices a new baby orca swimming along with the others – like her grandfather's spirit, leaping and swimming with the whales.

The understatement of the old man's romantic affinity for these wild creatures gives this story its emotional force. The close connection of death and life, understood in the relationship of grandfather and granddaughter, adult and baby orcas, is patent. Lightburn's static, airbrushed illustrations, warm with the browns of earth, point up the mythic qualities of the story. A good choice for children thinking about the death of a beloved adult.

McGugan, Jim. Illustr. Murray Kimber. *Josepha: A Prairie Boy's Story*. 1994. 5 to 7.
A boy recalls the departure of Josepha, a favourite school friend: Josepha is well into his teens but sits with the primary children in the one room schoolhouse because he hasn't yet learned English. Although he's intelligent and kind and could benefit hugely from education, in harvest season he drives off to the lure of a dollar a day for bagging grain.

There's an element of the surreal in this haunting story; Josepha's lack of ability with English makes him appear almost pre-lingual. But his great kindness and generosity with the young narrator reveal the unresolved tensions between capacity and need. Kimber's oil illustrations, with blocks of colour, angles, and smudges, are Cézanne-like. Vibrant teal, vermilion, and amber convey the intensity of prairie summer. A good story for discussing the experience of pioneers and new immigrants.

McKibbon, Hugh William. Illustr. Scott Cameron. *The Token Gift*. 1996. 6 and up.
Although set in India, this tale is of Persian origin. The inventor of the game of chess (or chaturanga, as it is known in the story), when offered a reward by the King, requests that he receive only a token gift: "Give me one grain of rice to represent the first square of the board, two for the second, four for the third, eight for the fourth, and so on, doubling each time." As the numbers mount to the millions, it becomes clear that the king cannot possibly honour his promise. The token gift destroys him.

Cameron's illustrations emphasize the exotic locale and the intriguing nature of the story. Children will examine and then delight in the illustration of the King's men, who review a chart of the vast amount of rice needed to honour the man's request. An afterword to the story supplies a little history of the game of chess.

McLerran, Alice. Illustr. Paul Morin. *The Ghost Dance.* **1995. 5 to 8.**
Over a century ago, Native spiritual leaders led sacred dances, calling
on the ghosts of times past to restore the world that had been lost
to them. "Nation to Native nation, the dream raced like a flame. The
people sang the vision-song, and danced." Yet the dance and its magic
failed, so McLerran, in her free verse, asks the reader to dream, sing,
and dance again.

The text demands careful attention, but Morin's illustrations and his
assemblages of artifacts make this a particularly beautifully designed
and illustrated book. The textures in the art let the reader almost feel
the earth, the buffalo, and the fabrics. Included in the art are wampum
beads, feathers, and even a ceremonial buffalo skull. Morin's work is
always remarkable: dark and brooding, it illustrates richly the connection between human and nature.

McNeil, Florence. Illustr. David McPhail. *Sail Away.* **2000. 2 to 5.**
A little boy with a model of a pirate ship gets it shipshape and ready for
sailing – in his bathtub. The young Captain wears his pirate hat and,
with the help of his stuffed animals, scrapes the bottom, rigs the stays,
battens the hatches, and sails away in the claw-foot bathtub at home.

McNeil uses colourful nautical language and provides a glossary at
the end to help landlubber parents get their young sailors to weigh
anchor prior to their journey. McPhail's pale watercolours, showing a
tousle-headed toddler and a crew of endearing stuffed animals, emphasize the action in the story.

Miller, Ruth. Illustr. Martine Gourbault. *I Went to the Bay.* **1998.
3 to 6.**
A boy investigates his bay and sights a variety of creatures in this brief
but successful story written in rhyming couplets. "I went to the bay to
look for frogs. / I saw a toad and some pollywogs," the boy begins. He
sees a loon, a heron, a turtle, and more; a pair of frogs go along as
hidden companions. Gourbault's pale coloured-pencil illustrations are
on paper so textured that they give the sense of looking through a
screen, so this has a very summery quality. A thoughtful conclusion
gets children to look at the world from a different point of view – "I
wondered if all the creatures would say / I saw a human being today!"

Mills, Judith Christine. *The Stonehook Schooner.* **1995. 4 to 7.**
Matthew's family have run a stonehook schooner in Lake Ontario for years, but the large, flat stones they raked from the bed and shores of the lake are almost all gone now and the family business is about to close. Matthew's father takes Matthew on the schooner's final voyage, and when the boat is hit by a squall, Matthew stands fast at his post as a lookout until he spots the dock they're heading for. When they arrive safely, a local ship-builder, impressed by Matthew's stalwart spirit, offers to take him on as an apprentice.

Matthew's bravery during the squall gives drama to this tale, which recalls the demise of the Great Lakes stonehooking trade in the early 1900s.

Mollel, Tololwa M. Illustr. Paul Morin. *The Orphan Boy.* **1990. 4 to 7.**
In Masai mythology, the planet Venus, called "Kileken," is an orphan boy who rises at dawn to herd cattle and returns each night for the evening milking. In this tale, Kileken helps an old man, bringing prosperity to him and health to his herd. When the man's curiosity leads him to uncover the secret of Kileken's identity, the boy disappears and the bright star returns to the sky.

Mollel's storytelling is direct, allowing the reader to imagine much more than is told, while Morin's richly textured art invites the audience to feel the heat of the sun and the dryness of the land.

Mollel draws on his African heritage in his retellings of several other traditional stories, including *The Flying Tortoise*, *Rhinos for Lunch, Elephants for Supper!* and *The King and the Tortoise*.

Morck, Irene. Illustr. Georgia Graham. *Tiger's New Cowboy Boots.* **1996. 4 to 7.**
Tiger's proud to have a new pair of authentic cowboy boots to wear when he heads off to help his uncle and cousin on a cattle drive on their ranch in Alberta. But even though he lovingly strokes the shiny leather, arranges his feet appealingly, and makes sure not to mar the new leather, nobody comments on his elegant footwear. Only when he forgets his feet and gets right in there, mucking up his boots and drenching them in the river, do his companions take notice.

A feeling of achievement comes through in this fairly quiet account of a cattle drive. Graham's photo-realistic illustrations transport viewers to a particular place and an event: the surging river, the wooded hills and distant, snow-streaked mountains are quintessential Alberta. The hard work, confusion, and noise of a real drive is apparent in Graham's carefully observed herd of cattle. Excellent for children interested in cowboys or ranches.

Morgan, Allen. Illustr. Michael Martchenko. *Matthew and the Midnight Tow Truck*. 1984. 2 to 6.
After playing with his cars and having a dessert that is not the red licorice he truly desires, Matthew goes to bed. He wakes at midnight to see a huge tow truck in front of the house; when he investigates, the midnight tow truck driver invites him to come and help. Together they tow cars for the driver's collection, trade them with other drivers, and eat red licorice ("You can never get enough red licorice, you know," the driver tells him. "It's good for you and it gives you big muscles"). In the morning Matthew wakes with a toy van in his pocket, very much like the big van he helped the driver hook.

This has the elements of a stereotypical boy's fantasy – an autonomous grown-up boy who collects cars and eats licorice for dinner, and a child protagonist who proves able to help out success-fully. Martchenko's cartoon-like drawings of the burly driver and his massive midnight tow truck are lively. Along with the cars and trucks, this shows a boy living with a single mother.

Subsequent titles by the same team repeat the grandiose fantasy formula and include *Matthew and the Midnight Money Van*, *Matthew and the Midnight Turkeys*, a compendium entitled *Matthew's Midnight Adventures*, and more.

Morgan, Allen. Illustr. Brenda Clark. *Sadie and the Snowman*. 1985. 2 to 5.
Sadie makes a snowman and he lasts a long time, but eventually various creatures eat his features and he melts into mush. The next time it snows, Sadie makes another snowman, using the old snow and a lot of new. But that snowman melts down, too. After repeated attempts and smaller and smaller snowmen, Sadie takes the basin of

water – all that's left of her snowman – and freezes it. The next winter, she has the beginning of the new season's snowman.

Morgan's story has the promise of continuity, ensured by ingenuity. The repeated pattern in the story and Sadie's devotion make this appealing for a young audience; Clark's fresh colours, her drawings of rosy-cheeked Sadie, suggest a pleasant, protected preschooler environment.

* **Muller, Robin.** *The Magic Paintbrush.* **1989. 5 to 10.**
Orphan Nib wants to be an artist and loves to draw with the bits of charcoal that he finds in the streets: "I want to paint pictures so real that people will think they are alive!" After a chance encounter with an old man he rescues from a ruthless gang, he's rewarded with a magic paintbrush that has the power of making real all that it paints. The old man tells Nib to use the magic paintbrush as long as he sees with his eyes, but he will not need it when he learns to see with his heart. A cruel King finds Nib and forces him to paint riches until Nib learns the truth of the old man's words and he's freed from this servitude.

Muller's own illustrations seem to have been painted with a magic brush – the story leaps to life in his glorious art. In one picture, while Nib paints a seagull, the reader sees the image of the bird coming to life, reflected in the pupils of Nib's eyes. The art is reminiscent of the fine style of nineteenth-century English fairy-tale illustrations, and readers will find themselves carefully examining each picture. Highly recommended.

Munsch, Robert. Illustr. Michael Martchenko. *The Paper Bag Princess.* **1980. 3 to 5.**
Munsch plays on fairy-tale conventions and gender stereotypes in this early and best of his popular stories. Princess Elizabeth is engaged to marry Prince Ronald; when a dragon smashes her castle, burns all her clothes, and absconds with Ronald, she heads off to rescue him. Clad in a paper bag, the only covering available, she searches out the dragon, tricks him into exhaustion, and frees Ronald. However, Ronald's only response is criticism of her dishevelled appearance and unladylike behaviour, so Elizabeth sends him packing: "You look like a real prince, but you are a bum."

Kids love the inversion of roles here, and the little *frisson* of the forbidden in the word "bum." Munsch's text is straightforward plot, swift and to the point. Martchenko adds the character in his cartoon-like drawings: furious, enterprising Elizabeth, besmirched with soot, carries the day.

Munsch's many subsequent works tend to celebrate the agitated ineptitude of adults and the persistent power of stubborn children. They're usually structured on single situations repeated with variation, giving small children the chance to predict what's going to be said and chime in. Martchenko, who illustrates many of these titles, accentuates the exaggerated emotion and frantic activity of the stories and takes care to reflect Canada's multicultural population. Titles are available singly (*David's Father*; *I Have to Go*; *Murmel, Murmel, Murmel*; and so on) or in collected volumes *Munschworks 1, 2, 3,* and *4,* and *The Munschworks Grand Treasury*.

Nichol, Barbara. Illustr. Scott Cameron. *Beethoven Lives Upstairs.* **1993. 6 to 10.**
Growing up in Vienna in the 1820s, ten-year-old Christoph finds the family's new lodger very disturbing. Mr. Beethoven pounds, howls, stomps, and generally creates mayhem. In a series of letters between Christoph and his Uncle Karl, a music student in Salzburg, we learn briefly of Beethoven's childhood, his deafness, and the passionate, complex music he makes despite his inability to hear. At the same time, Christoph's life unfolds, his pesky sisters grow a little older; he learns to like Mr. Beethoven (and even the two attendant sopranos); and he befriends a dog he names Metronome, in honour of Beethoven's musical influence.

Nichol's text is wonderfully restrained and nicely revealing. The directness of Christoph's observations and complaints engages children, while historical information seeps in painlessly. Cameron's art, with elaborately dressed figures and a world shadowed with browns and golds, suggests the formal, ornate atmosphere of the period. The character of Beethoven comes alive here in a story that engages even those who have no previous interest in music.

Nichol, Barbara. Illustr. Barry Moser. *Dippers*. 1997. 5 to 8.
Dippers is eerily authentic-sounding; it purports to be words reprinted from a letter found in the Toronto Archives. A young girl, Margaret, remembers the summer dippers emerged from the Don River in Toronto, a summer of excessive heat in which her sister Louise became seriously ill. In scraps of memory, she describes the dippers, with their little legs that look broken but aren't, and their small, leathery wings that go "clickety clickety." The dippers aren't dangerous, but somehow they're a disturbing sign that this summer is different, out of control.

Margaret writes with the remote voice of recall, not passionately, but curiously. This work isn't about plot so much as state of mind, the mysteries of adults and growth, and it is truly haunting. Moser's watercolour illustrations and the parchment colour of the pages add to the feel of the story's authenticity.

Oberman, Sheldon. Illustr. Ted Lewin. *The Always Prayer Shawl*. 1994. 6 and up.
Lewin's black-and-white illustrations of Czarist Russia set the stage for the story of Adam, who receives a precious Jewish prayer shawl from his grandfather and namesake prior to emigrating to North America. Adam grows up in the New World; as his prayer shawl wears out, he fixes it, adding a new fringe, cloth, or collar. Lewin adds colour to the illustrations as Adam grows to be an adult, emphasizing that the story is now coming into the present. When Adam becomes an old man, the only certainty is that he will pass the prayer shawl on to his grandson, who, according to family custom, is also named Adam. This story of traditions tells of the passing generations in a thoughtful and slightly sentimental manner. Lewin's illustrations give added poignancy to the story.

Oberman, Sheldon. Illustr. Les Tait. *The White Stone in the Castle Wall*. 1995. 4 to 7.
Within the wall that surrounds Casa Loma in Toronto, there is one large white stone: Oberman's story tells of how it might have got there. In 1904, young John Fiddich cares assiduously for his garden, but it yields only a large, white boulder. Still, he hears that stones are needed for Casa Loma, so he drags it there, only to be told that, because it is

white, it can't be used. In an amusing twist, Henry sells his stone for the wall, instead of the castle, and gets a job working with Sir Henry Pellatt, the castle's owner. Tait's paintings are historically accurate, and this story has the appeal of being about a "real" Canadian castle.

Oppel, Kenneth. Illustr. Terry Widener. *Peg and the Whale*. 2000. 3 to 6.
Seven-year-old Peg is "a big strapping lass" who is good at whatever she turns her hand to. Born on the sea and having caught every kind of fish, she decides she must catch a whale. Peg sets sail on a whaling ship and catches a whale, or at least ends up setting up a comfy living arrangement in the stomach of the whale.

The absurdity of this story won't be lost on children, and they'll enjoy Peg's feisty nature. Widener's illustrations portray Peg in her slicker and in all her glory – whether she's in the belly of the whale or sailing on the whale's back. The final illustration shows unsinkable, unstoppable Peg at eight, in mountain gear, looking for a new challenge.

Oppenheim, Joanne. Illustr. Barbara Reid. *Have You Seen Birds?* 1986. 3 to 6.
Reid's image of a cat, paws on the window, carefully watching a bird on a branch, makes a tantalizing entry to the rhyming text, "Have you seen birds?" Alluding to the seasons, the countryside, and the seashore – as well as the days and nights – Oppenheim asks her audience if they have seen town birds, marsh birds, barn birds, and so on. Birds scratch, wade, squawk, screech, and coo through the questions.

Reid's art answers each query with glorious, imaginative full-colour Plasticine illustrations. Flamingos, parrots, hawks, and seagulls soar through the pages, showing children the variety of birds living all around them. Reid's characteristic humour is evident in her final illustration: the cat leaves the window, watched attentively by a myriad of birds.

Oppenheim, Joanne. Illustr. Ron Broda. *Have You Seen Bugs?* 1996. 3 to 7.
Oppenheim's rollicking rhyme encourages children to pore over these pictures of bugs, looking for see-through bugs, winking, blinking bugs, swimming-under-water bugs, and so on. The insects are brought to life

spectacularly in Broda's paper-sculpture illustrations. Photographs of his three-dimensional sculptures in brilliant colours give the sensation that the bugs are about to leap off the page. Additional information about bugs and a list of all the bugs illustrated appears at the end of the book.

Orr, Wendy. Illustr. Ruth Ohi. *Aa-choo!* **1992. 2 to 4.**
Megan wakes up hot and groggy, but neither parent nor neighbour is free to stay home and take care of her. So Megan spends the day enjoying her illness in Mommy's office – making a fort, tasting the goodies at the big meeting, and making friends with an employee who knows where to find the bathroom. The next morning Mommy wakes up sneezing, and Megan knows just how to take care of her.

This is a slight story that addresses the problems of a sick day with humour. Ohi's watercolours, in full-page colour, show Megan's world from multiple visual perspectives.

Pearson, Debora. Illustr. Chum McLeod. *Load 'Em Up Trucks.* **Mighty Wheels Series. 1999. 2 to 4.**
With a very little bit of text Pearson points out the features of vehicles designed for lifting, loading, and hauling – cement-mixer, transport truck, fork lift, and more are here in splendour. McLeod's boxy style gives the trucks a light, clean look, but doesn't diminish their interest. Good suggestions for how parents can use a child's fascination with large vehicles to expand thinking are included in the introduction to each book in this series. Other titles in the series include *Rough, Tough Wheels* and *Hard-Working Wheels*.

Poulin, Stéphane. *My Mother's Loves: Stories and Lies from My Childhood.* **Trans. from French. 1990. 4 to 7.**
The title gives every indication that Poulin is not going to tell the truth about his childhood. Instead, he presents a wonderfully delicious fabrication about a mother with lots of children living in a tiny house – so tiny that it can hold either family or furniture, but not both simultaneously. One day, when the furniture is out in the yard, the garbage collector takes it away; the family chases after the truck and succeeds in bringing home both the furniture and a husband for their mother.

Poulin's illustrations of wide-eyed children are overshadowed by a vaguely sinister atmosphere. The absurd situations are bizarrely entertaining, and the difficulties of having so many children in such a tiny house make for some funny situations.

Pratt, Pierre. *Follow That Hat!* Trans. from French. 1992. 3 to 6.
Having finished putting together a scale-model tricycle, Leon Napoleon takes a relaxing stroll. A forceful wind snatches his hat, and away he goes in pursuit – by bicycle, taxi, plane, horse, balloon, and Rapido-Expresso-Transcontinental-London-Santa Fe-Istanbul train. Fields, farms, forests, and mountains whiz past in luminous green, indigo, cobalt, and black ("isn't there anything red in this scene?" asks the narrator), until Leon, now on a scooter, finally lands his hat. "Yup, his hat all right!" the narrator exclaims. Or is it?

Pratt's acrylics glow on a black background; the intense colours and distorted proportions reflect the frantic rapidity of Leon's journey. A playful, intrusive narrative voice invites children to speak back to the story.

* Reid, Barbara. *The Party*. 1997. 3 to 6.
A girl and her sister are all dressed up to go to the annual family party and, when they get there, it has all the elements it should: initial shyness with cousins, unwanted embraces, good food, wild games, and finally hiding from the grown-ups when it's all over. Reid's impeccable, lolloping verse captures all the impetuousness and enthusiasm of the event, from the first "claims to fame" ("I cut my own hair," Claire begins. "Mummy cried." / Sally has stitches: "I flew off the slide!") to the final, somnolent satisfaction: "Oh what a great time, / what a wonderful time, / such a very late time at the party."

Reid's Plasticine illustrations are full of intriguing detail, from the devilled eggs and the marshmallow salad, to the uncle whose large belly is covered with crumbs. Whirling kids are shown blurred with dizziness; an aerial view shows the various places the children hide from their mothers. Humour and character shine through: this conveys richly the intense, happy experience of a fun family event. Highly recommended.

Reynolds, Marilynn. Illustr. Stephen McCallum. *Belle's Journey.* **1993. 4 to 7.**

Belle is an old horse, earning her keep carrying Molly to school and to piano lessons on Saturdays, but one day Molly's father thinks it's time to sell her and buy a frisky pony. Molly is worried, because she wonders whether anyone will want the old horse. When a winter blizzard catches Molly and Belle unawares on their eight-mile trek back from piano lessons, Belle proves her worth by bringing Molly home safely. When they reach the farm, Molly's father has to cut Molly's frozen clothes from Belle's back, and there is no further discussion of selling Belle.

Reynolds chooses her words carefully, and this story builds suspense in a satisfying way. McCallum's illustrations communicate both the tension and the love within the tale.

Reynolds, Marilynn. Illustr. Laura Fernandez and Rick Jacobson. *The Magnificent Piano Recital.* **2000. 4 to 7.**

When Arabella and her mother arrive, complete with their piano and fancy clothes, at a small sawmill town on a northern lake, the townspeople are at first disapproving. Arabella is put at the back of the class with the shabby students, and the teacher comments, "Children shouldn't wear fancy party clothes and ribbons to school." But Arabella takes comfort in playing the piano at home, and her mother earns a living giving piano lessons. After a season of lessons, a recital is held, and Arabella shines, along with her mother. Everyone – from the Finnish lumbermen to the banker and even to Arabella's sour teacher – attends the recital. When Arabella finishes playing, they leap to their feet with applause.

Reynolds's story is enhanced by the ornate detail on the exotic clothes worn by Arabella and her elegant mother, which contrast with the simplicity of the life in the town. Fernandez and Jacobson show Arabella almost glowing as she plays, making her musical brilliance visually apparent.

Reynolds, Marilynn. Illustr. Don Kilby. *The Prairie Fire.* **1999. 4 to 7.**

Percy is told he's not old enough to help his father plough the fire guard around their sod house on the prairies, but he proves his courage and maturity when he spots a prairie fire, warns the family, and douses sparks that have landed on the haystack and buildings. Percy's reward comes when his father asks for his help, because his next task is "a job for two men."

The theme of strength in the story is matched by Kilby's dramatic illustrations: one can almost feel the fire's heat, and the family's fear is made palpable by views of roiling smoke clouds and raging flames. The cover image of Percy racing the fire as he runs home across the prairie emphasizes the imbalance of the "man against nature" contest in the story.

Rhodes, Timothy. Illustr. Stefan Czernecki. *The Singing Snake*. 1993. 4 to 8.
This Australian folktale is about the creation of one of the world's oldest musical instruments, the didgeridoo. An old man promises to honour the animal with the most beautiful singing voice by making a musical instrument that resembles the winner. In a contest, all the creatures vie for the honour. The snake, knowing he has only an average voice, decides to capture the Lark and use hers. Snake does win the contest, and the old man creates the long didgeridoo, but the snake is so embarrassed when his treachery is revealed that he forgets how to use his own voice.

Czernecki's illustrations here are greatly influenced by Australian Aboriginal paintings. Geometric patterns on a background of rich ochre, verdant greens, and quiet yellows dotted with white shine out on every page; stylized images of all the animals add to its myth-like quality. An image of the snake, the lark trapped behind his teeth, clarifies the story.

Czernecki and Rhodes have collaborated on other books with folk art illustrations, including *Nina's Treasures* and *Bear in the Sky*.

Richards, Nancy Wilcox. Illustr. H. Werner Zimmermann. *Farmer Joe's Hot Day*. 1987. 2 to 4.
Farmer Joe lives with his wife in an old house in the middle of a big field. One summer day he complains of the heat; each subsequent day his wife tells him to put on an additional piece of clothing, until finally

she advises him to take them all off (almost) – and he stops complaining. This version of a cumulative traditional tale, where repetitions mount up to a surprise conclusion, shows Farmer Joe to be agreeable, simultaneously flummoxed and vaguely in control. Repetition and lighthearted watercolour illustrations that emphasize Farmer Joe's haplessness give this storytime appeal.

Sequels include *Farmer Joe Goes to the City* and *Farmer Joe Baby-Sits*.

Robart, Rose. Illustr. Maryann Kovalski. *The Cake That Mack Ate*. 1986. 2 to 6.
Robart's minimal text is based on the pattern of *The House That Jack Built*, but focuses on the egg, the hen, the corn, the farmer, the cook, and so on, and ends with a shocking surprise when we meet doggie Mack of the title.

Kovalski's soft colours and rounded lines create a pleasantly comfortable look, perfect to evoke the homey atmosphere of a farm kitchen filled with the smell of a freshly baked cake. With its limited vocabulary and use of repetition, this is an ideal choice for children learning to read.

Roddie, Shen. Illustr. Kady MacDonald Denton. *Toes Are to Tickle*. 1997. Infant to 4.
This book of purposes looks at things from a preschooler's point of view: "Morning is for waking up. An egg is to dip. Bread is for more jam, please," begins the litany, and it continues on through all the pleasures of the day. "Boxes are to see what's in them . . . Books are to choose from," and finally, "Mommy is for one more cuddle . . . one more story . . . and kissing good night. Good night!" This simple text offers the comfort of an ordinary happy day with the imaginative, alternate purposes a child finds in mundane events such as dinner ("peas are for counting"). Denton's fresh colours and expressive lines show the smiling enjoyment of the whole family, the busy energy of preschooler and baby brother. This charming book will stand many re-readings.

Sadu, Itah. Illustr. Roy Condy. *Christopher, Please Clean Up Your Room!* **1993. 4 to 7.**

Christopher likes his room just the way it is, until the night cockroaches cover his walls and demand that he clean it up – it's too disgusting even for them! "The socks under the bed were cheesy / The sandwich behind the door grew fungi / The room was so untidy / The shoes smelled funky funky / And the fish bowl stank!"

This tall tale of the goldfish from the dirty fishbowl seeking help from cockroaches to frighten Christopher is outrageous fun. The West Indian lilt in the storytelling voice of the author resonates in the language; Condy's cartoon illustrations of cool Christopher, the messy bedroom, and the invasion of cockroaches maintain Sadu's enjoyably silly exaggeration. A sequel is available in *Christopher Changes His Name*, written and illustrated by the same pair.

* Schwartz, Roslyn. *The Mole Sisters and the Piece of Moss.* **1999. 2 to 5.**

The endearing, enigmatic mole sisters are a rare expression of the fully absorbing pleasure preschoolers can derive from the simplest, smallest things. Marching along in unison, noses pointed to the sky, these two moles of few words explore the pleasures of jumping on a piece of moss (BOINGA-BOINGA is the text for that page), swinging on wavy wheat, or investigating the possibilities of a cool breeze. With very few words, in this title and the other mole sisters stories Schwartz conveys a whole quality of relationship, humour (the occasional "hee hee hee" is infectious), and philosophical questioning. "The mole sisters were looking for something. But what? 'We don't know,' they said." Or, "The mole sisters were thinking. 'Who are we?' 'Good question,' they said." Like close friends with limitless ideas for play, these two explore and enjoy life with perfect mutual understanding. Schwartz's coloured-pencil illustrations of the shapeless, almost faceless pair are hilariously expressive. These little books (15 cm by 15 cm), with their tiny, inset pictures and few words per page, are full of riches – national treasures. Other titles include *The Mole Sisters and the Rainy Day*, *The Mole Sisters and the Blue Egg*, *The Mole Sisters and the Question*, and others. All are highly recommended.

Scrimger, Richard. Illustr. Gillian Johnson. *Bun Bun's Birthday.* 2001. 3 to 6.

Intense drama, tragedy, or amusement can erupt at any moment in the life of a 3-to-5-year-old, and do for baby Bun Bun's sister Winnifred, who is devastated when she realizes that the family is preparing to celebrate not *her* birthday, but that of one-year-old Bun Bun. She knows, from the toes of her striped socks to the tip of her tiara, that *she's* supposed to be the next party girl. Finally, Winnifred reaches an understanding that satisfies her: it's really *her* birthday, because Bun Bun is too young to remember it.

Scrimger conveys Winnifred's disturbance with complete conviction, never succumbing to bland moral example. This is a funny, affectionate treatment of one of those "life lessons" so seriously distressing to children. Johnson's ink-and-watercolour drawings, in the nicely detailed style of certain British illustrators, such as Helen Craig and Wendy Smith, reveal the humour and emotional trauma of the moment: Winnifred is shocked, devastated, or smug, as suits the occasion. Winnifred's adventures continue in *Princess Bun Bun*, when the family goes to visit an uncle in an unfamiliar apartment building, and Bun Bun and Winnifred end up alone in an ascending elevator.

Simard, Rémy. Illustr. Pierre Pratt. *My Dog Is an Elephant.* Trans. from French. 1994. 4 to 7.

When Hector meets a runaway elephant in his sandbox, he offers to hide him. But it isn't easy. Every time Hector's mother opens a closet or a drawer and finds the elephant, she faints dead away. Hector tries disguise instead; but the elephant as butterfly, dinosaur, or moose attracts collectors and more. Eventually, Hector disguises the elephant as a businessman and sends him home to Africa on a plane. Being alone again is hard, but it isn't long before a mouse befriends him. Or is it a mouse?

This tale's fun comes from its outrageousness; all the elephant's disguises seem perfectly reasonable, even up to his learning how to behave like a dog – to bark, fetch the paper, and lift a leg on the hydrant. Pratt's art is vibrant, lively, and funny, from the ruby-nosed dog to the massive double-spread elephant being measured for his first disguise. The elephant's look of apprehension as he tries out the butterfly costume, or the vision of Hector's mother's upturned feet as she faints repeatedly, are a hoot. Great offbeat, imaginative fare.

Additional Simard/Pratt collaborations, *The Magic Boot* and *Mister Once-upon-a-time*, provide similar fantastical humorous stories.

Smucker, Barbara. Illustr. Janet Wilson. *Selina and the Bear Paw Quilt*. 1995. 4 to 8.

Selina, a Mennonite girl living in Pennsylvania, learns of the impending Civil War and realizes that she'll be forced to flee to Canada with her pacifist family. Selina's grandmother, who has passed on her love of quilting to Selina, stays behind because she's too old to travel. As she starts her new life in Ontario, Selina treasures her grandmother's last gift, a quilt made in the traditional Mennonite "bear paw" pattern.

Smucker tells a story of family love and also offers a glimpse into the life of the Mennonites in the 1860s. Wilson's oil illustrations are bordered with different quilt patterns, each identified on the cover of the book. The tale gives children an appreciation for the stories and memories that are sewn into many quilts; it also shows the narrative purposes in this traditionally female domestic art.

* Stinson, Kathy. Illustr. Robin Baird Lewis. *Red Is Best*. 1982. 2 to 5.

"My mom doesn't understand about red," Kelly complains, and goes on to explain why "red is best." She can jump higher in her red stockings; her red boots take bigger steps; her red mitts make better snowballs; and juice even tastes better in a red cup. Kelly's vivid imagination soars when she wears red: she can be Little Red Riding Hood in her red jacket; her red barrettes make her hair laugh, and red paint puts singing in her head.

Stinson's brief text is perfectly matched by Lewis's simple line-drawn illustrations. The reader sees only Kelly, dressing, eating, and amusing herself: the exasperated voice of the mother is heard as she tries to get her daughter to wear something else, but only Kelly, delighted in everything red, is on view. This is an unpretentious gem of a story, and utterly true to preschooler fixations. Highly recommended.

Stren, Patti. *Hug Me.* **1977. 3 to 5.**
Porcupine Elliott Kravitz can't find anyone willing or able to hug him successfully. He spends "most of his time hugging telephone poles, parking meters and traffic lights," until the day he meets Thelma Claypits, another porcupine, who turns out to be a most satisfactory hugger.

First published twenty-five years ago, this story was a huge success and gave rise to a short film made by the National Film Board of Canada. Stren's line drawings and the wacky text have considerable appeal, showing that the desire for friendship is universal.

Stren re-illustrated the text in 2002 with comical full-colour art: unfortunately, what was subtle and endearing is now blatant and forced. But although Elliott isn't quite as cute as he was twenty-five years ago, new readers can still enjoy the story. It's best to find a copy of the original in a library, or to compare the current edition with the NFB film.

Stren, Patti. *For Sale: One Brother.* **1993. 7 to 10.**
This book strikes some adults as ugly, but it appeals to many children. Molly has a brother she wants to be rid of, so, much to the horror of her mother, she places a sign in the laundry room of their apartment building – "For Sale one brother. Price negotiable. No reasonable offer refused." Molly's punishment is to spend the whole week with her brother. She ends up losing him and has to put another sign in the lobby, "Lost one brother. Age 4. Enormous reward."

Stren uses silly stamps, watercolours, and a rapidograph pen to illustrate this tale of sibling rivalry in garish, chaotic (and ugly) manner – but one with "kid appeal." The story is full of non-stop comments and asides – in balloons, italics, highlights, and outrageous colours. Of great interest to a limited audience.

Thompson, Richard. Illustr. Martin Springett. *The Follower.* **2000. 4 to 7.**
"On Monday, dark as shut your eyes, it followed her home . . ." So begins Thompson's cumulative poem, perfect for readers or listeners not ready for truly scary picture books. Suspense builds as the young witch

passes more and more places – until the final picture reveals that the follower is the black cat that has been visible in all the previous pictures.

Thompson's eerie text is well matched by Springett's illustrations, mostly worked in carefully controlled dark shadows and silhouettes. The cat "hidden" on each page provides the story with a visual challenge for younger children. The design and page layout make this an elegant volume for fall reading.

Tibo, Gilles. *Simon in Summer*. Trans. from French. 1991. 2 to 4.
The simple texts of Tibo's Simon stories each develop one idea – in this case, "My name is Simon and I love summer." Simon wants summer to stay forever, so he tries to keep the things that mean summer to him: the singing frogs, the flowers and butterflies, even the sun. None of his tactics work, but he learns to celebrate something about the end of the season: the return of all his playmates.

Using paint and computer-generated art, Tibo depicts a country that feels safe, green, and dreamlike. The soft edges of the natural environment contrast with the precisely depicted wildlife and urchin Simon, with his cock-eyed cap and little smile. The contrast points out what's at the heart of most of the Simon books – the interaction of reality and imagination. These books focus on the simple make-believe games of preschoolers; there's always something to figure out, and animals and friends come into every story. Also available are *Simon and His Boxes*, *Simon and the Snowflakes*, *Simon and the Wind*, and more. Good texts for children beginning to read on their own.

Tregebov, Rhea. Illustr. Maryann Kovalski. *The Big Storm*. 1992. 4 to 6.
Jeanette's cat, Kitty Doyle, doesn't just catch mice for the family deli, she also escorts Jeanette to and from school every day. One wintry afternoon, Jeanette goes home with a friend after school; not until she's finished playing, eating latkes, and making her way back to the deli does she remember Kitty Doyle waiting in the whirling snow. The cat is listless and freezing, until Jeanette nurses her back to liveliness with a bowl of warm milk and honey.

Tregebov's pace is perfect for the age group. The matter of childish forgetfulness will resonate with many parents and children; so will the consoling conclusion. Jeanette's deli-operating Jewish immigrant family is warm and affectionate; Kovalski's soft colours and blurred and rounded lines communicate security and family love.

Tregebov, Rhea. Illustr. Leanne Franson. *What-If Sara*. 1999. 3 to 5. Sara has busy fingers and a penchant for daydreaming. She wants to help, but day after day, by the time her tailor father and homemaking mother have finished tidying up messes from her busy fingers and day-dreaming mind, they don't have time to teach her what she wants to learn: how to knead, how to sew. But one day, Sara's ability to read and write helps her Jewish immigrant father out; and when she returns from his errand to find Momma's dough swelling all over the kitchen, a little fantasy about beating down an invading army comes in handy.

Without a spare word, this affirming story shows that sometimes a child's special skills can save the day. Franson's illustrations depict what Tregebov's story evokes – the environment and qualities of a loving Jewish-immigrant family in urban Canada in the early 1900s.

Valgardson, W. D. Illustr. Ange Zhang. *Thor*. 1994. 40 pages. 5 to 8. Thor would rather watch superheroes on television than do just about anything else, but while visiting his grandparents for the Christmas holidays he is conscripted to help his grandfather set his ice-fishing nets on Lake Winnipeg. Thor thinks he's too small to help, and so does his grandfather, although his grandmother insists he's big enough. In the end, not only does Thor prove to be helpful fishing, but he also helps to save a foolish snowmobiler who crashes through the ice.

Valgardson warmly portrays the loving grandparents and the apprehension of young Thor. Zhang's illustrations show Thor's fear, excitement, and joy as he lives through his experiences. The cold out on the ice is visually apparent. The complex procedures of ice-fishing are made understandable in Zhang's careful drawings.

Valgardson, W. D. Illustr. Ian Wallace. *Sarah and the People of Sand River*. 1996. 6 to 9. Twelve-year-old Sarah doesn't want to leave her fishing-camp home on northern Lake Winnipeg, but her Icelandic-speaking father tells her she has to go to school in the city so she can learn English. Once she gets there, the woman who boards her forces her to do all kinds of drudgery. Lonely and often freezing cold, Sarah is mystified to meet a Cree woman who gives her gifts of deerskin clothing; but it seems this woman is a ghost from "the people of Sand River," a Cree family Sarah's grandmother nursed many years before.

The familiar literary situation of a vulnerable orphan beleaguered by a stingy, oppressive mother-substitute gives this story a fairy-tale feel; it's coloured Canadian by the symbols of Icelandic and Cree mythology, and real Canadian history. Wallace's pencil-and-watercolour illustrations are still but atmospheric; he emphasizes the supernatural aspects of the story. With its substantial text and many pictures, this is a good book for girls who are ready for more text but still appreciate pictures.

Van Camp, Richard. Illustr. George Littlechild. *A Man Called Raven*. 1997. 5 to 8.
Two boys abusing a raven are accosted by a stranger, who tells a cautionary tale of a mean old man who is changed into a raven because of his heedless cruelty to the bird. When the raven-man witnesses his own funeral, he is amazed by the number of people who come to mourn him, even though he was never kind or friendly. The care shown at his funeral inspires the raven-man to watch over and help his people for as long as he lives in his raven form. Hearing this tale, the two boys realize how disrespectful they've been; the stranger turns into a raven and flies away.

The patent moral here is cloaked in powerful Dogrib and Chipewyan imagery that makes concrete the connection between people and creatures, and also illustrates the importance of mutual care within the community. The prose has the directness of an oral telling. Littlechild's illustrations, collage, pastel, and paint in brilliant colours, radiate a surreal vividness that emphasizes the tale's symbolic qualities.

Van Camp, Richard. Illustr. George Littlechild. *What's the Most Beautiful Thing You Know About Horses?* 1998. 6 to 9.
On a day so cold "the snow is holding its breath," the author, who is a member of the Dogrib Nation, lives in the far north, and has never had much to do with horses, asks his family and friends, "What's the most beautiful thing you know about horses?" Their answers are surprising

and poetic – they flow over land; "I love their hair!"; they run sideways; "I love their breath." Van Camp's musings and questions in response to these comments turn this into a curiously thought-provoking exploration not only of horses, but also of humans.

Littlechild's illustrations, paint-on-paint and pastel, are brilliant with colour – fuchsia, teal, turquoise, scarlet, and gold – a modernist, stylized explosion of images and patterns that suits the fanciful nature and amusing conversational tone of the text. Not so much a story as a conversation, this is a good work to use to get children thinking about the qualities of any particular animal.

Von Königslow, Andrea Wayne. *Toilet Tales*. **1985. 2 to 4.**
The silliness of imagining different animals on the toilet is here directed towards who is *really* able to use the toilet, that is, "big kids like you." The hen tries to lay an egg; the lion won't get off his "throne"; the goat eats all the toilet paper. But the little girl looks just right, blushing prettily as she does her best. Amusing drawings and colourful toilets add to the message.

Von Königslow, Andrea Wayne. *Would You Love Me?* **1997. 2 to 4.**
Like *Toilet Tales*, this is an upbeat message story for younger children. Rhyming questions and answers lead the reader through to the final affirmation: "AND I LOVE YOU TOO!" Bizarre animal situations make this nicely funny, instead of sentimental ("Would you love a skunk that is stinky and smelly? Yes, I'd roll him over and tickle his belly.")

Von Königslow, Andrea Wayne. *Bing and Chutney*. **1999. 2 to 4.**
Bing and Chutney, a pig and an elephant, have lived together for three years. One day Chutney decides to pursue a career in dance in the city; Bing stays home and opens a baking school. Chutney dances to great acclaim, and Bing's cooking school thrives. But after a week, the two friends can't stand being apart.

Von Königslow's text is straightforward, stating the extravagances in the plot with such matter-of-factness that they seem no more amazing than the simple, human reunion at the end of the story. Her watercolour-and-ink drawings evoke a homey, pleasant world full of amiable creatures, good meals, and affection. This story teaches the days of the week; it's also one of the few for this age group that may be interpreted as depicting a gay couple.

Prequel *Bing Finds Chutney* and sequel *Bing and Chutney off to Moosonee* are also available.

Waboose, Jan Bourdeau. Illustr. Karen Reczuch. *Morning on the Lake*. 1997. 5 to 8.
Setting out early in the morning in a birchbark canoe, a young Ojibwa boy and his *mishomis* (grandfather) share their day, the quiet misty lake, a climb up a rocky cliff, and an evening walk through the woods. The young boy has deep respect for his grandfather, listening when he shares his knowledge, and sitting with him without talking. Both respect the silence, the earth, and the beauty around them.

This forceful reminder of how one can live in harmony with nature honours the traditions of the wise grandfather. Waboose's quiet, thoughtful prose celebrates the beauty of the Ontario landscape; Reczuch's art evokes nature's calming effects, and honours the wild creatures with beautifully rendered images of an eagle and a pack of wolves. Reading this is like a walk in the woods.

Waboose, Jan Bourdeau. Illustr. Brian Deines. *Sky Sisters*. 2000. 5 to 8.
Two Ojibwa sisters, Nimishe and Nimise, set off in the northern Ontario night to watch for the Sky Sisters, the northern lights. Their mother instructs Nimise to listen to Nimishe, who is older, and reminds the two of the words of their grandmother: "Wisdom comes on silent wings." In the quiet of the night, the sucking of an icicle rings loud, a rabbit startles, and the bounding of a deer makes the heart beat faster. In this silence the sisters dance, joined at last by the flickering, swirling shimmer of the Sky Spirits, a celestial reflection of the girls below.

Waboose's text evokes the cold and the delight of walking without an adult at night, and Deines's luminous blues, his purple-black sky thick with stars, create the austere, mysterious light of a clear winter night. Images of the two girls, their breath floating in front of them as they walk, climb, or simply look at the sky, allow the reader to enjoy the northern light experience vicariously.

Waldron, Kathleen Cook. *A Wilderness Passover.* **1994. 4 to 7.**
Having moved from an urban Jewish community to a farm in British Columbia's mountainous interior, Mama can't see how the family can get together the traditional foods and guests for Passover. But Louie and Susan show how local foods and greens can suit the feast admirably – and even supply a table full of guests, thanks to friendly neighbours.

This narrative is useful for showing the adaptation of traditional Jewish practices to the environment of British Columbia's wilderness.

Wallace, Ian. *Chin Chiang and the Dragon's Dance.* **1984. 4 to 8.**
Chin Chiang is to dance with his grandfather in the New Year's Dragon Dance, but instead of feeling excited, he's scared. The thought of being laughed at and ruining the dance is too much for him, and he takes refuge in the public library. There he meets a cleaning lady who tells him of her former days dancing the Dragon Dance, and Chin Chiang practises with her, hoping she'll take his place. When the two of them arrive at the event, they both pick up the dragon's tail and, in a glorious performance, dance with Chin Chiang's grandfather.

The excitement of Chinese New Year and the Dragon's Dance is vividly evident in Wallace's dragon, ornate in rich reds, greens, and blues, and bursting off the pages. The story, though slight, allows children to share in the excitement of learning to perform in Chinese New Year celebrations.

Wallace, Ian. *Boy of the Deeps.* **1999. 4 to 8.**
Wallace documents Canadian customs and history in picture-book format in this homage to the coal miners of Cape Breton. On James's first day as a miner, he and his father are caught when their tunnel collapses; the two struggle out and return home, knowing that dinner awaits and they will be down in the deeps under the Atlantic again the next day.

The modest story allows Wallace to detail the life of the miners. The darkness of the coal mine is almost oppressive in the glowing blue-blacks on every page, but the sense of life and camaraderie shines through in the miners' yellow lantern light. Wallace's luxurious sunrise and sunset endpapers remind readers that miners spent the entire day in darkness. A thoughtful book, and good for classroom use.

A similarly modest story, *Duncan's Way*, focuses on the end of the cod fishery in Newfoundland.

Waterton, Betty. Illustr. Ann Blades. *A Salmon for Simon*. **1978. 4 to 7.**
Last summer Simon caught minnows with a strainer, but this summer his father has given him a fishing pole of his own. All summer he fishes for salmon without any luck. While digging for clams one September day, he sees a large eagle fly overhead and accidentally drop a Coho salmon into a pool where he has been digging. Watching the magnificent salmon in the pool, Simon realizes that he wants the salmon to live and be free. He digs a channel to let the tide come in, and lets the salmon swim back into the sea.

This story will resonate with young fisherfolk; the illustrations, in Blades's child-like watercolours, show thoughtful Simon to be an Aboriginal boy.

Waterton, Betty. Illustr. Joanne Fitzgerald. *Plain Noodles*. **1989. 2 to 5.**
Mrs. Figg, an old lighthouse-keeper's wife, is miserable because she's lonesome for her little bambinos who have long since left home. While she's out painting on the beach, a boatful of babies, three-year-old Rosie at the helm, arrives. Mrs. Figg is delighted to serve the babies a breakfast of plain noodles, which is just what they like best.

Fitzgerald's sunny watercolours bring out the charm in this fanciful tale of the babies, the sea, Mrs. Figg, and the havoc they all wreak on the lighthouse – which is presented here as great fun. Children delight in the knowledge that this is a tall tale, and laugh with Mrs. Figg and Rosie as they care for the babies. The bizarre boatload of babies arriving at the lighthouse raises concerns for some parents, and the text is a little long for storytimes with large groups, but if a caring adult has time to discuss the story with a young child, this picture book offers a glorious romp.

Wishinsky, Frieda. Illustr. Linda Hendry. *Jennifer Jones Won't Leave Me Alone*. **1995. 4 to 7.**
The wild-haired protagonist of this story, a boy, laments the affectionate attention lavished upon him by irrepressible Jennifer Jones. When Jennifer's mother is transferred, and the boy has to be content with

receiving postcards from Europe instead of Jennifer's hand-delivered love-letters, he realizes that her attention was desirable after all, and he eagerly anticipates her return.

Wishinsky's story has a quick beat and strong rhyme, making it a good read-aloud or read-on-your-own for beginning readers. Hendry's cartoon-like illustrations, largely in light pinks and greens, emphasize the comic aspects of the tale.

Wishinsky, Frieda. Illustr. H. Werner Zimmermann, *Each One Special*. 1998. 4 to 6.
Harry is an extraordinary cake decorator, who makes each of his cakes a masterpiece. When his bakery closes, he loses his purpose in life. Young Ben knows that Harry just needs to find something to do, and introduces him to the joys of modelling clay. Soon Harry is sculpting clay instead of marzipan, and once again he creates and sells works that are "each one special."

Wishinsky shows the strength of intergenerational relationships in this compassionate story, which also deals with the difficulties that arise when an elderly employee suddenly loses a job – or an artist a medium. Zimmermann's loose lines and almost-gaudy colours illustrate the boundlessness of Harry's creativity, and the warmth in the friendship depicted.

Wishinsky, Frieda. Illustr. Michael Martchenko. *Oonga Boonga*. 1998. 3 to 6.
Baby Louise won't stop crying, no matter what her mother, father, grandma, grandpa, or neighbours try. It isn't until her brother is home from school and says "Oonga Boonga" in his own special way that she stops. Everyone is amazed, until she cries again, and won't stop until her brother comforts her with the phrase "Bonka Wonka." Clearly the element that most intrigues baby Louise is her brother, Daniel.

This story was previously issued in the United States, illustrated by Debi Stephenson, in 1990. Both Stephenson and Martchenko capture the frustration of the parents and the delight of the baby with her brother. Wishinsky's text works because it's straightforward and unadorned: ultimately the story is empowering for any child who has a unique (and successful) relationship with a younger sibling.

Wolfe, Frances. *Where I Live.* **2001. 3 to 6.**
Author/illustrator Wolfe depicts the pellucid beauty of a calm sea in this celebration of the intense pleasures of wading, berry picking, and firelit evenings on the Nova Scotia coast. "Engines push great ships through water and oars pull my small boat over the waves, where I live . . . Special treasures are found on sun-warmed sands and in the cool green waters, where I live . . ." Double-page illustrations draw children into the sensual experiences and the mood of summer. With ripples of light through green sea, toes in water, and clean sand, this is a great way to introduce the joys of the sheltered areas of the North Atlantic coast.

* Wynne-Jones, Tim. Illustr. Eric Beddows. *Zoom at Sea.* **1983. 4 to 7.**
Zoom the cat has always loved sailing about in the sink and the tub, and when he finds directions for "the Sea and how to get there," left for him by his sea-going Uncle Roy, he sets off at once. When he arrives at the house of a mysterious, silver-bangled woman named Maria, it's as if she's been expecting him. With the turn of a giant wheel, she lets in the sea, gulls, sandpipers, pelicans, and terns. Her house expands, the walls disappear, and Zoom is free to voyage until he's exhausted. "Thank you for a great day," he says. "May I come back?" "I'm sure you will," says Maria.

Zoom's fantastical adventures have the surreal quality of a dream, with all the imaginative richness that implies. Is this "real"? Or is it just Zoom and Maria, a nurturing, inventive caretaker, imagining adventures together? Beddows's shadowed, monochromatic illustrations under-score the mysteriousness of it all: Maria's house is full of tall pillars, dark arches, and everyday household items that behave in peculiar ways. An atmospheric, thought-provoking tale. Highly recommended.

In sequels *Zoom Away* and *Zoom Upstream*, Zoom and Maria visit the Arctic and Egypt in their quest for elusive Uncle Roy.

Wynne-Jones, Tim. Illustr. Catharine O'Neill. *The Hour of the Frog.* **1989. 4 to 7.**
At night, while pets Fred and Dreadnought, Mum and Dad, and the goldfishes Thunder, Frisco, and Lyle sleep, a little girl lies awake. It is the Hour of the Frog! Thlump! She hears that frog as he crosses the

living room, dances in the front hall, and makes himself a sandwich of eggs, mayo, peanut butter, onions, and flies! But when he tries to come up to her room, he'd better watch out! She's a match for him.

With minimal words and maximal imagination, Wynne-Jones conveys the anxiety of nighttime wakefulness and a child's control of her fear. O'Neill's playful illustrations pick up on Wynne-Jones's humour: the dancing frog, the expressive child, even the flies-on-a-sticky-bun sandwich convey a midnight nuttiness. Delightful.

Wynne-Jones, Tim. Illustr. Dušan Petričić. *On Tumbledown Hill.* 1998. 4 to 7.
A spindly gentleman artist and a nervous bunny head up Tumbledown Hill to paint. But what's this? Wicked faces poke out between the words; bodies leap, bounce, and fight as, bit by bit, colourful monsters take over Tumbledown Hill, threatening painter and the page itself.

Begun as a literary exercise, in which each of the twenty-six sentences is one word shorter than the last, and with the device always apparent (Petričić presents the type to mimic Magnetic Poetry, so the loss of a word a page is always clear), this amusing picture book has visual and literary vigour. The black and white of print peels away to purple, green, pink, and turquoise, to winks, leers, grins, and derision. Wynne-Jones's well-chosen words, with their occasional rhymes and echoes, convey the artist's anxiety and self-questioning with panache. This fantastical tale will appeal to young children, or it can be used to inspire writing games with older ones.

Further delights can be found in Wynne-Jones's picture books *I'll Make You Small*, illustrated by Maryann Kovalski, and *The Last Piece of Sky*, illustrated by Marie-Louise Gay.

Ye, Ting-xing. Illustr. Harvey Chan. *Three Monks, No Water.* 1997. 4 to 7.
Ting-xing invents this folktale-like story to explain the traditional expression of the title for times when people try to avoid their chores. A monk lives alone in a mountain temple, and his only bother is that it's tedious carrying water up from the creek below. When another monk asks to join him, the first is thrilled. But the two of them can't seem to carry water successfully together; and when a third monk

comes along, thinking his scholarship is too important for him to do menial chores, no one carries the water. A fire that threatens to destroy the temple helps the monks recognize their foolishness.

Chan's amber illustrations, paint on textured board, have the appearance of ancient paper and suit the invented antiquity of the tale. Chinese characters and a Chinese seal on the flyleaves add to the effect. The moral is universal.

Share the Sky, also written by Ting-xing, illustrated by Suzanne Langlois, tells of a Chinese girl's experience as a new immigrant to Canada.

Yee, Paul. Illustr. Harvey Chan. *Roses Sing on New Snow: A Delicious Tale*. 1991. 5 to 9.
Having immigrated to North America, Maylin works in her father's restaurant every day and is responsible for its wonderful reputation, but her father credits her two lazy brothers with her work. In a cooking contest, judged by the visiting Governor of South China, Maylin's dish "Roses Sing on New Snow" is the winner, and her father is forced to reveal that she is its creator. Maylin is commanded to share the recipe, so that it can be taken back to China, but she maintains that the dish is one of the New World and cannot be recreated in the Old. After cooking with the governor, Maylin asks, "If you and I sat down with paper and brush and black ink, could we bring forth identical paintings?" – thus pointing out that an artist's hand can't be duplicated, in food or anything else.

Thoughtful Maylin, studious and carefully drawn, both in Yee's words and Chan's watercolours, is delightfully different from the overweight, lazy male members of her family. The governor's anger and conniving are patent in his facial expressions, and – somehow – Chan manages to convey too the energy of Maylin's cooking. A delicious and intriguing tale.

Yee, Paul. Illustr. Harvey Chan. *Ghost Train*. 1996. 8 and up.
After her father leaves China to find work in North America, Choon-yi makes her living as an artist. When her father sends money at last, she travels anxiously to join him – only to discover that he has been killed

in a slide while building the railway. He comes to her in a dream, however, asking her to paint a picture of the fire-car, the train that runs on the section of tracks he built. Choon-yi travels on the train, and although she hears shrieks of agony and anguished wailing, she sees no one. When she has finished her painting, her father appears to her once again, showing her how to take the souls of those who have died building the railway back to China.

Yee's haunting tale is exquisitely illustrated by Chan, whose paintings stress the magical quality of the story, yet still show Choon-yi very much as a child of this world. This beautiful tribute to the Chinese immigrants who lost their lives building the railway alerts children to some of the less laudable moments in Canadian history; at the same time, it gives them a sense of Canada's shared-but-diverse cultures.

* **Yerxa, Leo. *Last Leaf First Snowflake to Fall*. 1993. 7 and up.**
This remarkable work, celebrating the secret moment when fall turns to winter, is both a visual and a verbal poem.

"Long ago, before time / before sunlight burst across the universe . . . before shadows were placed by the hands of the Creator across rabbit trails on moonlit snow . . ." So Yerxa brings us to the moment of an Anishinabe adult and child's departure for a secret place in the wilderness. By canoe and on foot, they travel the lakes and woods of northern Ontario, the child describing, with precise and noticing eye, the small and great beauties all around – up until that unseen moment of transition, the fall of the last leaf, the fall of the first snowflake.

Yerxa's collage illustrations in the bronzes, ambers, and deep greens of the northern woods draw the viewer into both season and place. Dyed tissue paper, wrinkled and textured like the veins of leaves or the surface of wind-touched water, give the landscape depth and mystery. This trek at the time of seasonal change becomes a mythic journey; the child's waking up to snow has the newness of a birth. An outstanding book to share with a thoughtful child, even an adolescent. Highly recommended.

Yerxa, Leo. *A Fish Tale, or The Little One That Got Away*. 1995. 6 to 9.
Now an "old, gray and dingy fuddie-duddie" fish, the protagonist of this odyssey tells how, as Small Fry, he was bored in dart school and

decided to find out whether all the tales of the sky, hooks, and upper reaches of the water were true. Lured away by knowing, not-to-be-trusted Jack, he finds out that being Small Fry saves his life. And though he discovers that all the stories are true, that "God answers prayers no matter what kind of fish you are," he realizes he can't really share his experience with anyone.

This wry fable brings up the big questions about life, and shows how terrifying but satisfying the results of a quest for knowledge can be. Yerxa's deep, luminous blues and greens make the water palpable in its endless depth and height and breadth.

Zagwÿn, Deborah Turney. *The Pumpkin Blanket.* **1990. 3 to 5.**
When Clee was born, the "Northern Lights shook their folds above her bed, but no one saw them." Clee now has a beautiful blanket, with sunny-coloured squares like a garden patch, and that blanket is a treasured companion. One night, when she's about to enter kindergarten, where her blanket will be out of place, Clee's father shows her that something else might need the blanket's squares – twelve pumpkins, ripening and threatened by frost. Clee gives up her blanket square by square to protect the pumpkins, and when the pumpkins are ready, the wind whirls the squares back up into the night.

Zagwÿn's soft watercolour-and-coloured-pencil illustrations suit this comforting tale of growing up, a story particularly appropriate for children attached to security blankets (or other things). Cosmic overtones soften the direct message of the narrative. Zagwÿn portrays Clee's emotions honestly and respectfully.

Subsequent stories *Turtle Spring*, *The Winter Gift*, and *The Sea House* deal with various moments of growth for Clee and her sibling.

Zeman, Ludmila. *The First Red Maple Leaf.* **1997. 4 to 6.**
When they emigrated from eastern Europe, Zeman's children asked, "Why is the maple leaf the symbol of Canada?" This story, told in the style of a legend, is her answer.

When the world is young, people know nothing but winter, and the evil Iceheart terrifies them. With the help of a goose, a boy leads the people south to where the trees are covered with leaves, only to see Iceheart shake these leaves off too. Birds from the south roost in the trees and are transformed into foliage, restoring the trees' former glory.

Zeman starts her story with dull beige, white, and grey, expanding her palette to include the rich reds and golds as people flee to the south. Her background as an animated filmmaker is everywhere evident: she fills the pages with as many as nine different vignettes, each allowing the reader to see a scene in the tale. The magnificent art has a European flair, reflecting the author/illustrator's heritage and her love of Canada.

Zimmermann, H. Werner. *Snow Day.* **1999. 4 to 6.**
Most children in Canada are familiar with the winter hope that school will be closed because of too much snow. Zimmermann shows the delight of two children, their dog, cat, and friends, as they enjoy the day off from school and the pleasures of deep snow. Making snow angels, catching snowflakes with their tongues, building forts, waving to the snowplough – everything that children do in a snowfall is lovingly and humorously portrayed. The adults are convincingly shown employed in more mundane activities, such as shovelling out driveways and cleaning up after the snowplough.

Zimmermann's illustrations have an exuberance that reflects the children's joy; his pale blues and greys illustrate the soft light of the winter day as it wanes into night, when the children are once again looking out the window and hoping for another snow day. The story is a great tool for classroom use during a snowy winter, and a fun story for reading aloud at home.

RECOMMENDED FOR OLDER READERS
The thoughtful stories and sophisticated illustrations in the following picture books invite the attention of older children and even teenagers.

Andrews, Jan	*Very Last First Time*
Bedard, Michael	*Emily*
Booth, David	*The Dust Bowl*
Butler, Geoff	*The Hangashore*
Carrier, Roch	*The Hockey Sweater*
Fagan, Cary	*Daughter of the Great Zandini*
Gregory, Nan	*How Smudge Came*

Hovey, Kate	*Arachne Speaks* (*See* Traditional Tales)
Jam, Teddy	*The Fishing Summer*
	The Stone Boat
Khalsa, Dayal Kaur	*Tales of a Gambling Grandma*
Khan, Rukhsana	*The Roses in My Carpets*
King, Thomas	*A Coyote Columbus Story*
Kusugak, Michael	*Baseball Bats for Christmas*
	Arctic Stories
Laurence, Margaret	*The Olden Days Coat*
Littlechild, George	*This Land Is My Land*
Major, Kevin	*Eh? to Zed*
Muller, Robin	*The Nightwood* (*See* Traditional Tales)
Nichol, Barbara	*Beethoven Lives Upstairs*
Oberman, Sheldon	*The Always Prayer Shawl*
Van Camp, Richard	*What's the Most Beautiful Thing You Know About Horses?*
Yee, Paul	*Ghost Train*
	Roses Sing on New Snow
Yerxa, Leo	*Last Leaf First Snowflake to Fall*
	A Fish Tale

Traditional Tales

The rich, multicultural makeup of Canada and a strong organization of storytellers have resulted in the production of many anthologies and picture books of retold, lavishly illustrated, traditional stories. Legends, folktales, and fairy tales from China, India, Russia, Africa, Europe, and Latin America are all represented here, in addition to many tales from the Aboriginal and First Nations cultures of North and South America. Because many of these traditional stories have been handed down through an oral tradition, and thus have strong plots, patterns of repetition, and often song-like language, they are extremely useful for storytellers. Their narrative patterns are especially successful with young children, who are gratified by stories in which "big guys" are outdone by fast-thinking, courageous "little guys."

Aldana, Patricia, ed. Illustr. Luis Garay. *Jade and Iron: Latin American Tales from Two Cultures*. 1996. 64 pages. 7 and up.
"Jade for the stone that was precious to the original inhabitants and iron, which was used by the Europeans for tools and weapons," Aldana writes of the title of this collection of tales told by a number of writers. Haunting, magical tales are gathered here: young Manioc asks to be buried alive because she knows her father wanted a boy child; the Enchantress of Cordoba never seems to grow old; a black ship sails through a tale dark, sinister, and foreboding. Nicaraguan artist Garay provides illustrations that focus on the crucial moment in each brief story; luminous colours in shadowed settings highlight the stories'

drama and emotional impact. Latin American culture is powerfully portrayed. With its brief stories (many of which don't appear elsewhere in English) and Garay's dark, forceful art, this is an excellent collection for the age group.

Andrews, Jan. Illustr. Simon Ng. *Out of the Everywhere: New Tales for Canada*. 2000. 4 and up.
"Out of the everywhere into here" is the saying that inspired this collection of folktales chosen from the heritage of Canada's diverse cultural communities. Andrews brings together ten tales – of Asian, Indian, First Nations, South American, and other origins – and sets them in the context of Canada. A mouse bride, the Twelve Months (twelve old men) who save the faithful girl, a woman who raises a mermaid, a wise daughter who fills her father's shop with light – these tales are full of fascinating characters, and extraordinary happenings that speak of human need.

The truths of the tales are burnished by years of imagination and retelling; Andrews lets their wisdom shine out in her direct, lucid prose. "Everyone brings something to a new country," she begins one tale. "Part of what Sayed brought was a terrible fear of not having enough." The human heart of each story is utterly clear in her renditions; Ng's illustrations, with rich, heavy colours and darkly shadowed, statuesque figures, emphasize the stories' mythic import. An excellent choice to read aloud or for stronger readers to enjoy alone.

Badoe, Adwoa. Illustr. Baba Wagué Diakité. *The Pot of Wisdom: Ananse Stories*. 2001. 63 pages. 7 and up.
Ananse, the trickster spider of some African traditions, is the protagonist of these ten tales, each illustrated with the thick, deep colours of glaze on ceramic tile. Vain, jealous, grasping, cocky, Ananse has all the human foibles to an extravagant degree. The stories play on both his ingenuity and his hapless lack of foresight. In one story he outwits a dwarf, a python, and an entire household of bees to become endowed as "the owner of stories." In another, he's shown up by his own sons, done in by his greedy stomach. Whatever happens, he's irrepressible, there to prevent us, like all trickster figures, from taking ourselves too seriously. These tricky, wise stories are perfect to share with young

children, who can see when Ananse's riding for a fall, boo him, laugh at him, and, at the same time, recognize human silliness. Badoe's tellings are deft and unobtrusive: she lets the story do the entertaining.

Barton, Bob. Illustr. Coral Nault. *Best and Dearest Chick of All*. 1994. 3 to 5.
Cheep-Cheep's always out of favour with his stepmother, Speckle, who cossets her own chick and bestows upon him a ridiculously long, fulsome name: "Little Yellow Fluffy Ball / Best and Dearest Chick of All / Not Another on the Farm / Boasts Such Beauty Wit and Charm." When a fox abducts "Little Yellow. . . ." etc., it takes so long for Cheep-Cheep and Speckle to relay who it is that's in trouble that "Little Yellow . . ." etc. almost meets his demise.

Barton's retelling of this funny, cautionary story is poetic and rhythmic: his ear for the fall and sound of words makes it an excellent read-aloud.

Clement, Gary. *Just Stay Put: A Chelm Story*. 1995. 4 and up.
See Picture Books.

Davis, Aubrey. Illustr. Dušan Petričić. *Bone Button Borscht*. 1995. 4 to 8.
When a ragged beggar arrives in a cold, bleak town, he shows that borscht made from buttons is indeed possible. In the synagogue – the only building with light – he cuts the buttons off his coat and says that if he had one more he could make borscht. In no time someone finds another button, then a pot, a spoon . . . little by little people bring a few carrots, some pickle juice, and finally the whole town has contributed to the steaming pot of borscht – made miraculously from buttons.

This charming version of the story of "stone soup" celebrates Jewish culture and is longer than most versions of the tale. Davis makes clear that the beggar's greatest miracle is that he has inspired the townspeople to share once again. Petričić's pencil-and-watercolour illustrations are gloriously evocative, showing the dark, seemingly uninhabited town with its single thin shaft of light from the synagogue blossoming into a row of lit houses and a friendly crowd of people at the story's end. This is one of the most satisfying versions of this tale.

Davis, Aubrey. Illustr. Dušan Petričić. *The Enormous Potato.* **1997. 2 to 5.**

Davis tells the popular "enormous turnip" tale with humour and wit, having honed it over years of storytelling to a tale of few words of great effect. In his rendition, the farmer, dressed in overcoat, boots, hat, and glasses, plants the eye of a potato, and it grows into the biggest potato in the world. He gets his wife, daughter, dog, cat, and even a mouse to help pull it out, and then everyone comes together for a potato feast.

The bright yellow background to Petričić's unusual, inventive illustrations commands attention; his exaggerated, sharp-nosed characters emphasize the story's fantastical elements. This is perfect for sharing with large groups of preschoolers.

Galloway, Priscilla. Illustr. Norman Cousineau. *Aleta and the Queen: A Tale of Ancient Greece.* **Tales of Ancient Lands series. 1995. 158 pages. 10 and up.**

Galloway retells tales of ancient Greece in a handsomely produced collection of large-format books, each illustrated by Cousineau. *Aleta and the Queen* contains stories from *The Odyssey* as though seen through the eyes of a serving girl in Ithaca. Galloway brings out the passion in this ancient tale, with its outlandish turns of plot, bizarre characters, and copious bloodshed. She doesn't temper the gruesome or libidinous aspects of the story, but simply makes it more accessible to young readers. She includes the complex lineage of the gods and goddesses where necessary, but doesn't swamp readers with too much background.

In three additional titles, *Atalanta: The Fastest Runner in the World*, *Daedalus and the Minotaur*, and *My Hero Hercules*, Galloway continues these "tales of ancient lands." *Atalanta* is the story of the girl whose father wants her killed at birth, and later wants her to marry against her will. *Daedalus and the Minotaur* includes the traditional story of the building of the labyrinth, the bond between Icarus and the Minotaur, and the inventions of Daedalus.

In *My Hero Hercules*, the mortal boy, Jason, provides a contrast to Hercules's great physical strength in a story likely to have special appeal to young male readers.

Each volume has a pronunciation guide and background information. Cousineau's stylized drawings are reminiscent of ancient pottery and friezes, and suit the stories' roots.

Gay, Marie-Louise. *The 3 Little Pigs*. 1994. 3 to 5.
Three little pigs set off to seek their fortunes; after a big bad wolf blows down the houses and consumes the first two pigs, the third one outwits him.

With great economy of language, Gay tells the traditional story, not shirking the consumption of pigs number one and two by the wolf. Her colourful, cock-eyed pen-and-watercolour drawings provide all the wind-whirling action and sly plotting tension a child could want. Puckering up to blow, his underlip whiskers quivering, this scrawny wolf has every air of the not-too-bright conniver. The pig's final smile of well-fed satisfaction says it all. An excellent rendition for young children.

Gay, Marie-Louise. *Rumpelstiltskin*. 1997. 4 to 7.
When a grasping father claims his daughter can spin straw into gold, the local monarch locks her up and says that if she doesn't do so, she will die. A little man appears and offers to perform the feat in exchange for the girl's first-born. When the king finally marries her and the little man eventually shows up again, the new queen doesn't want to lose her baby. She has to guess the little man's name within three days in order to save her child.

Gay's minimal text gets right down to the action in this tale of a woman caught between two grasping men. Graphite-and-coloured-pencil illustrations show everything there is to know about the cast – the king with a calculating eye and massive scarlet cape; the vulnerable girl, pigtails floating behind her; and little Rumpelstiltskin, with vigorously bristling eyebrows, and curling, pointy shoes that end in leafy twigs. The magical power of name is made dynamically apparent in the double-spread lettering of "RUMPELSTILTSKIN!!"

* Gilman, Phoebe. *Something from Nothing*. 1992. 2 to 8.
See Picture Books.

Hovey, Kate. Illustr. Blair Drawson. *Arachne Speaks.* **2001. 8 and up.**
Passionate energy propels this version of Arachne's fateful weaving
contest with Athena. Renowned for her skill at the loom, Arachne
refuses to credit the goddess as the source of her talents. Challenging
Athena to a contest, she weaves a peerless tapestry, depicting the
deities in shameful acts. Powerful Athena blasts her for her arrogance
and turns her into a spider.

Bold, commanding, with a deep sense of injustice, Hovey's Arachne
is determined to stand up for herself. An intricate scheme of rhyme and
rhythm gives the verse tension and force, and a tone of proud, outraged
exclamation. Youth defies age; the hard-working artisan defies privi-
lege and authority; daughter defies "mother" – this will resonate
particularly with middle-grade and adolescent readers. In his illustrations, Drawson echoes the clean lines and stylized features of classical
friezes, showing drapery defined as Greek columns, faces flattened and
angular. Arachne's turquoise dress, the deep azures of her tapestry,
leap out of the pale, sandy tones of marble with Mediterranean brilliance, bringing home the vivid personality of a girl who dares to stand
up to the gods – and is punished for it.

Hughes, Monica. Illustr. Brenda Clark. *Little Fingerling.* **1989. 4 to 7.**
In this traditional Japanese tale, a couple long for a child, even one "no
bigger than the tip of a finger." And that's what they get: Issun Boshi,
"Little Fingerling," who at the right time sets off to seek his fortune. He
falls in love with a nobleman's daughter and, after miraculously saving
her from two horrible demons, is turned into a handsome, human-sized
samurai with the blow of a magic mallet.

Hughes's narrative is fluid and clear. In the illustrations, Clark presents in accurate detail the architecture, household objects, and clothing
of the Japan of the period. The idea of a tiny person is always attractive
to children, and this has the added benefit of conveying information
about Japan.

Katz, Welwyn Wilton. Illustr. Laszlo Gal. *Beowulf.* **1999. 8 to 12.**
Katz's version of the Old English poem *Beowulf* is less a retelling than
a novel based on some of the original poem's characters. It revolves

around the coming-of-age of Wiglaf, a young warrior who comes into the original tale only at its end. Here, Wiglaf listens to his grandfather tell the story of Beowulf's famous struggle with the loathsome Grendel and his even more monstrous mother. Then he travels to Beowulf's court to take his place as a warrior. There, he helps Beowulf defeat a dragon in a final, fatal contest.

Katz replaces the stark, grand values of Beowulf's culture with psychological motives – a kind of emotional neediness on Beowulf's part – and with Wiglaf's constant interruptions, the story of the fight with Grendel loses momentum. Despite this, when Wiglaf arrives in Beowulf's court, the pace picks up immediately: his part in the dragon-slaying will have readers on edge. And Katz's psychologizing has the advantage of giving modern readers an avenue into this alien culture. Gal's illustrations, with glowing colours and textured backgrounds, are rather too refined for the tale's wildness.

Keens-Douglas, Richardo. Illustr. Marie Lafrance. *La Diablesse and the Baby*. 1994. 4 to 7.
See Picture Books.

Keens-Douglas, Richardo. Illustr. Stéphane Jorisch. *The Trial of the Stone*. 2000. 4 to 7.
When Matt takes a nap in the forest, he places his three coins under a stone for safety. Someone steals them, and when Matt wakes up and makes a commotion, the village judge orders the stone arrested and makes it stand trial for robbery. The proceedings are so silly that the villagers can't keep from laughing: the judge fines them each a penny for disrespect to the court, and Matt gets the proceeds.

Keens-Douglas's text is brief and almost like the script for a play, and the action is wonderfully farcical. Jorisch gives viewers a little sub-plot to think about: the real thief is apparent in every picture. This is excellent folktale humour, benign but clever justice.

King, Thomas. Illustr. William Kent Monkman. *A Coyote Columbus Story*. 1992. 4 to 8.
See Picture Books.

King, Thomas. Illustr. Johnny Wales. *Coyote Sings to the Moon.* **1999. 4 to 8.**
Coyote is an overweening fellow and always overestimates his own abilities, but here his incapacities actually end up saving the day – or rather the night. With his horrible singing he has driven Moon to the bottom of the pond, and all the choral harmony of Old Woman and the creatures can't raise her back to the sky. But Old Woman finally dreams up a plan in which Coyote's awful singing is the critical feature. "A solo?" asks Coyote, amazed.

Coyote's lolloping tongue and ears, his firm belief in his powers, and his inability to see his limits, make him an endearing, slapstick protagonist. What with his antics and King's direct, terse dialogue and tight dramatic plot, this story begs to be read with enormous expression. In Wales's watercolours, Coyote struts his paces, Moon is stylish in a wide-brimmed hat and shades, and the forest creatures, barred and speckled with shadow, eye the whole mess, appalled. Highly entertaining.

Langston, Laura. Illustr. Victor Bosson. *The Magic Ear.* **1995. 4 to 7.**
Honesty is rewarded in this tale based on a traditional Japanese story. A poor peasant, Hoderi, first saves a baby sea bream from a large angry fish. In fact, he has saved the life of the daughter of the king of Neriya, and he is taken into the sea to be rewarded. His reward is the magic ear – a shell that "will let you understand all the earth's creatures." With this treasure he helps solve the secret illness of a nobleman's daughter and wins her for his wife.

The tale is similar to many other folktales with poor and honest young men winning great positions and beautiful wives because of their kindness and honesty. This story is exquisitely illustrated by Bosson: each picture is framed in Japanese fabric. The style is very much reminiscent of antique Japanese art.

* Lottridge, Celia Barker. Illustr. Ian Wallace. *The Name of the Tree.* **1989. 2 to 8.**
Children are empowered by this Bantu folktale in which a tortoise helps the larger, older starving animals learn the name of the tree that will allow them to eat the fruit that is "as red as pomegranates, as

yellow as bananas, as green as melons, as purple as plums, as orange as mangoes and smelled like all the fruits of the world."

Lottridge's storytelling background is evident through her use of simple-but-effective language. Wallace portrays the drought faced by the animals with soft dusty illustrations in the muted shades of the Savannah: this is one of his most accomplished works. A perfect story to read aloud to young children and a marvellous tale for beginning storytellers. Highly recommended.

Lottridge, Celia Barker. Illustr. Joanne Fitzgerald. *Ten Small Tales*. 1993. 63 pages. 2 to 7.

These ten small tales, collected from around the world and polished to perfection, are ideal for telling or reading aloud to young children. Originating in Africa, Russia, Malaysia, Puerto Rico, India, and elsewhere, the stories include familiar tales, such as "The Old Fashioned Bed" and "The One Turnip Garden," as well as stories that may be new to the audience but have been passed down through generations of storytellers in other lands.

Fitzgerald's pastel watercolours enhance the spare nursery-tale text; each story has at least one full-page illustration. Additional smaller illustrations are scattered throughout the book and emphasize important elements in the tales. Fitzgerald's humans are particularly expressive – whether an old woman enjoying a cup of tea after outwitting a wolf or a dejected boy waiting for his father.

Lottridge, Celia Barker. Illustr. Harvey Chan. *Music for the Tsar of the Sea*. 1998. 4 to 7.

Sadko, a poor minstrel of Novgorod, one day pleases the mythic Tsar of the sea with his music. The water churns, the waves break, and the Tsar himself rises up from Lake Ilmen to offer Sadko a reward of jewels. In return, Sadko must promise that one day he'll play in the Tsar's underwater palace. But when he does return, as a successful sea-going merchant, his music is so powerful, the Tsar's dancing so wild, that it sets all the waters of the Caspian Sea in turbulence. Only with the help of the Tsar's daughter does Sadko manage to escape.

This tale has the allure of a fairy tale and the power of a creation story. Lottridge's telling is sure and compelling; Chan's oil-pastel illustrations are otherworldly. Deep, rich colours – amber, cobalt, and ultraviolet – glow in the dark regions of the Tsar's realm. Glimmers of gold, swirls of bronze, point up the drama of his frantic dancing, his monumental figure. An extremely successful collaboration.

* **Lottridge, Celia Barker. Illustr. Joanne Fitzgerald.** *The Little Rooster and the Diamond Button*. **2001. 3 to 7.**
Pecking away on the road outside the cottage, Little Rooster unearths a diamond button. But before he has a chance to claim it for his old, poor mistress, an imperial – and imperious! – sultan comes along, dripping with jewels, and takes it. Little Rooster isn't content to leave it at that: he follows the Sultan to his palace and, with the help of his obliging stomach and lots of persistence, manages to win the button, and much more, back.

This satisfying "swallowing" tale from Hungary shows that the little folk can win out over the big guys. Lottridge's sparing use of repetition invites the young audience to chime in at times; a carefully honed, understated storytelling style makes this a terrific read-aloud. Fitzgerald's illustrations are perfect for the story's style and its Hungarian origins, with soft yellows, rounded curves, and vistas of the green hills and villas of "once, long ago." And of course, the theme of swallowing and disgorging is one of particular amusement to the age group. Highly recommended.

Martin, Eva. Illustr. Laszlo Gal. *Canadian Fairy Tales*. **123 pages. 1984. 8 and up.**
In this handsome collection, storyteller Martin retells, in uniquely Canadian versions, twelve tales taken from various European backgrounds. Included are the familiar "Princess of Tomboso" and some well-known Ti-Jean tales, as well as others that may be completely unknown to readers. Some stories come with a new twist: in Martin's version of "Beauty and the Beast," the beast is a woman and the beauty a prince. Saint Nicholas makes an appearance in another tale, when he is summoned with a willow whistle by two children who escape being pickled by a butcher. What sets these tales apart from their European variants is the image of the powerful forest, an image that suggests the demands it must have made on early settlers in Canada.

Gal provides one elegant illustration for each story; Martin's story-telling is forthright and simple, a reflection of her years of telling tales orally. This is a marvellous book for storytellers, as the tales can be learned and told very easily.

Marton, Jirina, illustr. *Lady Kaguya's Secret: A Japanese Tale.* **1997. 4 to 7.**
Marton provides luxurious illustrations for this traditional Japanese story of a mysterious girl, who was found in a bamboo grove, raised by a peasant couple, and later courted by many, including the Emperor. Her depictions of Lady Kaguya are luminescent, a fitting quality for one who, it turns out, is the true daughter of the Moon King and only temporarily on earth. Rich reds, greens, and golds express Lady Kaguya's royal and ethereal lineage. The text, unfortunately by an anonymous author who can't be credited, is straightforward and succinct.

McKibbon, Hugh William. Illustr. Scott Cameron. *The Token Gift.* **1996. 6 and up.**
See Picture Books.

Muller, Robin. *The Nightwood.* **1991. 4 to 7.**
Based on the English fairy tale "Tamlane," this book focuses on the part of the story that happens in the woods – the Nightwood that is enchanted by the Elfin Queen, and where Elaine (burd Janet in "Tamlane") goes to dance and later save her lover from the Elfin Queen. "Beware of the Elves. / All children must learn: / If you stray in the woods / You may never return," is the portentous refrain.

A rather lengthy text gives viewers plenty of time to take in Muller's transporting illustrations. Elaine fairly radiates from the story, both beautiful and frighteningly possessed. The tale has a dark edge, and Muller picks up on this, showing the sinister elements of the Nightwood. The first illustration in this book, wonderfully reminiscent of Rackham in style, stands up to the best of fairy-tale illustration.

Muller's retelling of the traditional English tale *Mollie Whuppie and the Giant* is also notable because of Muller's illustrations – splatter-painted with toothbrush and Popsicle stick.

Reid, Barbara. *Two by Two*. **1992. 3 to 6.**
In rhyming couplets and complete with musical notation at the back, Reid tells the biblical story of Noah and his family building the ark, boarding all the animals by increasing increments – two pairs, three pairs, and so on. Reid's eye for detail – texture, expression, posture – gives her Plasticine illustrations great visual interest. Readers can find a monkey about to steal a banana, Noah's son on the verge of throwing up, and Mrs. Noah gathering eggs. With a focus on animals and a nicely rhyming narrative, this is a good choice for toddlers.

Reid, Barbara. *The Golden Goose*. **2000. 3 to 6.**
When the kind-but-downtrodden third son of a woodcutter's widow shares his food with "an old grey man," he's rewarded with a magical golden goose that leads him on quite a line dance through the country-side. Everyone who touches the goose is stuck to her – and all concludes with the rescue of a sober-faced used-car salesman's daughter and a happy ending.

Reid's Plasticine illustrations reach a fine pitch of fun and vivacity here. A schoolmistress in tweeds and sensible shoes, a lady with a million lawn ornaments, even the good-natured, unassuming hero – the whole cast is so lively, so full of personality that one feels a novel could be written about each of them. This has the typical strong plot of the Grimms' tale which is its source, but Reid has enhanced it with character.

Richards, Nancy Wilcox. Illustr. H. Werner Zimmermann. *Farmer Joe's Hot Day*. **1987. 2 to 4.**
See Picture Books.

Richardson, Bill. *After Hamelin*. **2000. 227 pages. 8 to 12.**
See Novels, 7 to 12.

* **Sage, James. Illustr. Pierre Pratt.** *Sassy Gracie*. **1998. 4 to 7.**
With a flair for dancing, new red shoes, and the cook off for the day, Gracie the maid has every chance to work up an appetite. And she does – so much so that she can't resist eating both of the chickens she roasted for her master's dinner party. When she sees her master's

dinner guest coming over the hill, she's filled with trepidation, until she thinks of a way to scare him off and absolve herself.

This traditional tale of a tricky, enterprising underdog outwitting the authorities comes through with great animation. The rhythm in Sage's language gives it the liveliness of an uproariously told oral tale; Pratt's oil-pastel drawings of the manic dancer, with her huge red shoes flying all over the pages and her enormous grin, show Gracie everywhere at once. Cock-eyed angles, heavy outlines, and shifting perspective match the bouncing energy and sassy spirit of ravenous Gracie. Highly recommended.

Setterington, Ken. Illustr. Nelly and Ernst Hofer. *Hans Christian Andersen's The Snow Queen*. 2000. 48 pages. 4 to 10.
Kay and Gerda have always been close friends, until the Snow Queen freezes Kay's heart and carries him off. It's up to Gerda to rescue her friend from the snow and the wind, and from his own icy heart – though it means outwitting a witch, escaping robbers, and travelling by reindeer to the far reaches of Lapland and Finland. A swarm of white bees, a message on a dried codfish, and a robber girl who bites her mother's ear all come into play in Andersen's blend of moral fairy tale and earthy language.

Setterington's telling is able and succinct: he tones down Andersen's rococo piety with his matter-of-fact tone and heightens the strangeness and fascination of Gerda's adventures. The Hofers' *scherenschnitt*, or cut-paper, illustrations bring out the ethereal, icy aspects of the tale. Snow crystals, rosy trellises, and the gabled houses of European folk art are precisely cut and presented as silhouettes, to remarkable visual effect.

Singh, Rina. Illustr. Farida Zaman. *The Foolish Men of Agra and Other Tales of Mogul India*. 1998. 48 pages. 5 and up.
In these ten stories handed down from the sixteenth-century court of Mogul emperor Akbar, Akbar's Hindu friend and advisor, Birbal, finds himself put on the spot repeatedly as he tries to save Akbar from making foolish judgements. In one tale, an ambitious courtier accuses a poor Brahmin of illegally warming himself by the palace lights a mile away, so Akbar sends the poor man away in disgrace. Birbal then

invites Akbar for dinner and puts the pot so far above the fire that the guests are kept waiting for hours. "How can the heat of this fire reach the pot so far away?" Akbar asks when he sees the cooking arrangements – and then suddenly gets the message.

Birbal's actions are clever parables that show up the weakness in Akbar's logic, a testament to the effective power of brains over brawn and its political equivalent. His wits keep readers guessing; Singh doesn't give away the logic until the last moment, so these funny, wise stories are excellent for making children think. Zaman's illustrations, in bright pinks, purple, and gold, shimmer like the festive silks, sashes, and embroideries of the courtiers.

Taylor, C. J. *Bones in the Basket: Native Stories of the Origin of People*. 1994. 5 to 10.
Mohawk artist and storyteller Taylor tells and illustrates eight tales of human origins in this collection drawn from a variety of North America's First Peoples: Osage, Zuñi, Mohawk, Cree, and others. Father Earth and Mother Sky, a magical raft, a rolling Elk, bones in a basket – in terse, economical prose Taylor unfolds these enigmatic stories. Deeply coloured, almost-surreal oil illustrations in yellow-green, cobalt, and scarlet underscore the powerful fertility of the moment the stories address. Rising land and emerging creatures against the blue darkness of space show form coming out of formlessness. Effective, succinct storytelling.

Additional thematic collections can be found in Taylor's *The Monster from the Swamp: Native Legends of Monsters, Demons and Other Creatures* and *How We Saw the World: Nine Native Stories of the Way Things Began*. The sources for the stories are listed in each volume. Most of them come from American compilations and retellings.

Taylor, C. J. *The Messenger of Spring*. 1997. 5 to 8.
Taylor retells, from a version recorded in an American collection of Native legends, the story of the encounter of spring messenger New Dawn and the formerly mighty Ice Man, whose strength has now diminished to puddles of ice water. When the aging Ice Man has finished his description of wintry power, he invites New Dawn to sing and dance his own story. As New Dawn dances, the trees bud and flower, the birds

return, and green floods the forest. The little flower known as the "Spring Beauty" is the only sign of winter's former presence.

Out of the blues and whites of winter, Taylor shows the pervading greens and red-browns of spring coming forth. The visual effusion is effective here; beams of spring light streak New Dawn as he grows to mythic stature. Simply and economically told.

Taylor's version of an Abenaki story of the origin of corn can be found in *How Two-feather Was Saved from Loneliness* and a Seneca legend in *Little Water and the Gift of the Animals*.

Thornhill, Jan. *The Rumour: A Jataka Tale from India.* **2002. 3 to 6.** A nervous, bristly hare hears a mango crashing down and assumes the world is breaking up. She alerts all the other hares, who in turn alert the pygmy hogs, the swamp deer, the tigers, and the Indian rhinos, all of whom flee in panic. The wise Asiatic lion finally forces the animals to re-examine the situation.

Thornhill tells this Buddhist moral tale without verbal embellishment, but her illustrations glow with light and colour. Patterned borders of mangoes and flowers frame each picture; the clear colours of the animals (all endangered species) shine in the detailed foliage of a fairytale Indian forest depicted with all the intricacy of a knotted carpet.

Toye, William. Illustr. Elizabeth Cleaver. *The Loon's Necklace.* **1977. 4 to 8.** Toye has retold several Aboriginal legends, deriving his text from *Canadian Wonder Tales* by Cyrus Macmillan. It's because of Cleaver's innovative collage illustrations, however, that these versions of the legends have come to have a place in Canadian children's literature. *The Loon's Necklace*, *The Fire Stealer*, *The Mountain Goats of Temlahan*, and *How Summer Came to Canada*, which derive from First Nations peoples in various parts of Canada, are all stories about the origins of nature – the world as it is – emphasizing the close relationship between human beings and the earth. The Trickster figures of Nanabozho and Glooskap figure in the origin of fire, fall colours, and summer; in *Mountain Goats*, shape-changing animals punish wasteful hunters. Cleaver uses collage, paint, prints, and even leaves and bark in her vivid illustrations. Rough prints evoke the carving of the Haida.

These tales have the strong structure of traditional stories; the collage shows children some possibilities for making their own art.

White, Ellen. Illustr. David Neel. *Kwulasulwut: Stories from the Coast Salish.* **1981. 76 pages. 6 to 8.**
White is an experienced Salish storyteller, and here she tells five stories, a mixture of traditional tales and original stories that use traditional themes. The most memorable one is "The Stolen Sun," in which Seagull tries to lord it over the world by imprisoning Sun in his cedar box. It takes the combined efforts of the ants, Raven, and Sea Urchin to let Sun back out into the world, so that humans and creatures can live and hunt as they should.

White has a robust, direct storytelling voice – Seagull laughs "so hard he could hardly stand up"; the ants "smack their little lips and pick their little teeth" when they've finished a good meal, an image that has to provoke a smile. The strong Trickster theme makes this both entertaining and educational. Poor production values make this a resource, or read-aloud book, rather than one children might pick up on their own.

A second volume of Coast Salish stories, *Kwulasulwut II: More Stories from the Coast Salish*, explores "training" – the experience of visions, among other things.

Ye, Ting-xing. Illustr. Suzanne Langlois. *Weighing the Elephant.* **1998. 4 to 7.**
Hei-dou's whole village loves Huan-Huan the elephant, because he's so talented and helpful. The Emperor hears of Huan-Huan's great resourcefulness and demands that Huan-Huan come to court, but the elephant refuses to perform for him and his demanding family. When the Emperor threatens to punish Huan-Huan with hard labour unless the villagers can answer a riddle – how much does Huan-Huan weigh? – it's Hei-dou's clever thinking that saves the day.

Like the best folktales, this pivots on logic and wisdom, and like the best folktales, it shows the arbitrary power of authority upset by the resourcefulness of the powerless. It presents a good mathematical puzzle, as well.

Zeman, Ludmila. *Gilgamesh the King.* **1992. 4 to 8.**
This most ancient Mesopotamian epic (over five thousand years old in its written form) makes an excellent fantasy adventure. Gilgamesh, a god-man, is sent by the Sun God to rule the people of the city Uruk. But when Gilgamesh expresses his power by acting cruelly, the Sun God creates another man, Enkidu, and sends him to live with animals. Enkidu becomes strong and compassionate; when beautiful Shamhat is sent to lure Enkidu to the city, so Gilgamesh can destroy him, Enkidu ends up teaching Gilgamesh the value of compassion and mercy.

Zeman's telling is clear and unadorned: the mythic meanings of this powerful epic are there for child and adult to pluck. What does it mean to be human? the story considers. In later adventures (*The Revenge of Ishtar* and *The Last Quest of Gilgamesh*), the meaning of human mortality and friendship come into play. Since this story is one of the ancient origins of the conventions and standards of epic heroism that children see in fantasy today – from Tolkien to *Star Wars* to Harry Potter – it's a good way to start them thinking about parallels between fantasies. Zeman's luxurious, tapestry-like illustrations, with borders featuring cuneiform script, offer a golden vision of an ancient kingdom. Like the friezes they imitate, these pictures tell an intricate story.

* Zeman, Ludmila. *Sindbad: From the Tales of a Thousand and One Nights.* **1999. 4 to 7.**
Sindbad the Merchant tells Sindbad the Porter of the first of his eventful journeys. Shipwrecked, Sindbad drifts for days clinging to a wooden barrel, only to find that the first island he lands on is home to a rapacious bird called a Roc. He escapes by tying himself to its foot, and when he finally steps off, he's in a valley that's full of diamonds, but haunted by vultures. And more!

Zeman bases her illustrations on the art and calligraphy of Persian books, carpets, and miniatures. Every page is a visual feast, from the intricately populated borders to the vigorous action at centre stage. Exotic colours illuminate the lands of Sindbad's adventures, and he stares wild-eyed, terrorized, and exhausted by turns. Despite the elegant orderliness of the pictorial borders, life in the middle is extreme, tumultuous, and entrancing. Zeman's prose supports the art, rather than the other way around; her text is brief and unembellished. This makes *Sindbad* a good picture book for young children, who will read depth and subtlety into the pictures. Highly recommended.

The sequel ***Sindbad in the Land of the Giants*** is similarly eventful and lavish.

Zimmermann, H. Werner. *Henny Penny*. **1989. 2 to 6.**
The story of Henny Penny, Cocky Locky, Ducky Lucky, Goosey Loosey, and Turkey Lurky's visit to tell the king the sky is falling is well known, successful because of its strongly patterned narrative and the fact that the young audience is in the know when the characters are not.

Zimmermann's watercolour illustrations make this rendition a winner with preschool children: his bumbling birds look downright silly, with an assortment of pots, pans, bags, and cups on their heads as they rush down the lane to the castle. The face of Foxy Loxy first shows consternation, then great satisfaction after his tasty meeting, so disastrous for the birds. Zimmermann also includes other farm animals and small creatures of the forest, who seem to understand just how ludicrous the whole episode is. The squirrel who dropped the acorn in the first place ends the story carrying a stack of nuts past a very full Foxy Loxy. Some children may find the fate of the foolish birds upsetting.

Poetry and Rhyming Stories

anada's voices in poetry for children include poets Dennis Lee,
Robert Priest, Jean Little, and Loris Lesynski, as well as a host
of others whose works are represented in anthologies. Collections of
poetry by individual poets are listed here, along with themed anthologies that include writings by many poets. Rhyming picture books
are reviewed in the chapter on picture books, but they are cross-
listed here. This list does not include anthologies published by
educational publishers.

Of all the kinds of literature produced for children, poetry is the
easiest to share. A single poem can take only a moment to read aloud,
but the sound and song of the language, the colour and quirkiness of the
image, can stick in the mind forever. In these collections and anthologies, you'll find poems heartbreaking and gut-busting, ethereal and
earthy. In many cases, art and illustration point out and enhance the
subtleties and humour in the language – from Kady MacDonald
Denton's gleeful toddlers in *A Treasury of Nursery Rhymes* to the art of
Ontario's Group of Seven, which illustrates *Images of Nature*.

* **Booth, David, ed. Illustr. Kady MacDonald Denton.** *Til All the*
Stars Have Fallen: Canadian Poems for Children. **1989. 94 pages.**
6 and up.
Sound patterns, pictures, emotions, memories, and stories prompted
Booth to include the particular poems in this anthology, which brings
together work by Dionne Brand, bpNichol, Tim Wynne-Jones, Susan

Musgrave, Dennis Lee, and others. Ranging from the clever, bouncing rhythm and rhyming of the section "When Your Ears Sing" to incisively worded, non-rhyming poems that capture moments of intense perception and feeling, each of these works speaks to a child's experience. Good soup, the fearsome Wendigo, a bed in a tree ("he says that it's worth it to lie in his bed and see folks go past in a jet") are all celebrated. So too is the courage of a girl with allergies who has to say "no" to an invitation to play with kittens. MacDonald Denton's illustrations, in a variety of media ranging from ink and watercolour to collage, express the sometimes quiet, sometimes uplifting, beauties of nature, as well as the busy joy of play and human interaction. A visually appealing anthology with much to offer. Highly recommended.

Booth, David, ed. Illustr. Michèle Lemieux. *Voices on the Wind: Poems for All Seasons.* **1990. 32 pages. 6 to 10.**
Booth brings together twenty-eight poems by poets of various places and periods in this anthology, which focuses on seasons and nature. John Ciardi, Rose Fyleman, and Naomi Lewis rub shoulders with Christina Rossetti, William Blake, and Emily Brontë, among others. Some are wistful, some funny, some celebrate quiet pleasures. Most are sharp and memorable, excellent for drawing children's attention to moments of brilliant perception or sensual awareness.

* Booth, David, ed. Illustr. Maryann Kovalski. *Doctor Knickerbocker and Other Rhymes: A Canadian Collection.* **1993. 72 pages. 2 to 7.**
Any decent collection of schoolyard rhymes can only be full of sheer, mad delight, and this is no exception. Exuberant rudeness, bizarre fantasy, weird wisdom, and cautionary advice are all preserved in these ditties collected from Canadian schoolyards, but originally deriving from the lore of Canada's British, Scottish, Irish, and Welsh heritage.

"If you think you are in love, and still there is some question, / Don't worry much about it, it may be indigestion," reads one piece of advice. "As I sat under the apple tree, / A birdie sent his love to me, / And as I wiped it from my eye, / I said, 'Thank goodness cows can't fly,'" another recounts philosophically. Queen Anne, Salome, "little Annie," Charlie Chaplin, and Julius Caesar ("the Roman geezer") each have a part to play here.

Kovalski's wicked, sly, rambunctiously knowing illustrations show a world in which children are clearly in control. Elements of Victorian architecture, costume, and advertisements, drawn in fine pen and ink, have an Edward Gorey–like air – a sort of sinister humour – that suits the strange world of nursery-rhyme language and silly puns. Gentlemen in top hats, ladies with bustles, and little girls with spindly, nimble legs populate the pages; little boys in suspenders blow up their teachers' underwear. Highly recommended fun for all the family.

Booth, David, ed. *Images of Nature: Canadian Poets and the Group of Seven*. 1995. 32 pages. 8 and up.
Booth has juxtaposed poetry by a variety of Canadian poets with images painted by the men who made up the Group of Seven, with the understanding that these paintings have come to mean "home" to Canadians. With their predominantly Ontario landscapes, the pictures are bound to have different meaning for children to whom deciduous hardwood forests and low rocky hills are unfamiliar, but the art here is powerful and beautiful, and can only enrich a child's aesthetic experience.

The poetry, however, spans the breadth of Canada, from the foggy white silence of Rona Murray's "The Foghorn" to the fragile harebells and fat cod of Earl Birney's "Ellesmereland." M. Nourbese Philip, Elizabeth Brewster, Leonard Cohen, George Swede – this collection gives children a chance to sip the heady language of some of Canada's accomplished wordsmiths. Much of this poetry is so visual that further illustration seems superfluous: "stripped of leaves, surprised – the trees / scrape the grey winter sky / with veined brittle arms," reads a poem by Philip. "Dropping stone after stone / into the lake I keep / reappearing," reads Swede's Haiku. These outstanding words can be shared by an audience from 8 to adulthood.

Burdett, Lois. *Shakespeare Can Be Fun!* series. 1995– . 64 pages. 6 to 8.
The eight titles in this series comprise a "portrait" of Shakespeare and retellings of seven of his plays. Burdett has been teaching Shakespeare to her grade two classes for years in Stratford, Ontario. She does this by simplifying the language and giving the children the benefit of a heavily rhythmic text in rhymed couplets. Deathless poetry this is not,

yet it is lively and understandable and covers all the characters and elements of the plot. The text can be used when staging kids' own productions (with permission) or as a starting point for creating a new version – or simply as an introduction to the story.

Drawings, letters, and diary excerpts invented by children in the voices of the *dramatis personae* give these versions extra depth and humour – and they're witness to the fact that young children are well able to empathize with many of the issues in the plays. "Dear Benvolio," writes Lady Capulet in the words of one child, "What am I to do to get Romeo to reveal his pain? . . . the truth stays jammed in his heart."

Available titles are *A Child's Portrait of Shakespeare*, *Much Ado About Nothing*, *Hamlet*, *The Tempest*, *Romeo and Juliet*, *A Midsummer Night's Dream*, *Macbeth*, and *Twelfth Night*.

Carpenter-Davis, Sandra, and Celia Barker Lottridge, eds. *Bounce Me, Tickle Me, Hug Me: Lap Rhymes and Play Rhymes from Around the World*. 35 pages. 1998. Infant to 4.
Thirty rhymes from almost as many countries are collected here. Thanks to Lottridge's adaptations, these verses seem to heed no boundaries, and here they are, with words and directions for accompanying actions, destined to end in a parent-and-child giggle most of the time. Mosquitoes and hot callaloo, a little rabbit going "sippity sip" and tickling a baby's ear, rhymes for eating, sleeping, bugs, toes, and fingers, are all to be found here, enhancing babies' exposure to sound, language, and physical fun. This book shares generously the warmth of parent and baby play; it's intended less for reading with children than it is for teaching adults the rhymes. Its broadly multicultural content makes it particularly enriching.

Dalton, Sheila. Illustr. Kim LaFave. *Doggerel*. 1996. 3 to 6.
See Picture Books.

* Denton, Kady MacDonald, ed. and illustr. *A Child's Treasury of Nursery Rhymes*. 96 pages. 1998. Infant to 6.
A populous, eventful world is presented in this treasury of nursery rhymes, familiar songs, children's poetry, and schoolyard ditties.

Dividing it into sections for babies, toddlers, nursery-scholars, and slightly older schoolchildren, Denton includes rhymes to laugh at, bathe to, cry to, even argue with. From "Dance Little Baby" to the concluding nonsense poem, "The Owl and the Pussycat" by Edward Lear, here's the strong rhythm, bouncing rhyme, comfort, tragedy, silliness, and rebellion of the inimitable nursery-rhyme world. Most of the verse is of British origin, but there are a few verses from China, Africa, India, and elsewhere.

Denton's ink-and-watercolour illustrations show the drama and humour, but especially the strong-minded, eccentric population of this relentlessly active world. Each small person emanates character with a capital C, from the pensive timidity of little Jumping Joan to the pleased interest of the boy who pulls a fish from his ear. Visual narratives sneak along the upper and lower margins, where babies crawl, schoolboys taunt, and animals holler and hoot across the pages. This volume brings together all the rich, imaginative abundance associated with the nursery-rhyme world. Highly recommended.

DeVries, John. Illustr. H. Werner Zimmermann. *In My Backyard*. 1992. 2 to 4.
See Picture Books.

Fitch, Sherry. Illustr. Marc Mongeau. *There Were Monkeys in My Kitchen!* 1992. 32 pages. 4 to 8.
Lunacy and mayhem result when monkeys invade the kitchen of young Willa Wellowby in Fitch's mad, rhyming tale. Monkeys bounce basketballs, gorillas cavort in fishnet socks, orangutans tango, and Willa cries, "Woe begone is me!" She calls for the police, the RCMP, even Scotland Yard, and by the time a woman appears with forty-nine Mounties and says, "Well Welluh Willa Wellowby" all the monkeys have disappeared (but elephants are on the roof).

The story doesn't make much sense, nor is it intended to, but the crazy antics of the monkeys should have children laughing. The rhythm and beat of Fitch's rhyme doesn't come easily, but once it's established, the story bounces along. Mongeau's illustrations in bright reds and yellows make for liveliness: he captures the insanity of the story with frantic, overly busy pictures. Fitch has written other rhyming stories, including *Toes in My Nose*, *Mabel Murple*, and *Sleeping Dragons All Around*, but they're best listened to on tape with Fitch's voice providing the bounce, rhythm, and beat.

Gilman, Phoebe. *Jillian Jiggs.* **1985. 3 to 6.**
See Picture Books.

Heidbreder, Robert. Illustr. Kady MacDonald Denton. *I Wished for a Unicorn.* **2000. 2 to 4.**
See Picture Books.

Johnson, Gillian. *My Sister Gracie.* **2000. 3 to 6.**
See Picture Books.

Lee, Dennis. Illustr. Frank Newfeld. *Alligator Pie.* **1974. 64 pages. 3 to 8.**
Lee invented these verses expressly so Canadian children could have verse (especially nursery rhymes) with identifiably Canadian settings, names, and sensibilities. *Alligator Pie* was taken to children's hearts immediately. With Mississauga rattlesnakes, Kamloops, Trois Rivières, ookpiks, and Kempenfelt Bay included in the rhymes, Lee managed to help Canadian parents and teachers introduce this country to their children. Aside from the attractions of the Canadianisms within the verse, the poems are impeccably rhymed and faultlessly rhythmic – features which make them almost instantly memorable. Short, snappy verses alternate with longer ballad-like stories, and the occasional allusion to matters vulgar and disgusting seizes some children's attention at once. While some of the shorter verse is easy for children to read on their own, some is accessible only to older readers – but, indeed, most of it begs to be read aloud. Newfeld's illustrations have not aged well: the 1970s designs and colours may have been innovative when the book was first published, but now it looks dated and uninviting. Subsequent similar collections by Lee are *Garbage Delight*, illustrated by Frank Newfeld, *Jelly Belly*, illustrated by Juan Wijngaard, and *Garbage Delight: Another Helping* (see below).

Lee, Dennis. Illustr. Gillian Johnson. *The Cat and the Wizard.* **2001. 3 to 6.**
See Picture Books.

* **Lee, Dennis. Illustr. Maryann Kovalski.** *Garbage Delight: Another Helping.* **32 pages. 2002. 3 and up.**
Lee's collection *Garbage Delight*, originally published in 1977, is re-issued with seventeen new verses and a few deletions from the original in this edition, newly illustrated by Kovalski. Lee's poetry remains at once rollicking, robust, and sometimes deliciously thoughtful: "I see the moon and the moon sees me / And nobody sees as secretly / Unless there's a kid in Kalamazoo, or Mexico, or Timbuktu, / Who looks in the sky at the end of day, / And she thinks of me in a friendly way – / 'Cause we both lie still and we watch the moon; / And we haven't met yet, but we might do, soon."

In a style reminiscent of Rosemary Wells, Kovalski populates these pages with a cast of raccoons, bandit-masked, rotund, and cute as can be. The soft watercolour-and-pencil illustrations are full of interest and character – a recurring alligator bathes luxuriously and composes new verses to "Alligator Pie." This is much more appealing as a picture book than *Alligator Pie* (see above); the raccoons bring it right into the world of preschoolers. Highly recommended.

Lesynski, Loris. *Boy Soup, or When Giant Caught Cold.* **1996. 4 to 7.**
See Picture Books.

Lesynski, Loris. *Catmagic.* **1998. 4 to 7.**
See Picture Books.

Lesynski, Loris. *Dirty Dog Boogie,* **1999, and** *Nothing Beats a Pizza,* **2001. 32 pages. 5 to 11.**
Lesynski's ear for rhythm and mind for rhyme make these Seuss-like, bouncing verses irresistible to the ear. "A *boogie* is a dance and a *boogie* is a jive and a *boogie's* just another way of saying I'm alive," one poem begins, inviting kids to sing and stomp along. Humour and a spirit of solidarity with children characterize both these collections,

which range from observing the quality of sunlight as it drips down the stairs to the familiar experience of sock fluff between the toes ("Blue socks make blue fluff and red socks make red. / Striped socks make some of each colour instead"). Lesynski's verses point out the great pleasure and fun of language; often, too, she nudges readers to look at the world from a different perspective. With cartoon-like, infectiously silly illustrations, both of these volumes make good read-aloud or read-on-your-own, read-at-school or read-at-home.

Levert, Mireille. *Rose by Night.* **1998. 3 to 5.**
See Picture Books.

* Little, Jean. Illustr. Sue Truesdell. *Hey World, Here I Am!* **1986. 88 pages. 8 to 12.**
These funny, perceptive, and often moving poems all derive from Little's fictional character Kate (to be found in *Kate* and *Look Through My Window*). They focus on those odd moments of recognition and feeling that come during childhood and early adolescence – from sheer fatigue ("Today I will not live up to my potential"), to the wondering moments of first holding a newborn baby, to the disquieting experience of having to understand a mother's hurt feelings. Friendship, family argument, an annoying sister, this is the stuff of childhood, and Little treats it insightfully and cleverly, her compassion patent and complex feeling glittering between the lines. Excellent for girls, and good for boys, too. Highly recommended.

MacLeod, Elizabeth. Illustr. Louise Phillips. *I Heard a Little Baa.* **1998. Infant to 3.**
See Picture Books.

Nichol, Barbara. Illustr. Philippe Béha. *Biscuits in the Cupboard.* **1997. 32 pages. 5 to 12.**
Nichol's dog poems, both humorous and thoughtful, present the world from a canine perspective, as in "Lazy Dog": "My grievance is so very small / I'm tempted to forget it. / But when it's you who threw the ball / Why must I go and get it?"

Nichol celebrates the joys of leaving scent on a tree, of annoying one's fleas, and of trips to the park that will be remembered when the dog grows too old to leave home. Poems vary in length from brief two-liners to the lengthy "The Legend of Chicken Bones." There's something to grab every dog lover. Béha's humorous line drawings capture the antics as well as the "emotions" of Nichol's many dogs.

Priest, Robert. Illustr. Tineke Visser. *The Secret Invasion of Bananas: Poems for Kids.* **2002. 159 pages. 5 to 12.**
Priest, a poet and songwriter, demonstrates his considerable talent with this collection of works from the last twenty years. Concrete poems, pithy sayings, songs, and poems are included here – on topics ranging from aliens and robots to knights and dragons. Nature and mutual respect are underlying themes. The poems are funny and clever ("Oh a peach is sweet / and a pear is fair / but the orange orange / is best to share") and deserves to reach a wide audience; unfortunately, the poor production values of this book make it less attractive than it should be. Priest's work also appears in an earlier, more appealing-looking volume, *Day Songs, Night Songs*.

Reid, Barbara. *Sing a Song of Mother Goose.* **1987. 32 pages. Infant to 5.**
Reid brings together some very familiar and some not so familiar – and thus all the more rewarding – nursery rhymes here. Mother Hubbard, Georgie Porgie, and the ten o'clock scholar are represented; so too are the lesser known Jack-a-nory story, Solomon Grundy, and My Pretty Maid. Reid's Plasticine art, in rosy trellis borders at the top and bottom of the pages, interprets these cryptic, strange little verses with spirit and vivacity. The horrid little girl glares with crossed eyes and stuck-out tongue, and the pretty maid stalks off in high dudgeon. There's plenty of scope for toddler investigation here.

Reid, Barbara. *Two by Two.* **1992. 3 to 6.**
See Traditional Tales.

* Reid, Barbara. *The Party*. 1997. 3 to 6.
See Picture Books.

Service, Robert W. Illustr. Ted Harrison. *The Cremation of Sam McGee*. 1907/1986. 32 pages. 7 and up.
Travelling through the frozen Yukon, the narrator has to fulfil the last request of his shivering companion Sam McGee: he must make sure Sam is cremated once he has died of the "cursèd cold." After hauling Sam's corpse for miles on a dogsled, the narrator finally cremates him in the boiler of a sunken, ice-locked barge. When he checks to make sure the job is done, there's Sam, sitting happily, warm enough at last.

Service's heavily rhythmic, gruesome-but-funny verse has come to represent the Yukon gold rush for some; the story's sufficiently strange that children find it creepily entertaining. No one can forget the opening line. "There's strange things done in the midnight sun by the men who moil for gold . . ." Harrison's stylized, vibrant art, with its ribbons of colour, comes out of his close observation of the Yukon and makes a good companion piece to the extreme story. Unobtrusive notes explain matters of local interest in the illustrations – a cache, ice-fog, ravens, and more.

Harrison has also illustrated Service's poem *The Shooting of Dan McGrew*, the story of two jealous lovers. His art can also be found in *O Canada*, a bilingual version of the Canadian national anthem, in which Harrison expresses his impressions of each province and territory (with the Northwest Territories and Nunavut as one).

Thomas, Dylan. Illustr. Murray Kimber. *Fern Hill*. 1945/1997. 32 pages. 8 and up.
Thomas's unforgettably poignant and vivid poem about the loss of childhood is interpreted visually here in Kimber's acrylic paintings. In a style evoking that of Cézanne or Van Gogh, Kimber shows trees like shrouded human figures and cobalt streams luminous in moonlight. The red dark horses of the poem fly through shadowed landscapes like mythical beasts; blocks and shapes of colour and shadow stand in visually rhythmic relation to one another. The power of Thomas's stringent, forceful language, his lilting Welsh rhythms, can only enrich children;

Kimber's art gives an idea of the possibility of the play between visual art and language.

Wynne-Jones, Tim. Illustr. Dušan Petričić. *On Tumbledown Hill.* **1998. 4 to 7.**
See Picture Books.

Books for Beginning Readers

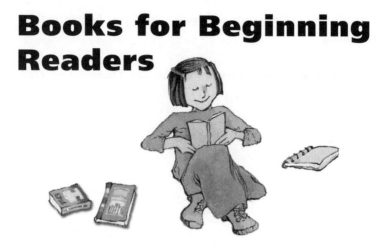

Controlled vocabularies, simplistic plots, and uninspired illustrations often characterize stories given to children who are learning to read on their own. These stories are usually fit to be read once or twice, but can never become beloved, read, and re-read stories that earn the place of personal favourites. Few books marketed to the emergent reader (or to the parent of the reader) have the freshness and character that invite repeated readings.

Many publishers, recognizing the demand for "easy to read" or "beginning readers," have produced books and series geared to specific grade and reading levels. Usually these books are slightly taller and wider than mass-market paperbacks; often they're clearly marked, according to reading level of series, and are easily identified as "easy to read" books. These are the bridge between picture books and children's novels or fiction, and one usually finds them shelved between these two sections in a library. In this category, there are a few Canadian gems, and we have highlighted some titles from publishers' series. But apart from "easy to read" series books, there are a number of picture books that are ideal for children learning to read. For example, some of Maryann Kovalski's works, first successfully published as picture books, have recently been reissued as "First Flight" books (an "easy to read" series published by Fitzhenry and Whiteside). The new books are smaller than the original editions, but the stories and illustrations remain the same. A child's enjoyment of the book *Jingle Bells* will not be different if he or she reads it in picture-book format or in its new format as a "First Flight" Book.

A number of picture books are listed in this section to remind parents that there are many books outside "beginning readers" series that have an "easy to read" text that will not intimidate children. Some are perfect for a child to read to a younger sibling or friend. Reading out loud to a younger child (even if the book does not appeal particularly to the reader) gives the reader a sense of accomplishment and pride. The many books by Gilles Tibo may seem to appeal to children who are not old enough to be reading on their own, but the text in some of these stories is also ideal for beginning readers.

When examining books to suit that crucial period when a child is developing reading confidence, it is important to look closely at both text and illustrations. The illustrations may extend the text, but they should definitely represent what is written on the page, so that readers will be able to use them to confirm their understanding of the words.

It is essential for children who are learning to read to continue to have the opportunity to hear stories read aloud. "Easy to read" texts are often below a child's emotional and intellectual capacities and interests, so it is even more critical for parents, teachers, and adults who are engaged with children to give them the opportunity to relax and get lost in a story that will feed their imaginations and emotional abilities. Children's listening comprehension is much more developed than their reading ability at this time. KEEP READING ALOUD.

The following books are enjoyable and accessible for children beginning to read on their own; as always, you need to check the text and content to make sure it matches the child's interests and abilities. *Early Readers* are within the reading levels common to children from kindergarten through grade two. *First Novels ("Chapter Books")* include short novels, usually with some illustration, which are appropriate for children who have gained some reading fluency, that is, from grades two through four.

EARLY READERS

Charles, Veronika Martenova. Illustr. Leanne Franson. *Don't Open the Door!* Easy to Read Spooky Tales Series. 2000. 56 pages.
With its spooky cover and enticing title, this will appeal to readers wanting slightly scary stories. Three friends having a sleepover

provide the framework for the story: each boy tells a spooky tale inspired by the host's mother, who has admonished them, "Don't open the door! Not for anybody!" Charles uses international folktales as the basis for the stories the children share with each other, and the tales are satisfying but not too frightening. Other titles in the series are ***Don't Go Near the Water*** and ***Don't Go into the Forest***.

DeVries, John. Illustr. H. Werner Zimmermann. *In My Backyard.* **1992.**
See Picture Books.

Ellis, Sarah. Illustr. Ruth Ohi. *Next Stop!* **2000.**
See Picture Books.

Ellis, Sarah. Illustr. Kim LaFave. *Big Ben.* **2001.**
See Picture Books.

Godkin, Celia. *Flying Lessons: A First Flight Level Two Reader.* **1999.**
A straightforward text and clear, accurate illustrations describe the growth and maturation of a baby robin up until the moment he flies.

Kovalski, Maryann. *Omar on Ice.* **1999.**
See Picture Books.

* Kovalski, Maryann. *Rain, Rain: A First Flight Level Two Reader.* **1999.**
Kovalski illustrates her stories of Jenny and Joanna visiting their New York grandmother with endearing, soft watercolours. When it pours on the day the three planned to go to the beach, lovable, cushiony Grandma transforms her apartment into a beach. Kovalski's illustrations are exuberant with the infectious energy that emanates from Grandma. With its repetition of simple words and phrases, and illustrations that extend the story, this is an excellent first reader with character. ***Jingle Bells*** and ***The Wheels on the Bus*** (reviewed in Picture Books) also feature Grandma, Joanne, and Jenny. Highly recommended.

Little, Jean. Illustr. Jennifer Plecas. *Emma's Magic Winter.* **1998. 64 pages.**
In this tale, veteran writer Little provides a fast-moving plot and a limited text perfect for young readers. Emma, shy about making friends in her new neighbourhood, pretends her boots are magic, and so finds the courage to play with a new neighbour. A sequel, *Emma's Yucky Brother*, shows how Emma adjusts to a new, adopted brother.

Robart, Rose. Illustr. Maryann Kovalski. *The Cake That Mack Ate.* **1986.**
See Picture Books.

Spicer, Maggee, and Richard Thompson. Illustr. Barbara Hartman. *Fishes in the Ocean: A First Flight Level One Reader.* **1998.**
"Fishes in the ocean, sharks in the sea, We all go swimming with a 1 2 3." The story counts up to ten and then reverses and counts backwards. Rhyme draws the reader through the text.

Spicer, Maggee, and Richard Thompson. Illustr. Kim LaFave. *We All Go Sailing: A First Flight Level One Reader.* **2001.**
LaFave's bright, bold colours and Katzenjammer-kid–like children help readers find more here than the text indicates. Three children discover an array of sea creatures on their voyage through colourful waters in a rhyming text. Words such as barracuda will challenge some beginning readers, and the authors show little regard for biological accuracy in their allusions to marine life, but the story is energetic and has lots of useful repetition. A sequel by the same trio, *We'll All Go Flying*, has similar strengths and weaknesses.

Thompson, Richard. Illustr. Barbara Hartman. *Then and Now: A First Flight Level One Reader.* **1999.**
This concept book shows the effects of time in the process of change and growth, with minimal words in a rhyming text: "Then was a seed. Now is a flower." Hartman illustrates each page with two small pictures showing a girl experiencing then and now. Thompson uses familiar concepts and his text rhymes, but very beginning readers need help discovering the rhyme as they struggle their way through this.

Tibo, Gilles. *Simon in Summer.* **1991.**
See Picture Books.

Wishinsky, Frieda. Illustr. Linda Hendry. *Jennifer Jones Won't Leave Me Alone.* **1995.**
See Picture Books.

Wishinsky, Frieda. Illustr. Linda Hendry. *No Frogs for Dinner: A First Flight Level Two Reader.* **1999.**
Melvin has great plans when he visits Aunt Rose in New York, but Aunt Rose has planned completely different, and rather boring, activities. It isn't until Melvin rebels at eating frog's legs that Aunt Rose changes her plans. Wishinsky's text captures the fear and annoyance of visiting a caring-but-domineering relative. Hendry's amusing watercolours illustrate Melvin's disappointment and incredulity when his plans go awry. This is a rewarding book, with a stronger story than most early readers.

FIRST NOVELS ("CHAPTER BOOKS" – GRADES TWO TO FOUR)

Bellingham, Brenda. *Princesses Don't Wear Jeans.* **1991. 63 pages.**
See Novels, 7 to 12.

Bingham, Deanne Lee. Illustr. Kim LaFave. *Andrew's Magnificent Mountain of Mittens: A First Flight Level Three Reader.* **1998. 45 pages.**
Every child knows what it's like to lose mittens, and Andrew's solution to his lost mitten problem will cause great hilarity. Bingham's text is surprisingly energetic given the limitations of the basic-reader format. The story is divided into very short chapters, giving children a sense of accomplishment as they read through the book. Sequel is *Andrew, Catch That Cat.*

Gilmore, Rachna. Illustr. Gordon Sauvé. *Fangs and Me.* **1999. 54 pages.**
Maisie's best and only friend moves away, and the boy who moves into the house next door turns out to be a bully. Maisie's love of spiders helps her tame, and become friends with, this new boy and gain

enough confidence to establish other friends in the neighbourhood. A slight, but satisfying story.

Lang, Audrey. Illustr. Wayne Lynch. *Nature Babies* series. 2001. ca. 36 pages.
See Non-Fiction.

Lottridge, Celia Barker. Illustr. Elsa Myotte. *Berta: A Remarkable Dog*. 2002. 99 pages.
See Novels, 7 to 12.

***Our Canadian Girl* series. 2001– . 60 to 90 pages.**
See Series Books.

Roberts, Ken. Illustr. Leanne Franson. *The Thumb in the Box*. 2001. 95 pages.
See Novels, 7 to 12.

Staunton, Ted. *The Kids from Monkey Mountain* series. 2000– . 60 pages.
This series revolves around the kids in one grade-five class in a small Ontario town. Each volume is written from the point of view of a different child in the class – sometimes that child experiences the same events that happened in the volume before, so that readers are given multiple perspectives on the motives and effects of the children's interactions.

Staunton's a writer of humour, but these aren't just a series of slapstick jokes and stock characters, despite the falling-off bathing suit and pie in the face that play a role in #5 *Second Banana* – and also in *Forgive Us Our Travises* and *Princess*, #3 and #4. Sharp observation and a compassion for the difficulties of age allow the author to walk the fine line between humour and human understanding. The kids are lively, believable, and distinctively conceived; the stories are funny and psychologically realistic. They also show how point-of-view can change entirely the meaning and direction of a story, and our understanding of human character behind it.

Tibo, Gilles. Illustr. Louise-Andrée Laliberté. *Naomi and Mrs. Lumbago.* **2001. 86 pages.**
See Novels, 7 to 12.

Wiebe, Trina. Illustr. Marisol Sarrazin. *Abby and Tess, Pet-Sitters* **series. 2001. 95 pages.**
Abby and her younger, usually annoying, sister Tess share a love and enthusiasm for pets. Abby not only looks after pets for people, but she also must contend with the antics of Tess, who likes to pretend that she's a dog and follows Abby everywhere. The combination of the frustrations of sibling responsibility and humorous animal stories makes Wiebe's series successful. Children learn about various pets and animals through these stories, and the fast-paced plots hold their interest. A Web site, www.abbyandtess.com, is available for children who want to get more involved with the pair. Titles include *Goldfish Don't Take Bubble Baths*, *Lizards Don't Wear Lip Gloss*, *Hamsters Don't Glow in the Dark*, *Piglets Don't Watch Television*, and *Goats Don't Brush Their Teeth*.

Novels, 7 to 12

The titles included in this section are suitable for most children aged 7 to 12 to read on their own. However, a great many of them are excellent for reading aloud, either to children in this age group, to younger children with listening stamina, or with the whole family. Perusing the titles will reveal those that might pique the interest of a four-year-old who enjoys sharing chapter books with older brothers and sisters or simply one-on-one with an adult. Please note, too, that the age levels assigned here take into account both advanced younger readers and slower older readers: your knowledge of the child will determine whether the story will "take" or not.

Barkhouse, Joyce. *Pit Pony*. 1990. 116 pages. 8 to 12.
Willie – or Wee Willie, as he is affectionately known – has just turned eleven and has no desire to follow the family tradition of working in the coal mines of Cape Breton. But when an accident sends his father into the hospital and cripples his brother, Willie must go down into the mine so the family can keep their house. Willie's love of horses is rewarded when he's promoted to "Driver" of a coal cart drawn by the small pony "Gem." The constant threat of an accident in the mine is less frightening to Willie than the oppressive presence of Simon, another boy working in the pitch-black tunnels with him. Disaster strikes, giving Willie the chance to prove his heroism.

Barkhouse recreates the dank, oppressive atmosphere of the mine, the choking, dusty air, and the ever-present fear of disaster in the tunnels in this brief novel for readers who are just beginning chapter books. The addition of a few Gaelic phrases adds authenticity to the text, but doesn't hamper the flow of the otherwise clear language and simple plot. The book provides a gripping story from a little-known chapter of Canadian history. *Pit Pony* has been made into a film.

Bastedo, Jamie. *Tracking Triple Seven*. **2001. 215 pages. 10 to 14.**
The natural world of the Canadian tundra comes alive in the story of Benji, a city boy who is working with a team of bear biologists employed at his father's diamond mine. Benji's experiences, and those of his stereotypically overly busy father, provide the framework for the novel; but the most compelling reading here is in a parallel plot concerning the bear the team is tracking, a female grizzly, Triple Seven, and her three cubs.

Bastedo's writing is most assured when he's writing of the wilderness and the grizzlies. Benji, his father, and the biologists provide an interesting side story, but the account of Triple Seven's life as she fights to survive with her cubs is what catches the reader's attention. A story for those interested in the outdoors and animal stories.

Bellingham, Brenda. *Princesses Don't Wear Jeans*. **1991. 63 pages. 6 to 9.**
Tilly Perkins arrives in her grade three class with baggy tights, uncombed hair, a hole in her sweater, and an unevenly hemmed skirt. She's unlike anyone Jeff has ever met, and her stories of bears, dragons, and mice intrigue him – even when he knows they derive, at least partly, from her active imagination. When Jeff's classmates label Tilly a liar, Jeff has to decide if being friends with her is worth losing all his old friends. In the end, he invites the whole class to his birthday party, and everyone waits to see if Tilly really will bring him the mice she has promised.

In this delightful novel for those who are beginning "chapter books," Bellingham explores the difficulties of peer pressure and creates a character well able to stand up to the ridicule of the popular members of the class. Her direct, humorous prose shows understanding and respect for the concerns of her readers.

Bodger, Joan. *Clever Lazy: The Girl Who Invented Herself.* **1979. 201 pages. 8 to 12.**

Born in a fictional ancient China, "Clever Lazy" is so named by parents who hope their daughter will be "clever enough to be lazy and lazy enough to be clever." After a childhood filled with love, exploration, and invention, Clever Lazy is orphaned; she then finds work as a clerk in a cousin's shop in the Imperial City. Although her happy childhood becomes a distant memory, Clever Lazy continues to invent, and soon designs a better spout for the teapots her cousin sells. Her fame spreads, and eventually she is appointed inventor to the Emperor. Clever Lazy makes many spectacular inventions – including gunpowder and fireworks – but in the end, she, her husband and baby must flee to the Dancing Mountains to seek aid from "the Goddess," where they find the reward that comes to the good at the end of all fairy tales.

Bodger delights in the details of Clever Lazy's inventions; she explores, too, the difficulties of dealing with the jealousy, greed, and envy provoked by those with new, good ideas. An experienced story-teller, she weaves together elements from many folktales into this clever, witty story. An excellent choice for convincing girls of the interests of science.

Bradford, Karleen. *There Will Be Wolves: The First Book of the Crusades.* **1992. 214 pages. 10 to 13.**

It's 1096 and Ursula, an apothecary's daughter, is accused of witchcraft in Cologne, Germany. She's sentenced to burn at the stake, unless she will join the People's Crusade led by mad Peter "the Hermit," and march to win Jerusalem back for the Christian Church. Horrified as she is by the violence the Hermit excites with his rhetoric, Ursula and her friend Bruno are even more disgusted by the brutality that becomes the norm among their fellow travellers. When Turkish soldiers take revenge and decimate the marauding Crusaders, Ursula and Bruno finally turn back in sorrow and shame.

Bradford gives anything but a romantic picture of the People's Crusade in this highly readable story. Although Ursula and Bruno have ideas that are somewhat anachronistic to the Middle Ages, today's readers will get a good sense of modern views on this disastrous religious war. Bradford oversimplifies medieval Christian attitudes, but as an introduction to the period, this is a fine start. Ursula's a sympathetic character, and the story moves quickly, making it a good choice for reluctant readers.

Bradford, Karleen. *Shadows on a Sword: The Second Book of the Crusades.* **1996. 195 pages. 10 to 14.**
In 1096, having just become a knight, seventeen-year-old Theo joins the First Crusade and begins the march towards Jerusalem, full of idealism. Frustrated with the many delays as the Crusaders travel on to Constantinople, he nevertheless takes pleasure in hunting sprees with a friend and in conversations with spirited Emma, a servant of the nobility. When the Crusaders begin to fight with the Turks as they press on after Constantinople, Theo proves he's a fine warrior, but the blood-shed and looting sicken him. By the time Jerusalem has been captured and every Jew and Muslim within it killed, Theo is thoroughly ready to give up his knightly duties.

Bradford's account of the sorties, hardships, and skirmishes of this complicated, dispiriting three-year journey moves at a good pace. The "glory" and action of war is balanced by the development of Theo's relationship with Emma (who eventually survives by disguising herself as a boy), and his growth in both wisdom and dismay. Though Theo's liberal-mindedness is rather anachronistic in a man of his upbringing, it gives readers access to important questions about religious wars then and now. An engrossing read for both girls and boys.

Bradford, Karleen. *Lionheart's Scribe: The Third Book of the Crusades.* **1999. 175 pages. 10 to 14.**
Lame, fifteen-year-old Matthew takes up his quill in the year 1190 to begin an account of his days as a scribe in Sicily. Shortly after he begins his journal, King Richard the Lionheart sails into the harbour, en route to win Jerusalem back from Muslim leader Salah-uh-din. Matthew wheedles a place on board and is soon promoted from horse-boy to scribe. He tells of the disheartening, traumatic events of the ill-fated Third Crusade, of his friendship with a Muslim girl whom he rescues from the sea, and of Rashid, son of a great Muslim warrior.

Despite the anachronism and limitations of the diary form and its lack of dialogue, this is eventful and engaging. Dealings with kings and queens and descriptions of sickness and political intrigue are enlivened by Matthew's confiding voice as he shares his own doubts and inadequacies. The "I'll wagers" and "I warrants" smack of nineteenth-century romantic "medievalese," but Bradford successfully introduces the still painfully relevant issues of bias and interpretation. Matthew's two Muslim friends provide a useful counterpoint to the medieval Christian attitudes Bradford invites readers to critique.

Buffie, Margaret. *Who Is Frances Rain?* **1987. 192 pages. 10 to 14.**
Lizzie and her brother and sister expect their usual happy summer with Gran on a remote lake in northern Manitoba, but even before they're out the door the summer's threatened. Lizzie's mother and fairly new stepfather have decided to come too – even though they're not speaking to one another. Driven away from Gran's by family friction, Lizzie decides to explore nearby Rain Island. When she finds the ruins of an old cabin and digs up a pair of spectacles that seem to make her see ghosts, she's caught up in a mystery that has implications for the unhappiness in her own family. But it takes dear Gran's failing heart to bring the family to its senses at last.

Lizzie's colloquial style ("the present generally stunk") and forthright expression of adolescent discontent will engage even reluctant adolescent readers, and the twists and turns of the ghost story – as well as the dysfunctional family dynamics – will keep pages turning. The feeling of summer wilderness and romance is everywhere here, and it's refreshing that the ghost is that of a female prospector. Buffie's resolution of family difficulties is pat, but still satisfies; her description of Lizzie's near-possession is deliciously eerie.

Buffie explores the supernatural and the adolescent psyche in additional novels for this age. Titles include *My Mother's Ghost* and *Angels Turn Their Backs*.

Buffie, Margaret. *The Watcher.* **1999. 260 pages. 11 to 14.**
Fifteen-year-old Emma is entering what her mother calls "the Borderland – a territory between childhood and adulthood . . . a vast world of change, some good, some not so good." But Emma isn't just exploring adolescence: in vivid, waking dreams she sees forests of writhing, serpentine vines and roots, and the green of underwater

caverns. Is this all related to her strange new neighbours, who have taught Emma to play the ancient boardgame Fidchell? Are her dreams and Fidchell somehow related to her sickly sister, Summer? Before Emma can sort out her own identity, much less anyone else's, she discovers that Summer is in a terrible danger that only she can avert.

Although Emma's realistic problems seem stereotypical, Buffie's brilliant imagery of the Celtic Fomorii and Blue Celtoi is unforgettable and enriching. Aspects of Celtic mythology and some peculiar characters (including the handsome young man who turns into an owl every night) make this memorable. Emma's story continues in *The Seeker*.

* **Burnford, Sheila.** *The Incredible Journey.* **1961. 152 pages. 9 to 12.**
This is the well-known and oft-filmed tale of three domestic house pets that travel across 250 miles of Canadian wilderness to reach their loving "home" and family. Luath, a young, powerful Labrador retriever, leads old Bodger, a battered, English bull terrier, and Tao, a Siamese cat, on their trek across country. Each animal acts in the manner of its breed: Luath, gentle and civilized, struggles to catch game; Bodger summons his fighting skills when faced with a bear; and Tao, who appears to be pampered, turns out to be lithe, hard, and canny.

Burnford writes with the authority of first-hand knowledge of animals. Instead of endowing the animals with the powers of speech – as some of the film versions do – she draws the reader into the fearful journey through her gripping descriptions, so that the strength of the tale rests in the animals themselves and the powerful bond exhibited between them. Tao hunts for food for wounded Bodger; Bodger rescues Luath when he's attacked by another dog; and Luath struggles to help Tao cross a raging river. Encounters with bears, lynx, hunters, and wolves make for many suspenseful moments: Burnford's energetic writing keeps readers on the edge of their seats. Good read-aloud. Highly recommended.

Chan, Gillian. *A Foreign Field.* **2002. 184 pages. 11 and up.**
It's the autumn of 1942, and fourteen-year-old Ellen Logan worries about her brothers overseas; one is missing and the other is about to see action. When British Stephen Dearborn, an RAF pilot in training at the

local airfield, shows up on the doorstep, Ellen and her family befriend him. For Stephen, who lied about his age to join up (he's only sixteen), the Logans' hospitality means the world, and he comes to love Ellen for her reserve and serious mind. The two become close, sharing their aspirations and hardest fears. When Stephen goes back to Britain and begins flying his own missions, they continue to correspond – until one day Ellen hears he's been killed in action.

Chan paints a convincing picture of life at the airfield and in the small Ontario town where Ellen lives. Stephen and Ellen are complex, fully realized characters – both a little plain, Stephen rather stiff and self-absorbed, they're neither glamorous nor beautiful. Stephen's frequent letters home are vivid and revealing; a recurrent nightmare, sparingly reiterated, haunts the reader. Chan shows poignantly Ellen's necessary sudden maturation as she realizes the weight of Stephen's attachment to her and responds to the demands of the war. A multi-layered, compelling read.

Clark, Joan. *The Hand of Robin Squires.* **1977. 145 pages. 10 and up.** The mystery of the "money pit" and the possibility of buried treasure on Oak Island in Nova Scotia have intrigued many since a hand was first found at the bottom of an old mining shaft in 1795. Clark offers a fictional account of how the hand came to be there: English Robin Squires and his father, an inventor and land surveyor, are drawn into a mysterious plan by Robin's uncle to construct an elaborate shaft and series of tunnels in North America. After his father's death, Robin convinces his uncle to take him to Oak Island, only to realize that his uncle's plan is to bury stolen treasure, and Robin along with it.

Clark delivers adventure, suspense, and excitement, as well as an understanding of the Aboriginal peoples and the horrors of the slave trade. Robin's friendship with Actaudin, a young Mi'kmaq, allows the reader to see the contrast between Mi'kmaq beliefs and the cruel ruthlessness of Robin's uncle and his cohorts. This fast-paced adventure story of a boy's courage in friendship also describes the complexities of building a shaft. The title makes it clear that there will be a gruesome ending, but even so, readers are shocked by the force Clark brings to the final chapters. A must-read for anyone visiting Oak Island.

Clark, Joan. *The Dream Carvers*. **1995. 226 pages. 10 to 13.**
Caught at the moment of his first bear kill, Greenlander Thrand is kidnapped by hunters from the Osweet, a branch of the red-ochre people, or Beothuk, of Newfoundland. As he learns their ways and gets used to his new name, "Wobee," he realizes he's there to replace a young Osweet man the Greenlanders captured and killed on an earlier expedition. And although he takes his replacement duties seriously, and comes to like life among the Osweet, he still longs for contact with home.

Thrand/Wobee's struggles to understand his identity are at the heart of this fascinating, dream-like story. Clark conveys feelingly the disorientation caused by Wobee's first recognition that his own culture isn't necessarily normative, or even preferable – a leap of understanding that's timelessly applicable. The boy's intense longing and his mysterious, dream-related bond with Abidith, an Osweet girl, make this much more than a memorable depiction of life among the eleventh-century Beothuk. Reading this is like visiting another world.

Cook, Lyn. *Pegeen and the Pilgrim*. **1957. 278 pages. 9 to 12.**
Cook was one of the first to write popular children's stories with Canadian settings. *Pegeen and the Pilgrim* was first released in 1957, a few years after the inaugural season of Ontario's Stratford Festival. It was reissued in 2002 for the Festival's fiftieth anniversary.

Twelve-year-old aspiring actress Pegeen is getting ready for life in high school and hoping to get into the school play. Life for Pegeen isn't simple: she and her mother have little money and run a boarding house. Cook weaves the ups and downs of a school play, a new school, new friends, and the continual work associated with a boarding house (including an interesting assortment of boarders) together with the excitement of the Shakespeare Festival in Stratford.

Well-structured and nicely told, this isn't the story of how a young girl gets to act on stage, but rather describes how Pegeen becomes caught up in the general excitement of the theatre. In some ways the fact that this story is dated makes it more interesting. Children who have experienced Stratford will be interested to learn when the first theatre was built, or when Festival performances were moved out of the tent.

* Cumyn, Alan. *The Secret Life of Owen Skye.* **2002. 6 to 10.**
Eight-year-old Owen Skye and his brothers Andy and Leonard always
have good ideas for entertainment, whether it's visiting a house haunted
by the Bog-man's wife (they want to ask her how men can have babies),
tearing out of the creek stark naked to steal bicycles, or making sure
Uncle Lorne makes it to his own wedding. But aside from all the expe-
ditions, accidents, and illnesses the boys share, Owen has his own
secret: he's in love with his classmate Sylvia, and the only thing he can
think to talk to her about is the family superhero, Doom Monkey the
Unpredictable and his Atrocious Hat.

This episodic story of the strange contortions of boys' brains has
moments of absolute mirth and mayhem, but underneath it's a thoughtful, sound portrayal of sweet, painful moments of growth. Cumyn's
short sentences and sure prose give the story a brisk pace; even better
is his language, which reflects the odd way kids' minds work when they
don't quite know everything – like Leonard, who surmises that aliens
look like tin foil and must have two heads. Every moment of this story
is interesting; it makes a great read-aloud. Highly recommended.

* Curtis, Christopher Paul. *The Watsons Go to Birmingham – 1963.*
1998. 210 pages. 10 and up.
Sibling problems beset ten-year-old Kenny, middle child of the Weird
Watson family of Flint, Michigan. Brother Byron, at thirteen, has tried
his parents and brother in every way – playing with matches, buying
sweets on family credit, and, at last, dying his hair. Kenny's parents
shave Byron's head and decide it's time for serious action. They pile into
the car and head for Birmingham, Alabama, where Byron can learn
what's what from his strict, traditional grandmother. But it's really the
outbreak of racial violence that turns Byron around, and makes Kenny
look at him differently.

Told in the voice of Kenny, *The Watsons* has enormous energy and
authenticity when it comes to the tensions and humour of family
rivalry. The image of Byron with his lips frozen to the side-view mirror
is unforgettable, and so is Curtis's description of the paralyzing effect
of winter clothing. All the hilarity that precedes the trip to Alabama
deepens the emotional impact of the events that follow. An amusing,
compelling read for both girls and boys. Highly recommended.

* Curtis, Christopher Paul. *Bud, Not Buddy.* **1999. 8 to 12.**

It's 1932, Bud's ten years old, and he's been in and out of foster homes in Flint, Michigan, since his mother died when he was six. Despite it all, he hasn't lost his spirit, and when the latest foster home becomes unbearable, he grabs the suitcase containing all his mother left him (five flyers for a jazz band, some rocks, and a blanket) and goes "on the lam." He's sure his flyers, advertising "Herman E. Calloway and the Dusky Devastators of the Depression!!!!!!" will lead to his unknown father. His encounters with "Hooverville," early union organizers, and, finally, jazz, do indeed lead to the fulfilment of his dreams.

This tale is eventful, and Curtis writes with a rare, delightful vigour and spirit. Bud's direct, boyish voice is believable and highly entertaining: "There was a real old smell that came out of it too," he says of an old saxophone case, "like dried up slobber and something dead. It smelled great!" A funny, dramatic adventure story, this also gives insight into the lives of African-Americans at the time of the Depression. A great read for both girls and boys. Highly recommended.

* Doyle, Brian. *Angel Square.* **1984. 125 pages. 9 and up.**

It's Christmas, 1945, in Lowertown, Ottawa. The war is over, the soldiers are back, and, in Angel Square, Tommy Lamont and his schoolmates fight daily battles – Irish Catholics versus Jews versus French Canadians, in every combination. But this frantic daily warfare takes on a nastier face when the father of Tommy's Jewish friend Sammy is brutally assaulted. As Sammy's father lies in the hospital at death's door, Tommy and his friend Gerald turn sleuths to find the person who was twisted enough to do such a thing.

Doyle combines the suspense and tension of mystery with a humour that's part-slapstick, part-carnival. Tommy's forthright voice, pointed observations (even about such lesser characters as Toe-Jam Laframboise), and his tense, forceful account of the confrontation with the repulsive evildoer keep the story bounding along. With its short, sharp sentences, abundant dialogue, and small pages, this is a great choice for reluctant readers, boys or girls, and a colourful and unforgettable portrayal of 1940s Ottawa by one of Canada's unique voices for children. Also available, with its sequel *Up to Low*, in the compendium *The Low Life: Five Great Tales from Up and Down the River* (see below). Highly recommended.

Doyle, Brian. *Easy Avenue*. 1988. 180 pages. 10 and up.
Hubbo has recently moved to the Uplands Emergency Shelter with his guardian, Mrs. O'Driscoll. He's starting a new school, too – imposing Glebe Collegiate Institute, where Mrs. O'Driscoll works as a cleaning lady. The best thing in his life is Fleurette Featherstone Fitchell, "a girl who is proud although she wears a rag in her long curly black hair." The worst things are the confusing courses, the snooty boys of the Hi-Y, and his shame that Mrs. O'Driscoll cleans at his school. When an unknown benefactor starts giving Hub monthly funds, and he lands a job on Ottawa's swanky Easy Avenue, things look pretty good – until Hub realizes where his real loyalties lie.

The Ottawa of the late 1940s comes alive in this ironic, loving, coming-of-age story. Doyle's world is peopled by oddballs – a family of six generations of women (all living) named Doris, for example; or Mr. and Mrs. Blank, whose dog, Nerves, always mirrors their own faces. Hub's guileless observations about the poor and the rich point out the ironies of his culture in a way that's both funny and bittersweet. A great read-aloud, and a wonderfully compassionate portrayal of the perils of adolescence. Hub's adventures continue in *Covered Bridge*. Both volumes are included in *The Low Life: Five Great Tales from Up and Down the River* (see below).

Doyle, Brian. *Spud in Winter*. 1995. 140 pages. 8 to 13.
Standing outside his house on an afternoon of the coldest winter on record, Spud Sweetgrass sees something he shouldn't see. It's the face of a man who loves his hair. It's the face of a murderer! And Spud saw the murder. Did the murderer see him? Spud isn't sure, and he doesn't want to tell the police what he saw and endanger himself and Connie Pan, his girlfriend – because the man with the beautiful hair is one of Connie's beauty-salon clients. It takes Spud, Connie, "Dink the Thinker," and an entire ESL class on skates to bring the big-haired man to justice.

Doyle's a master at storytelling: suspense rises and falls and rises again in this short, eccentric mystery. Spud's clipped, candid voice keeps the story moving rapidly, and sharp observations about a raft of endearingly quirky characters make Spud's world funny and unforgettable. (Who won't remember Connie, the girl with "the most beautiful philtrum on the planet earth"?) Doyle emphasizes and celebrates Ottawa's multicultural population – and its deep, dark winters. This is a good read-aloud, and a good choice for reluctant readers, boys or girls. A previous volume, *Spud Sweetgrass*, is similarly entertaining.

* Doyle, Brian. *Uncle Ronald*. 1996. 138 pages. 10 and up.
Terrorized by an abusive father, Mickey McGuire flees Ottawa and travels to the small town of Low to stay with his Uncle Ronald, a kind giant of a man who runs a small farm. Mickey loves Uncle Ronald and his aunts, famous identical twins known as the O'Malley sisters. It seems strange that the O'Malley sisters are clunking around in the dead of night, though – and when Mickey learns that someone is sabotaging the soldiers the government has sent to collect taxes from the reluctant citizens of Low, he has a good idea who's behind it.

The comic antics of the O'Malleys and the penniless people of Low provide a poignant contrast to the serious, even tragic, undercurrents of Mickey's and his mother's vulnerability to the violent father. On the one hand, this is a lively burlesque – the celebration of the people's wacky victory over a paternalistic, authoritarian government in 1895. On the other hand, Mickey's fear, his profound sense of safety once he hears Uncle Ronald's kind voice, is palpable. Populated by a cast of Doyle's trademark eccentrics – Second Chance Lance (a horse), Even Stephen, and manifold McCooeys. This is included in the compendium *The Low Life: Five Great Tales from Up and Down the River* (see below). Highly recommended.

Doyle, Brian. *The Low Life: Five Great Tales from Up and Down the River*. 1999. 397 pages. 9 and up.
This compendium brings together five of Doyle's novels of the Gatineau River and Ottawa, arranged according to the chronology of the stories' events.

Uncle Ronald (Where they found us in 1895). See above.

Angel Square (Who we were when the war was over in 1945). See above.

Easy Avenue (When we tried to climb up in 1948). See above.
Covered Bridge (How we almost tore it all down in 1949)
Up to Low (Why we clung to the magic from 1950 on . . .)

* **Doyle, Brian.** *Mary Ann Alice.* **2001. 160 pages. 9 to 13.**
Mary Ann Alice McCrank, daughter of Fuzzy and Frank McCrank, has
the soul of a poet. That's what her teacher, Patchy Drizzle, says. And
her poet's soul has plenty of fodder for inspiration in 1926, the year the
government decides to build a dam at Paugan Falls, near her hometown
of Martindale on the Gatineau River. The population of the entire area
converges to work on the dam – from the brawny farmers, who blast
and haul stone, to Mary Ann Alice's own schoolmates, who run
errands, cook, and serve food. Tragedy, miracle, and the comeuppance
of a stuffy lawyer or two mark this fateful year of growth, which concludes with a kiss and a sonnet.

Tall tale, carnival, skit, lyric – once again, Doyle's writing defies
convention. The direct, guileless voice of the narrator, a colourful,
almost-caricatured cast, and a brisk pace give this story a vivacity
that's irresistible. A lesson on rock formation becomes dramatic and
funny as relayed by Mary Ann Alice; her account of a bitter, isolated
war bride is rife with understated emotion. Full of incident, this tale
moves from comedy to suspense and back again repeatedly. At the
same time, Mary Ann Alice's growth from adolescence to adulthood is
deeply felt. A good story for both boys and girls, and an excellent candidate for read-aloud. Highly recommended.

Ellis, Deborah. *Looking for X.* **1999. 132 pages. 9 to 12.**
Eleven-year-old Khyber (a name she has given herself out of her
interest in becoming an explorer) lives in Regent Park or, as she
calls it, "Pauper Park," in downtown Toronto. She knows her
small family is labelled: "They think that because we're poor and
my brothers are autistic and my mother used to be a stripper that I'm
doomed to a life of crime and failure." Life at home is difficult, with
twin autistic brothers and no money, but Khyber and her mother
make a strong team, until her mother decides that the twins need
the structure of a group home and Khyber is accused of a crime she
didn't commit.

Khyber is a carefully drawn character, clever and sure of herself, but still vulnerable and in need of her mother's love underneath her bravado. Ellis explores the difficult and challenging world of the poor and homeless with compassion and humour; and she includes a rich cast of secondary characters: X, a sad homeless woman afraid of secret police; Valerie, a rude waitress with a heart of gold; and a whole vanload of women dressed as Elvis.

* **Ellis, Deborah.** *The Breadwinner*. **2000. 176 pages. 10 and up.**
Caught under the Taliban regime in Kabul, Afghanistan, Parvana is unwilling at first to take on the role of the "breadwinner" for her family. But because her father is imprisoned and her mother and sister are not allowed out without a male escort, she knows that only her courage and her earnings can keep her family from starvation. She disguises herself as a boy so she can sell her reading and writing skills to earn money and buy food – and as much as she first fears her role, she soon grows to enjoy the freedom her disguise allows.

The Breadwinner reveals a great deal about the life of women and their families under the Taliban: readers will be swept up in the fear, excitement, and horror of everyday life in Kabul. A scene in which Parvana and her friend collect bones for pay is unforgettable for its strangeness; at the same time, Ellis shows that Parvana has the same pleasures and difficulties as many girls – an irritating older sister, for example. A strong, compelling story. Royalties from the sale of this book support the education of Afghan girls in refugee camps in Pakistan. Highly recommended. A sequel, *Parvana's Journey*, is discussed below.

Ellis, Deborah. *Parvana's Journey*. **2002. 197 pages. 10 and up.**
This sequel to *The Breadwinner* begins when Parvana buries her father and then escapes the villagers who befriended her, for fear that they will sell her off to the Taliban as a soldier. Still disguised as a boy, she journeys through Afghanistan and searches for her mother and sisters, but without any sense of the direction she should take. She rescues a baby from an abandoned village, is joined by Asif, a cantankerous boy with only one leg, and finds shelter with a little girl and her grandmother, only to have it all destroyed in an air strike.

Forthright and uncondescending, Ellis depicts a "big, sad land" in which horror and heartbreak are now so commonplace that they're barely worth mentioning. Yet Parvana's story is told with hope, for, as Ellis remarks, it is the courageous children in Afghanistan today who will rebuild their country. *Parvana's Journey* gives children some understanding of the horrors of this recent war. All royalties from the sale of the book support the education of Afghan women.

Ellis, Deborah. *A Company of Fools*. 2002. 191 pages. 9 to 12.
The Plague of 1349–50 provides the historical setting for this tale set in France. When ragamuffin Micah is first brought to join the choirboys of the Abbey St-Luc, Henri, the chronicler of the story, is first shocked by his flamboyant irreverence for order and discipline. But Henri is soon caught up in Micah's high spirits, and when the Plague begins to devastate the people of France, the boys form a company of entertainers with some of the monks. Jesting and clowning, they bring laughter to the sick and dying, until one day Micah's beautiful singing voice seems to "cure" a child, and Micah becomes an instant celebrity.

This novel has all the elements needed to make it supremely readable – energy, laughter, choristers who are happily rude to each other, and a strong friendship between two realistic, appealing boys. Ellis conveys much information about medieval society in a tale that invites readers to consider serious issues, but at the same time remains highly entertaining.

Ellis, Sarah. *The Baby Project*. 1986. 144 pages. 9 to 12.
Jessica is overjoyed when her parents announce to her and her older brothers that Jessica's mother is pregnant. Jessica and her friend Margaret Lee instantly switch their sixth grade animal project from "duck-billed platypus" to "human baby," and when Lucie is born, Jessica can't believe how much she loves her. Even prickly, teenaged Simon sneaks into Lucie's room at night to read *Motor Trend* to her when he thinks no one is looking. In a very short time, though, Lucie dies of SIDS, and Jessica feels her whole family – even life itself – has lost its direction.

This short novel is a potent combination of deep feeling and delightful humour. Jessica's and Margaret's efforts to please Lucie are truly strange (they try to record "womb sounds" at a local beach, using a sponge mop and an illicitly borrowed tape recorder). So too are the quirks of the family in general – and of their flamboyant tenant, an aspiring country and western singer. But within the clever fun and almost-caricature of popular culture, Ellis offers wisdom with real tenderness; there's no false resolution of tragedy. A rich, appealing story of friendship and family.

Ellis, Sarah. *Pick-Up Sticks*. **1991. 124 pages. 9 to 12.**
Polly and her single mom have always lived in the same apartment in an old house, and Polly's mother's work as a stained-glass artist has always been enough to support them. But when the house is sold and they have to find a new apartment, Polly is suddenly infuriated with everything – that her mother isn't more financially successful, that she's never had a father, even that her loony friend Vanessa is obsessed with their English teacher. It takes a couple of weeks with wealthy Uncle Roger and his family to give Polly perspective on what's satisfying about the eccentricities in her own life.

Ellis has the knack of pointing out the funny side of humanity and material culture, and that humour is everywhere apparent here – from the man who collects postal codes to the vacuous sayings of the library janitor ("things are more like they are now than they've ever been before"). But it's Polly's inner struggles that give the story emotional momentum, and her discontent will be all too familiar to readers. Ellis celebrates humanity's quirks with compassion and flair.

Ellis, Sarah. *Out of the Blue*. **1994. 120 pages. 10 to 14.**
Megan thinks her parents are planning a big surprise for her twelfth birthday – a sailing adventure. Instead, she's dumbfounded when she discovers that she's going to meet the "baby" her mother gave up for adoption twenty-four years ago. And while Megan's parents and her little sister welcome newly announced half-sister, Natalie, with enthusiasm, Megan feels her world has just been turned upside-down. No one seems to share her reservations and resentment towards this young woman who suddenly claims a place in her family's life.

Ellis gives a vivid portrayal of Megan's difficulties in accepting her new sister. We see and feel the confusion, anger, and resentment she feels towards Natalie, and also towards her parents and her younger, more accepting, sister. In her customary manner, Ellis gives a sharp, funny, and sympathetic look at family life, all the while dealing with a subject rarely treated in children's fiction. There's no simplistically happy conclusion here, but rather one that allows Megan to remain true to herself and still show compassion and acceptance.

Ellis, Sarah. *A Prairie as Wide as the Sea: The Immigrant Diary of Ivy Weatherall, Milorie, Saskatchewan, 1926.* **2001. 205 pages. 8 to 12.**
Eleven-year-old Ivy keeps an account of her family's move from post-First World War England to southern Saskatchewan, where her family hopes to get rich by farming. But farming isn't as easy as it looked in *Canada West*, with its pictures of enormous vegetables and exaggerated stories of wheat yield. Ivy's brother has to pay off a relative's debts by working in a local store, and her father can't find any sustained employment. The Weatheralls finally decide to run a hotel in town, and Ivy learns she has a knack for midwifery.

Ivy observes with lively style the characters and events of her surroundings – snooty Nyla Muir; glamorous "no better than she should be" Miss Lorayne Lamott; the joys of Chautauqua and early radio. One gets a real sense of the details of the period, from the yellow celery dishes Ivy considers so elegant to the literary inadequacies of the Canadian children's classic *The Backwoods of Canada*. Ivy's pithy comments give an entertaining view of the dynamics of her family. One of the more spirited volumes of the **Dear Canada series** (*see* Series Books).

Fagan, Cary. Illustr. Cybèle Young. *Daughter of the Great Zandini.* **2001. 64 pages. 7 to 10.**
See Picture Books.

* **Foggo, Cheryl.** *One Thing That's True.* **1997. 128 pages. 10 to 14.**
Roxanne is thirteen years old, it's the last day of junior high, and suddenly her life is changing. A horrible boy tries to assault her and her brother Joel beats him up. Her parents decide Joel has to see a psychologist. Joel thinks their father is having an affair. Roxanne can't stop thinking about Michael, who, even though he's good-looking and a

great athlete, happens also to be a really good person. What is going on? Suddenly, Roxanne's loving family and beloved brother seem to be in turmoil – and when her parents reveal the mystery of their recent arguing and announce that Joel is adopted, he disappears altogether.

Roxanne's frank, articulate voice makes this short-but-substantial novel a work of art; she has a humour and wisdom that are entirely true to her age. "I really needed to think about what to do," she says when Joel is missing. "I couldn't go on throwing up in front of strangers and doing things I really didn't want to do just because I felt so awful." Foggo explores serious matters with a deceptively light hand. Roxanne and her family are the descendants of American slaves (her uncle has eccentric ideas about counteracting black stereotypes), and their race is an integral part of the story, but never its object. A thoroughly delightful story of adolescent growth. Highly recommended.

* Gardam, Heather. Illustr. Julia Bell. *Life on the Farm*. 2001. 157 pages. 7 to 10.
Patti suffers the difficulties of most kids: competition with her brother, frustration at not being big enough to do things, puzzlement at adult behaviour. On her tenth birthday she wakes up, hoping against hope that she'll get a horse; but before her family can think of birthday presents, a mink is wreaking havoc in the henhouse. All the chicks but one are dead, and disaster takes precedence. Patti has to be content to get the horse's mechanical equivalent, a bike.

In each chapter Patti experiences a surprising, memorable moment of growing up – her first bike, her first pet (a chicken), a fist fight, a grass-fire, a disconcerting encounter with a friend's mother. Gardam celebrates the "getting of wisdom" in subtle, thoughtful stories, mixing drama with inner growth in a way that's completely believable. Patti's inner resourcefulness – her recollection of what she's been taught and her ability to act on it – is the foundation for her growing independence, but it's a resourcefulness that's available to any child. With self-contained chapters and occasional illustrations, this is a great read or read-aloud for young girls. Sequel *Little Guy*, in which Patti does begin to look after a horse, is a worthy successor, a thinking alternative to series horse books. Highly recommended.

Griggs, Terry. *Cat's Eye Corner.* **2000. 163 pages. 7 to 11.**
Countless rooms, locked doors ("portals with personality") and a step-step-stepgramma (is she a witch?) greet Olivier when he arrives at Cat's Eye Corner for the summer. Good thing he relishes the suspicious and finds the inexplicable invigorating, because there's nothing here that *isn't* inexplicable or invigorating, from the topiary man kept trim by Gramps (when he isn't locked up) to Stepgramma's Poets (they used to be "pets" but then some Inklings stuck a letter "O" in). But Olivier's adventures really get going with a scavenger hunt that lands him in a mysteriously leafy, threatening world, where Mr. Mirific has locked up the Inklings, Captain Sputum's So-So Gang is on the rampage, and Olivier must return a sword to its proper owner.

A story should unfold "with a certain amount of dash," Olivier thinks, and *Cat's Eye Corner* does exactly that. Griggs writes with a liveliness of mind that never falters; her story is unpredictable but logically satisfying, full of adventures, puns, and sparkling imagination. All this sheer, reasoned nonsense is wrapped up in a fantasy that's eventful, unexpected, and peopled by cleverly weird creatures. Reminiscent of Norman Juster's *The Phantom Tollbooth*, this is one of Canada's best fantasies for children.

Haig-Brown, Roderick. *Starbuck Valley Winter.* **1944. 272 pages. 11 to 14.**
See Novels, 12 and Up.

Harrison, Troon. *A Bushel of Light.* **2000. 244 pages. 10 to 13.**
Maggie and her twin, Thomasina, are orphaned, then separated at age eight. Maggie's sent from St. Ives, Cornwall, to become a Barnardo Home child; eventually she comes to live on a farm near Peterborough, Ontario. The Howard farm is a poor one, and Maggie's responsible for all the housework, much of the farmwork, and the care of four-year-old Lizzy; Mrs. Howard spends her days in depressed seclusion. Maggie longs to be reunited with her twin, but she knows she must work on the farm for another seven years. Furthermore, she doesn't have any money, and she can't leave Lizzy. After an unsuccessful attempt to run away, Maggie learns that Thomasina has also become a Barnardo child and is living not far away.

Harrison writes with passion of the hardships of Maggie and later her sister, Thomasina, conveying the difficulties and sense of bondage many Barnardo children experienced. Maggie's frustration with the Howard farm and Mrs. Howard's reluctance to assume responsibility for her family is palpable, and a close attention to regional flora and fauna give this story a refreshing sense of place. *A Bushel of Light* seems to be a bleak story, but Maggie's spunk and drive pull it along to a satisfying, realistic ending.

Haworth-Attard, Barbara. *Love-Lies-Bleeding*. 1999. 140 pages. 10 to 14.
Thirteen-year-old Bobby records the ins and outs of ten months during wartime in London, Ontario, starting in September 1943. She writes of the agonies of puberty, her unwillingness to make friends with the minister's spunky, irreverent daughter, her impatience with her older sister and annoying brothers. But soon her diary is full of deeper concerns: her brother has arrived home, wounded and empty-eyed with shock; her uncle has been killed. Bobby is forced to spend time at the veterans' hospital and to come to grips with things she would rather not look at.

Bobby's diary entries are interspersed with excerpts from real letters written home by the author's father during the war. An eloquent contrast to life in a small city in Ontario, his descriptions offer a vision of the emptiness and devastation in parts of bombed-out Britain – a vision that becomes increasingly clear to Bobby. Haworth-Attard's writing is deft and convincing, and Bobby's faults and concerns make her realistic and likable. A good additional read for those who enjoyed Kit Pearson's *Guests of War* (*see* Pearson, *The Sky Is Falling*, below).

* Heneghan, James. *Wish Me Luck*. 1997. 197 pages. 10 to 14.
Britain is at war, and Jamie Monaghan welcomes the excitement when bombs start dropping in his Liverpool neighbourhood. He certainly doesn't want to leave, but his parents decide to evacuate him to Canada for "the duration." Travelling towards Canada with Bleeker, the tough kid from next door, and his own little sister, he finds that life aboard the ship *City of Benares* is luxurious: there are showers, stewards, and all the food he can eat. But the safety of all aboard *City of Benares* is

threatened when it's torpedoed by a German U-boat and the passengers have to take to lifeboats.

Heneghan's story, based on the actual sinking of *City of Benares*, is a remarkably successful work of historical fiction. The strong dialect of children from Liverpool and from Ireland and of the "toffs" (upper-class English), combined with vivid descriptions of the clothing, food, rationing, and continual cups of tea give the reader a strong sense of time and place. Clashes between Jamie and Bleeker, seen long before they share a cabin on board ship, make their forced companionship tense, and the gradual growth of mutual respect gratifying. When the ship is torpedoed, Heneghan's energetic pace and sharp account of terrifying hours in a lifeboat in the Atlantic keep the reader enthralled. Highly recommended.

Hewitt, Marsha, and Claire Mackay. *One Proud Summer.* **1981. 159 pages. 11 and up.**
See Novels, 12 and Up.

* **Holubitsky, Katherine.** *Alone at Ninety Foot.* **1990. 169 pages. 10 to 14.**
See Novels, 12 and Up.

Holubitsky, Katherine. *Last Summer in Agatha.* **2001. 185 pages. 11 to 14.**
See Novels, 12 and Up.

Horvath, Polly. Illustr. Wendy Halperin. *The Trolls.* **1999. 136 pages. 7 to 11.**
When the Andersons' babysitter in Ohio comes down with a "mild case of bubonic plague," Mr. and Mrs. Anderson call upon Aunt Sally. Aunt Sally arrives from Vancouver Island and Mr. and Mrs. Anderson take off for Paris – leaving Aunt Sally to care for and entertain Pee Wee (6), Amanda (8), and Melissa (10). And entertain she does. During the day, she plays walrus by sticking green beans in her nostrils and tells weird, surprising family stories; at night, when despised Pee Wee is asleep, she tells the girls what she did to their father, *her* little brother, and what has come of it.

Aunt Sally's tall tales, each headed with an exclamatory title ("Clam Bite!" "Greens!") and peopled with egomaniacal nuts, are hilariously refreshing. "I've seen many, with minds diseased from lack of greens, hauling their loved ones down to meet the trolls," Great-Uncle Louis, vegetable enthusiast, remarks direly. But within the fun and offbeat caricature, Horvath offers a serious reflection on the perils of sibling jealousy. With the exception of the chapter "Fat Little Mean Girl!" this is the best of inventive, moral humour for children, and vastly entertaining for both girls and boys. An earlier novel, *When the Circus Came to Town*, is also excellent for this age group.

* Horvath, Polly. *Everything on a Waffle*. 2001. 179 pages. 8 to 12.
This eccentric, optimistic story tells of eleven-year-old Primrose Squarp as she deals with the loss of her parents off the coast of Vancouver Island, British Columbia. Primrose knows her parents will return; but no one shares her belief. Candid and direct, she relates how her (temporary) orphanhood causes her to go into the custody of ancient, mothball-ridden Miss Perfidy, then to the care of flashy Uncle Jack (he lives off TV dinners), and then on to loquacious foster parents, Evie and Bert – all the while dodging the interfering plots of a school counsellor. A flamboyant cast surrounds her; preposterous chapter headings entice readers with their promise of drama – "I Am Almost Incarcerated"; "I Lose All My Sweaters"; "I Lose a Toe"; and "I Set Fire to a Guinea Pig." And Miss Bowzer, owner of the restaurant The Girl on the Red Swing, serves everything on a waffle.

Horvath includes a recipe for every chapter: a group of girls described as "crushed together like a bunch of asparagus" gives rise to directions for cooking asparagus at the end of the chapter. Primrose is frank and lovable, an independent-minded, perceptive narrator, and her journey towards understanding results in explicit, unabashed wisdom: "The only really interesting thing about someone that makes you want to explore them further's their heart." The story's a great romp, with many laugh-out-loud moments, but readers will long remember Primrose for her love and care for others and her unwavering belief that her parents will return. As Primrose says, "Haven't you ever just known something deep in your heart without reason?" Highly recommended.

Houston, James. *Frozen Fire*. **1977. 149 pages. 10 to 14.**
Matthew Morgan had hoped his father would give him clothes that
would cover his gangling limbs for his birthday, but instead he got a
pair of steel-toed climbing boots and a copy of *Geology Made Easy*.
Now he and his geologist father are off to Baffin Island, to prospect.
When Mr. Morgan goes to investigate what he thinks will be a major
copper find, his helicopter goes down; when Matthew and his new Inuit
friend, Kayak, set off to find him, a series of mishaps has them struggling for their own survival. Kayak's traditional knowledge of hunting
and negotiating the North allows the boys to survive storms, hunger, and
even a spell drifting on an ice-pan.

Houston's brisk, undemanding prose and the suspenseful adventures he describes make this a good choice for reluctant boy readers,
particularly. Houston's knowledge of and respect for the people of the
North is always apparent: this is both engaging and educational
(despite the dated use of the word "Eskimo"). This is a good alternative
for children hooked on series mysteries or adventures. Sequels, ***Black
Diamonds*** and ***Ice Swords***, are also available.

Hughes, Monica. *The Keeper of the Isis Light*. **1980. 191 pages.
10 to 13.**
Olwen Pendennis, Keeper of the Isis Light, has lived with her Guardian
on the uninhabited planet Isis all her life, and she loves it. She's never
felt the need for other company – until a group of colonists from Earth
arrive, and handsome Mark London wins her confidence. But even as
she's getting to know Mark, there are things she can't understand. Why
are the colonists so rude to Guardian? Why do they find the atmosphere
of Isis dangerous, when she doesn't? And why does Guardian insist she
wear a full body suit and mask whenever she meets with them? In one
moment of revelation, Olwen's whole life is changed forever.

With wonderful unexpectedness Hughes forces her readers to confront "the Other," to consider our prejudices and where they come
from. In this case, science fiction works as a perfect medium. And
while Hughes's depiction of Earth colonist Mark is a bit stiff and two-
dimensional, intelligent, responsive Olwen engages readers' interest
and sympathy and holds it. Hughes's style here is unremarkable, but
this is a satisfying, fast-paced story of surprises and depth. Sequels *The*

Isis Pedlar and *The Guardian of Isis* are also available, although neither has the punch of the first volume.

Hughes, Monica. *The Seven Magpies.* **1996. 148 pages. 10 to 14.**
Maureen Frazer is more than a little nervous when she is sent to the Logan Academy for Young Ladies in the remote Scottish highlands. Britain has declared war on Germany, Maureen's father has been sent to the Front, and her mother is working with the Wrens. Logan seems the safest place for Maureen. However, she's the last to arrive and she's the eighth girl in her dorm – and the girls have already formed a secret society called "The Seven Magpies," based on the old rhyme, "One for sorrow, Two for joy, Three for a Girl, Four for a Boy, Five for Silver, Six for gold, Seven for a Secret that can ne'er be told." Excluded from the club, Maureen pursues her own interests, and discovers a strange stone with an ancient face carved on it, much different from the stone to which the Seven Magpies, under the auspices of domineering Kathleen, deliver late-night offerings.

Hughes has written numerous children's and teen books and this is one of her most assured novels. Readers quickly identify with the feelings of exclusion that plague Maureen and the brave front she puts on while pretending that she doesn't mind. Celtic mythology, the theme of the insiders/outsider, and a subplot involving a possible spy make for a slightly fantastical story. Additional titles by Monica Hughes include *Hunter in the Dark*, *Devil on My Back*, and *Where Have You Been, Billy Boy?* among others.

Hunter, Bernice Thurman. *That Scatterbrain Booky.* **1981. 8 to 12.**
Booky is the nickname of Beatrice Thomson, a young girl growing up in Birchcliff (Scarborough, Ontario) in 1932. Booky's spunk and optimism carry her through tough times in the Thomson household: her father is out of work; she has three siblings; her mother is expecting another baby; and eviction from their house seems inevitable.

The *Booky* stories are full of simple details of everyday life: bringing home leftovers from a wealthy friend's house, going to the "Ex" (the Canadian National Exhibition) on Kids' Day, visiting the Annex at Eaton's, riding the streetcar downtown, and watching the Santa Claus parade are major events for Booky. Readers empathize as Booky makes bad decisions (she says the new shoes fit, although they're two sizes too small) or delight with her when she gets simple treats, such as the free cashews at her aunt's store. Told in the first person, these stories are captivating in their truth and energetic spirit. Photos from Toronto's hungry thirties attest to the authenticity of this historical novel based on the author's childhood.

Sequels *With Love from Booky* and *As Ever, Booky* follow Booky's growth into adulthood. The trilogy is also published in a single volume, entitled *Booky: A Trilogy*.

Hunter, Bernice Thurman. *Amy's Promise.* **1995. 192 pages. 8 to 12.** Twelve-year-old Amy Phair sometimes finds life unbearable: ever since her mother died, her irascible father has been drinking heavily, her Gramma has been cantankerous and bossy, and Amy has been stuck doing all the drudgery, while her three brothers seem to enjoy life. Not only that, Amy's baby sister, Janey – the baby her mother made her promise to take care of – has been taken away to stay with relatives. As Amy struggles through this period of family grief, deprived of both school and music, she sometimes can't believe she'll ever be able to fulfil her mother's promise.

Set in 1920s Toronto, this story has the warmth, down-to-earth writing, and domestic interest that Hunter is best at. Amy is a stalwart, loving protagonist; her tense, motherless family is honestly portrayed. Hunter incorporates the concrete details of the period – Amy bandages Gramma with glycerine, camphor, soft cotton, and a gold safety pin – in a way that makes both the social and the physical setting entirely clear. This is an engaging read for girls. The sequel, *Janey's Choice*, is equally satisfying.

Huser, Glen. *Touch of the Clown.* **1999. 223 pages. 11 to 14.**
See Novels, 7 to 12.

* **Jam, Teddy.** *The Charlotte Stories.* **Illustr. Harvey Chan. 1994. 48 pages. 4 to 7.**
In these three stories Charlotte, about five years old, makes friends with a boy who is always attired in hockey gear ("when he grows up he's going to be an animal," Charlotte's friend Miriam remarks with

devastating conclusiveness), has a difficult birthday party, and tries to make a pet of a mouse her parents want to trap.

The simple language and modest situations in these stories are deceiving – Jam conveys brilliantly the eccentric-but-infallible logic of children in a way that is entirely true to the child's perspective. Charlotte is sharp and observant; her intense experience of the "now" is what always governs her. "I am a terrible little girl and I wish it wasn't my birthday," she states grandly; fortunately her mother has enough good sense to understand that something scary is troubling her. Jam writes with compassion and the light touch of humour; he has the knack of using ordinary words to say extraordinary things. A perfect read-aloud for those in kindergarten, with the added advantage that Chan's illustrations make clear that Miriam is Chinese Canadian. Highly recommended. Sequel *TtuM* discussed below.

Jam, Teddy. *TtuM*. Illustr. Harvey Chan. 1999. 110 pages. 4 to 8.
As summer begins at the end of grade four, Charlotte's thrilled to rescue a cute puppy abandoned in a rainstorm. She and her friend Mimi deduce that this dog understands only backwards talk; he's named "ttuM" (Mutt) and becomes part of Charlotte's family. When she and her parents head to Lake of Bays for a summer holiday, ttuM comes too – but he soon takes to running away, barking outside a neighbouring cabin, and whining after a black-clad canoeist who passes by occasionally. Charlotte and Mimi have a mystery to solve, and it's one Charlotte feels darkly morose about.

Charlotte's strong feelings and delightfully stubborn outlook give this realism and warmth. Aside from the ever-popular topic (wanting a dog), the story appeals because Jam writes so unerringly from a child's-eye view. Charlotte, for example, can't leave behind her hatred of long division; it becomes the point of comparison for every unpleasant circumstance. Sharper readers will be entertained by Jam's understated prose, which reveals worlds of feeling and family dynamics. But even those who aren't used to reading – or listening – between the lines will enjoy this funny, sympathetic novel.

Jocelyn, Marthe. *The Invisible Day.* **1997. 167 pages. 7 to 10.**
Invisibility presents a number of challenges for fifth-grader Billie in this lively, funny story. Billie finds herself invisible after trying out some "vanishing powder" that she finds in an abandoned knapsack. Havoc ensues as she evades her mother, bluffs her way through the school day, invisibly crashes a movie set, pees in the street, and avoids difficult situations. Finally she manages to track down the teenaged inventor of the potion and discovers the disgusting antidote (which includes a great deal of chewing-gum juice and dog biscuits).

In subsequent volumes, *Invisible Harry* and *Invisible Enemy*, Billie's pup, Harry, and then her class enemy, Alyssa, become invisible. Each story is filled with Billie's escapades with her stalwart friend Hubert and the inventive Jody, who together manage to correct the situation without adult help or knowledge. The thoughts and motives of Billie and Hubert reveal a theme of kindness that isn't always present in fast-paced humorous books for this age group. Good for read-aloud.

Jocelyn, Marthe. *Earthly Astonishments.* **1999. 179 pages. 9 to 12.**
Twelve years old and twenty-nine inches high, Josephine is used to being picked on. But when the cook at McLaren Academy for Girls beats her with a ladle, Josephine decides it's time to seek employment elsewhere. She hitches a ride on a horse-bus (this is 1884) and ends up at the Half-Dollar Saloon in the employment of impresario R. J. Walters of the Museum of Earthly Astonishments. Overnight, Josephine becomes "Little Jo-Jo of Bavaria," moving from drudge to celebrity, enjoying fame, and celebrating her small stature. But one day that's not enough; she and her new friend, Charlie ("the Albino Boy, A Ghostly Phenomenon"), realize they can live independently.

This has a snappy pace, an exciting plot, and flavourful dialogue that's fun to read: "You skeered my guts through a hole," says one boy. Josephine makes a clever, courageous heroine. With verve, wisdom, and honesty Jocelyn explores the realities of human curiosity, friendship, and life with a physical trait that will always have to be accommodated.

* **Johnston, Julie.** *Hero of Lesser Causes.* **1992. 178 pages. 11 and up.**
See Novels, 12 and Up.

* **Johnston, Julie.** *In Spite of Killer Bees.* **2001. 253 pages. 11 and up.**
See Novels, 12 and Up.

Kacer, Kathy. *The Secret of Gabi's Dresser.* **1999. 128 pages. 8 to 12.**
Life for Gabi changes dramatically when the Nazis invade Czechoslovakia. She no longer has friends; she's not allowed to go to school, and her parents begin to fear for her safety as they hear rumours that young Jews, especially girls, are being rounded up and sent away. Gabi's mother wants Gabi to go away and stay safely with some friends; but Gabi's desperate to stay with her family and convinces her mother that she can hide in a large dresser if Nazis come. Sure enough, the dresser proves a safe hiding place when soldiers come looking for Gabi – even though her kitten almost gives her away.

Kacer tells this tale through the voice of a grandmother telling her grandchildren of her childhood in Czechoslovakia. While the story gives children some understanding of the plight of the Jews and the brutality of the Nazis, it doesn't dwell on the horrors of the Holocaust, making it an excellent story to share with younger readers ready to consider such matters. In a foreword and in endnotes, Kacer provides additional information about the war and the fate of the Jews. The story, though fiction, is based on a true personal story from Kacer's mother; pictures of the family, as well as the dresser, make readers recognize that the fear described in this gripping story was very real.

Katz, Welwyn Wilton. *Witchery Hill.* **1984. 244 pages. 10 to 14.**
Mike's summer holiday with his father on the island of Guernsey turns into a horrifying battle against a coven of witches in this surprisingly frightening book. Mike and his father visit Guernsey to help his father find a setting for his next book, and stay with a family friend. Lisa, the friend's daughter, shows Mike around the island, pointing out Trepied Hill and explaining that witches have gathered there for centuries. She also confides her fears of her beautiful stepmother, whose appearance and kind actions, she claims, are deceiving. Soon Mike is

drawn into the horror of Trepied Hill: he knows that a human sacrifice is planned, and only he can stop the power that will be unleashed.

Katz has put as much terror into a book for young readers as is possible. Fear grows in Mike from the first time he walks into the tomb by the hill and feels the cold there; by the time he finds the body of a sacrificed puppy on an altar, it's clear that the story is going to become more gruesome. Katz's characters each have complex lives and personalities: it's hard for Mike – and the reader – to predict who really is the ascending witch. Readers are rewarded with a truly scary story. Not recommended for the faint-hearted and to be read in daylight hours.

Katz, Welwyn Wilton. *False Face*. **1987. 155 pages. 10 to 14.**
Life for Laney is altered forever when her dog discovers an ancient Aboriginal burial site in a local bog, and she uncovers a miniature face mask. The mask, half-red and half-black, shows a pain-filled face, and is used to temper the power of a full-sized mask that still lies buried in the bog. Tom Walsh, struggling with his own half-Native heritage, finds the larger mask and a body beneath it, but because he is afraid of its energy, he leaves it. However, Laney's mother, ignorant of the mask's power, unearths it, unleashing horrifying powers that could kill Laney. This exciting tale of terror is mixed with family dramas in both Laney's and Tom's lives.

Tension mounts as Tom and Laney begin to understand the power of the masks; Laney fights with her sister and mother; Tom grapples with his Aboriginal father's death, and tries to come to grips with his life off the reservation with his white mother. All of this brings added suspense. The story is steeped in Indian mythology, giving the reader some understanding of Native lore.

Kertes, Joseph. Illustr. Peter Perko. *The Gift*. **1995. 39 pages. 8 to 10.**
As Toronto takes on the sparkle and magic of Christmas, Jacob Beck, a Jewish boy growing up in the city in 1959, longs to participate in Christmas celebrations. He wishes he were a British Canadian, not a Hungarian Jew. Jacob's world opens up when Larry Wilson invites him to Christmas lunch. After begging his family to let him miss the family's Hanukkah celebrations, Jacob goes off for lunch with what he

thinks is a suitable Christmas gift – a plaster cast of the Last Supper. Larry is not delighted with the present, and embarrassed Jacob ends up fleeing home to watch his family light the Hanukkah candles from outside on the porch.

Kertes's tale of the young immigrant longing to fit in and being embarrassed by his foreign parents will resonate with readers no matter what their background. The frustration of trying to do the right thing and getting it wrong is told beautifully. Perko's illustrations are in black pencil, with soft colours used only on Christmas decorations, showing the magical appeal of Christmas amidst Jacob's seemingly bleak everyday world. The last illustration of the Hanukkah table surrounded by Jacob and his family is, in contrast, finally radiant with colour.

Kogawa, Joy. Illustr. Matt Gould. *Naomi's Road*. 1986. 82 pages. 8 to 12.
Joy Kogawa based her story of young Naomi Nakame with "black hair and lovely Japanese eyes and a face like a valentine" on her acclaimed novel for adults, *Obasan*. After the Japanese attack Pearl Harbor, the Canadian government deports Naomi and her Japanese Canadian family from Vancouver to an internment camp in the interior of British Columbia, and later to a farm in Alberta. Written from Naomi's perspective, this story recounts how she copes with the multitude of changes in her life. It's a tale of bereavement and hardship, though Kogawa provides a kernel of hope in the form of Naomi's friendship with the blonde girl, Mitzi, thus keeping the young readers involved in the story.

Kogawa writes of Naomi and her brother Stephen to document a tragic part of Canada's past. Naomi is quite young at the beginning of the novel, making it difficult for older children to engage quickly in her story. However, those interested in the Japanese Canadian experience or the historical time period will find this a powerful, yet painful, narrative. *A Child in Prison Camp*, by Shizuye Takashima (*see* Non-Fiction), is an excellent companion to this.

Korman, Gordon. *Radio Fifth Grade*. 179 pages. 1989. 9 to 12.
Benjy Driver is mad about radio, and he and his friends run a radio show for their school. The pet-shop owner who sponsors the show

insists that, each week, the kids sell their "mascot of the week," but when they're given a taciturn "talking" parrot to sell, the parrot thwarts every sales pitch. To top it off, an enthusiastic teacher starts giving the "fifth grade seminar" massive amounts of homework, including a list of hard questions to answer each week. When Benjy has the great idea of including the questions in a phone-in quiz show, ratings skyrocket and the class does brilliantly. But the ornery parrot threatens to do them in – if the teacher doesn't catch on first. Or perhaps fearsome Brad Jaworski, the "Venice Menace," will bring about their demise with his on-air stories about two homicidal kittens.

Korman's wacko humour works on ludicrous and inventive situation comedy – the kids' efforts to avoid disaster involve one hare-brained scheme after another, including teaching the parrot French, running a blow-dryer outside the teacher's apartment at strategic moments, and chasing a runaway plaster truck. This story, and other titles by Korman, such as *The Twinkie Squad*, *The Toilet Paper Tigers*, and *Losing Joe's Place*, have the appeal of obvious humour, simple, accessible language, and a quick pace. School and family situations (especially little brothers and sisters) dominate most of Korman's stories. Particularly appealing to reluctant readers, this is entertaining without being challenging. *See* Series Books for further entries by Korman.

* **Lawrence, Iain.** *The Wreckers.* **1998. 196 pages. 10 to 14.**
"For seven days we ran before the storm," recounts fourteen-year-old John Spencer; "chased by a shrieking wind . . . she went like a witch." John's first sea voyage ends cataclysmically, when his father's brig is wrecked off the coast of Cornwall. But worse than the wreck is John's discovery that the vessel was lured onto the rocks by local villagers – "wreckers," who have a vested interest in ensuring there are no survivors. John does survive; but even under the protection of the local girl Mary and her violent, temperamental guardian, Mawgan, his life is in peril. Pursued by the odious, legless "Stumps" and threatened by Mawgan, John and Mary risk their lives to save John's father and thwart the murderous wreckers.

Set in 1799, this has the high drama and gruesome horror of R. L. Stevenson's *Treasure Island*. With a few well-placed words, Lawrence creates a deliciously ghastly atmosphere; his evocation of storm, terror, and grand, foundering ships is unforgettable. Mawgan and Stumps make Long John Silver look tame. Multiple mysteries and relentless suspense propel the plot. An excellent choice for "reluctant" readers – both boys and girls. John's career at sea continues to be highly fraught in sequels **The Smugglers** and **The Buccaneers** (the "High Seas Trilogy"). All three titles are highly recommended.

Lawrence, Iain. *Ghost Boy.* **2000. 328 pages. 11 and up.**
Fourteen-year-old albino Harold Kline has lived his life as an outcast in his small prairie town. "He's ugly and stupid, / He's dumb as a post, / He's a freak and a geek, / He's Harold the Ghost," the local boys taunt him. But after years of jeers and ridicule, everything changes for Harold the day the circus comes to town, for he decides to follow it in order to meet the featured attraction – the Cannibal King, who is also an albino. Harold finds a new and loving family with the sideshow performers of the circus, and he proves to have a knack teaching the circus elephants how to play baseball. But he soon realizes that being one of the "freaks" limits his opportunities: Flip, the first girl to show any interest in Harold, makes it clear that she won't have anything to do with him if he continues to fraternize with the "freaks." In a bitter lesson, Harold has to decide where he belongs.

Lawrence has created a rich cast of multi-faceted characters who bring the excitement of the circus to life, while showing the dreary underbelly of relationships beneath the big top. Harold's journey to self-acceptance is fraught with peril; eventually, he learns to accept not only himself, but also the frailties of others.

* Lawrence, Iain. *Lord of the Nutcracker Men.* **2001. 212 pages. 10 to 14.**
Johnny loves playing war with the nutcracker soldiers, Tommies, and Frenchmen his toymaker father has whittled for him. But when the Great War begins and his father enlists, Johnny's world changes. His mother sends him from London to stay with crusty Aunt Ivy in the country. His dad's letters reveal that combat is sordid, not glorious. The wooden soldiers he whittles and sends to Johnny take on the disturbingly abject features of men in the trenches. Even worse, Johnny

comes to suspect that the wars he fights out in the garden with his toy soldiers are horribly related to the fate of his beloved father. ·

This is one of the most poignant, potent novels of the First World War written for children. Ten-year-old Johnny is very true-to-life ("he talked about books in a way that wasn't too terribly boring," he concedes of a teacher), Aunt Ivy a masterpiece of tart rectitude. The increasingly wrought emotion comes across vividly, even visually, in this uncompromising exploration of the political and physical realities of the war. Somehow, realism and rationality touch on eerie mysticism; children will be completely engrossed by the story, but pushed to think deeply. Highly recommended.

* **Lemieux, Michèle.** *Stormy Night*. **Trans. from German. 1999. 240 pages. 9 and up.**

This unusual book, which presents philosophy graphically, is perfect even for children and adolescents who have an intense aversion to text. In the first pages, Lemieux shows a girl getting ready and climbing into bed. Once she gets there, her mind is flooded with questions and imaginings. "Where does infinity end? Is there life on other planets? Sometimes I feel like I don't fit in my body! When I dream at night, where am I? I'm scared of being abandoned, being separated from every one I love! Can we each see our own soul?"

Conflicting emotions, fears, and existential queries are expressed one by one on the left-hand page; on the right, Lemieux illustrates the comment with a line drawing, expressing visually what the girl is wondering. "Sometimes I feel as if my eyes can see inside of me," the girl remarks, and we see a thoughtful character, his cranium taken over by a figure with a lantern emerging from the attic of his brain. With its witty drawings and abundant questions, this unique work contains a wealth of humour and wisdom; it both comforts and inspires questioning. "You are not alone in having these questions, these fears," it seems to say. Highly recommended.

* **Little, Jean.** *From Anna*. **1971. 201 pages. 9 to 12.**

Although her four older brothers and sisters are clever and athletic, eleven-year-old Anna is clumsy and can't seem to learn anything.

When Papa decides in 1933 that the family will move from Frankfurt, Germany, to Toronto – partly because they inherited a grocery business, but mainly because Papa is worried about the Nazis – "Awkward Anna" is sure that school will be horrible. But a friendly doctor realizes that Anna can barely see; he prescribes glasses and sends her to a special program for the visually impaired. Soon grumpy, lonely Anna has started to smile and make friends; when Christmas rolls around, she makes the best Christmas present for her parents and wins the admiration of her family.

Anna's stubborn, courageous spirit, feelingly conveyed, is at the heart of this absorbing novel. Little taps into familiar emotions – fear of change, sibling jealousy, desire for parental approval – but she does this within the context of Anna's adjustment as a new immigrant and her slow blossoming in the special class, elements that give the story added depth. An unusually moving novel for readers who love family stories, this also reflects some of the author's own experiences as a visually impaired child. Highly recommended.

A sequel, *Listen for the Singing*, relates Anna's experiences as she starts high school without the aids of the special class. With the outbreak of the Second World War, Anna and her family have to struggle with Canadian anti-German sentiment, and when Anna's handsome brother Rudi joins up and is blinded, Anna has to call on all her resources to help him adjust to the change. Excellent and informative reading.

Little, Jean. *Mama's Going to Buy You a Mockingbird.* **1985. 213 pages. 10 to 12.**
Jeremy Talbot's summer begins badly, when his father has to have an operation and Jeremy and his sister Sarah have to go to the family cottage with fussy Aunt Margery. But when Jeremy's parents finally do arrive, the summer seems to get even worse – Jeremy learns that Mr. Talbot has cancer. As summer turns to fall, Jeremy must adjust to his father's illness, and then his death. Hanging onto his father's last gift to him, a stone owl, and making friends with one of his father's favourite students, a girl named Tess, help Jeremy find some stability and hope.

This is not a story to hand on to a bereaved child, but it will give young readers some inkling of the emotional traumas of losing a parent. Little writes with sensitivity of the larger feelings that are often behind children's petty anger, and shows Jeremy finding the courage to move beyond his own feelings in order to respond to the needs of others in his family.

Little, Jean. *Willow and Twig.* **1999. 227 pages. 9 to 12.**
Abandoned on the streets of Vancouver by her drug-addicted mother, ten-year-old Willow knows that the only haven for herself and her younger brother, Twig, lies with Gram. Once they're installed in Stonecrop, Gram's old Ontario farmhouse, Willow feels she's come to the right place at last: now memories of privation and abuse can be spoken of and resolved. The aunts, uncles, dogs, cats, and other pets make Stonecrop a hectic but happy haven, and as she makes friends and adjusts, Willow is finally able to entrust her brother's care to nurturing adults.

Little writes with great understanding of the comfort of finding family love and stability after the trauma of abandonment and privation. Twig, who suffers from hyperactivity, stands out for his personality and not only for the "issue" of ADHD; but it is sensitive, indomitable Willow with whom readers engage. Little introduces serious, difficult matters within the context of a comforting family story that will be particularly appealing to girls. Uncle Hubert, who is blind, will give readers some insight into Little herself.

* **Little, Jean.** *Orphan at My Door: The Home Child Diary of Victoria Cope, Guelph, Ontario, 1897.* **2001. 221 pages. 8 to 12.**
When Victoria's mother presents her with a diary, it comes with an injunction: "No embroidery, Victoria. Just write down what really happens each day. When you grow up you will love having the true story of your twelfth year." For Victoria it turns out to be a big year, beginning with the arrival of pug Snortle, the sudden departure of the maid, and the arrival of a Barnardo girl – Mary Anna, whose "smiles are gone so fast they are like hummingbirds." Unwanted relatives, the revelation of family secrets, and a burgeoning friendship with Mary Anna bring Victoria a new awareness: although the world is a wonderful place, it can also be sad or dangerous.

Among Little's many novels, this contribution to the **Dear Canada series** ranks among her best. Victoria's intelligent, lively commentary is utterly engaging; generous use of dialogue allows readers to see the peculiarities and funny side of every friend and family member. The excitement of hiding Mary Anna's runaway brother, dealing with a villainous farmer, and witnessing the death of a grouchy aunt give the story dramatic momentum that keeps pages turning. This is wry, poetic, and often poignant. Best of all, it feels *real*. Victoria and her family are people we might really want to know. Highly recommended, especially for girls. (*See also* Series Books.)

Little, Jean. *The Jean Little Collection.* **2002. 358 pages. 5 to 9.**
Jean Little's ability to address the concerns of young children with simplicity and respect has won her a large audience of loyal readers, mostly girls. Problems with peers, making friends, and overcoming fears and family expectations are some of the difficulties treated in the three short novels in this collection. Comfortable, stable families and undemanding circumstances allow the protagonists' small-but-important trials centre stage.

In *Different Dragons* (129 pages), Ben is sent to stay the weekend with Aunt Rose. This is supposed to be a special treat, but it's not: Ben's afraid to say goodbye to his father, afraid to sleep alone in the dark, and when an overly enthusiastic Labrador retriever shows up, he has to deal as well with his fear of dogs. But when Ben sees that both he and Gully, the dog, are afraid of thunderstorms, he starts to believe they might have something in common after all.

Lucy, of *Lost and Found* (80 pages), feels lonely and nervous about making friends in her new neighbourhood. When she finds a stray Maltese terrier, she falls in love with it and brings it home, wanting to keep it forever. But her parents and the girl next door persist in sleuthing out the owners, and Lucy has to give it up. A sad little Papillon at the animal shelter, however, touches Lucy's heart; she takes it home for keeps, realizing that the dog needs her love.

Ten-year-old Janie of *One to Grow On* (140 pages) has a penchant for embroidering the truth – at least that's how she sees it. To her family she's just telling lies, and her stories can never be trusted. Janie's thrilled when popular Lisa makes friends with her, but then she finds that Lisa is also telling lies, and these lies hurt Janie. It takes a special adult friend who believes in Janie to give her the confidence to give up lying and be herself.

Many additional titles by Little are available; of particular interest are *Kate*, *Look Through My Window*, and *The Belonging Place*. Little's autobiography is available in *Stars Come Out Within* and *Little by Little* (*see* Non-Fiction).

Lottridge, Celia Barker. *Ticket to Curlew*. **1992. 144 pages. 8 to 12.** Eager to help his father build a house and barn before the rest of the family arrives, twelve-year-old Sam Ferrier travels by train to Curlew, Alberta, where the family has acquired land. Sam and his father finish the buildings, the family comes, and Sam explores the prairie, finds a friend at school, and gets used to the new farm. He learns to love his horse, Prince (who is renamed "King" after a winter in the wild), and he helps a Ukrainian neighbour boy learn English.

Told from Sam's perspective, the story covers the family's first year on the farm. Readers will relate to Sam's pleasures – finding a friend in the new school, or a buffalo skull out on the prairie; but the story's richness lies not so much in drama and incident as in Lottridge's ability to show a family building a new life on the Canadian prairie at the beginning of the last century. Historical details – the neighbour's sod house, the price of lumber, the lack of books, or the boredom of eating sausages packed in lard, day after day – give an understanding of life in Alberta one hundred years ago. Lottridge provides details that appeal to children in a tale rewarding in its simplicity.

Lottridge, Celia Barker. Illustr. Daniel Clifford. *The Wind Wagon*. **1995. 46 pages. 7 to 11.** In 1859, Sam Peppard decides to harness the strong winds that blow across the prairies and builds a "wind wagon" to take him to the Rocky Mountains. Everyone laughs at his idea, but he sets sail for the Rockies and – travelling up to 25 miles per hour – passes many of the carts pulled by oxen.

This short book is ideal for readers who are not ready for long chapter books. The quick pace, intriguing illustrations, and the idea of the story appeal to children interested in the past as well as those who are interested in machines. More like a vignette than a full-blown story, this is based on an historical incident.

Lottridge, Celia Barker. *Wings to Fly.* **1997. 209 pages. 8 to 12.**
Life in Curlew, Alberta, in 1918 for eleven-year-old Josie Ferrier, sister of Sam in *Ticket to Curlew* (see above), offers many challenges. Her wishes for a friend are answered when Margaret, a new English immigrant, moves with her family to a nearby farm and "soddy." Life is hard; there's an outbreak of influenza and Margaret's mother is desperate to return to England. But life for Josie is just unfolding, and she's filled with excitement for the future. Will she be a teacher like Miss Barnett, who had to fight to get paid? Or perhaps a pilot like the amazing Katherine Stinson?

Lottridge writes with a sure voice and a sense of humour. In one touching scene, a tea party is held in a sod house and, when it rains, muddy drops fall on the women's white dresses, almost ruining the party. That episode and many others ring with authenticity, partly because they're derived from real family stories. Lottridge gives readers a sense of the obstacles put in the way of women who wanted to try something different in the early 1900s. She also celebrates the women who truly tested the boundaries and pursued their dreams.

Lottridge, Celia Barker. Illustr. Elsa Myotte. *Berta: A Remarkable Dog.* **2002. 99 pages. 4 to 8.**
Marjory can't figure out why dachshund Berta, whose favourite pastimes are "eating, sleeping, and, if necessary, taking short walks," suddenly shows an interest in grooming chicks and kidnapping a baby kitten. When a local sheep farmer asks Marjory's family to look after a lamb, all becomes clear – Berta wants a baby. She takes over the care of lamb Patrick with great success, washing him, waking the family for his night feedings, and protecting him from outsiders.

Marjory is an intelligent, candid protagonist, straightforward in her opinions and interesting in her ideas; Berta is a gently eccentric, ordinarily remarkable dog. Lottridge's realism is quiet but amusing, with characters of animals and humans coming through succinctly, so that what is quite a simple story becomes funny and charming. Part of the magic lies in Lottridge's sure, storyteller's voice and her accessible but nicely unpredictable language. A good read-aloud for 4-to-7-year-olds ready to listen to "chapter books."

Lunn, Janet. *Double Spell*. 1968. 134 pages. 8 to 12.
As soon as twins Jane and Elizabeth see the old doll in the antique shop on Toronto's Yonge Street, they know that they have to have it. They are long past the age of playing with dolls, but the antique doll seems to have a power over them. "What do you think the doll is – a witch doll or something?" asks one. The two soon discover that they are sharing dreams and develop an unrelenting desire to track down the history of the doll, not knowing they will solve a mystery that has been hidden in their family.

This enchanting and suspenseful mystery turns into a ghost story, combining Lunn's passion for making history come alive for children with her ability to tell a good story. The history is hidden within the realistic family story, with its intriguing aunts, difficult brothers, and new puppy. The book was written over thirty years ago, but the dialogue is still fresh and true to life: the twins argue and bicker with each other, and the parents incorrectly blame children. Lunn leads readers carefully into the world of the supernatural, showing the power that family history holds.

* Lunn, Janet. *The Root Cellar*. 247 pages. 1981. 10 and up.
Twelve-year-old Rose has lived a quiet life, the ward of her urbane American grandmother. When Grandmother dies suddenly, Rose has to live with Canadian relatives on an island in Lake Ontario. Trying to escape the chaos of the large family, she ducks into an underground cellar and finds she's gone back in time – to the 1860s. Will and Susan, whom she meets in the past, become her friends; when Rose discovers that Will has gone to fight in the American Civil War and hasn't returned, she and Susan set out to retrieve him from a military hospital in Washington. The difficulties of travelling disguised as a boy, of surviving on what she can earn, and especially of learning to be a good friend, transform Rose's self-understanding and her appreciation for her present-day relatives.

Lunn writes with a strong, engaging voice; her depiction of spoiled Rose is complex and sympathetic. Her exploration of moral issues – in the friendship between Susan and Rose, and in the matter of Canadian involvement in an American war – is honest and demanding. "Being a person's too hard," Rose thinks as she views the devastated landscape and populace in Washington. "It's just too hard." With suspense, depth, and a protagonist that strikes a chord with modern readers, this is an enormously successful time-travel story. Highly recommended.

Lunn, Janet. *Shadow in Hawthorn Bay*. 216 pages. 1986. 10 and up.
Mary Urquhart has always had "the second sight," and when she hears her beloved cousin Duncan calling her from his new home in Upper Canada, she knows she has to leave Scotland and go to him. But it's 1815, travel to Canada is slow, and by the time Mary arrives at Hawthorn Bay on Lake Ontario, Duncan is dead. Mary takes over the family claim and struggles to make a living by teaching and weaving, and she's befriended by local farmers, even though they don't believe in her "second sight," her Scots fairies, or her ghosts. When kind, generous Luke Anderson wants her to marry him, Mary has to confront at last the true nature of Duncan's death.

Lunn blends the folklore and magic of Scotland with the down-to-earth practicality of uneducated Loyalist settlers in Upper Canada. Mary has a passionate, enterprising spirit that makes her appealing, and the drama of a barn fire, a blizzard, and the taunting voice of the ghost give the story satisfying momentum. The hardships and customs of this period of settlement are realistically presented. This makes up the middle volume in Lunn's stories of Hawthorn Bay, which include *The Hollow Tree* and *The Root Cellar*, both reviewed in this chapter. Particularly appealing to girls.

* Lunn, Janet. *The Hollow Tree*. 1997. 260 pages. 10 and up.
Gentle, quiet Phoebe Olcott, fifteen-years-old, is caught between sides in the American Revolutionary War. Her father is killed as a Patriot; her cousin is hanged for a Loyalist spy. Trying to make amends for her part in her cousin's hanging, Phoebe sets off into the Vermont woods to complete his mission, crossing the Appalachians and hiking up along Lake Champlain to Upper Canada.

This story has the excitement of the danger of the wild, and the worse threats of the ignorant company Phoebe falls in with, but

Phoebe's inward journey is what makes it satisfying. She's "stubborn as a bear," her Mohawk friend observes – steady, kind, both fearful and tenacious. Her slow, convincing passage of growth reaches its climax when she dares to free a soldier captured by Loyalist refugees. In a moment of clarity she realizes that she, too, is held captive – by her own fears and, especially, by the strong wills of her father and cousin.

Phoebe's journey to independence and self-knowledge is multi-layered and touching. Lunn depicts the nastiness of both parties in the Revolution, showing that comfort can be found on neither side: this isn't Phoebe's war. A deft, confident storytelling voice and Phoebe's strong spirit make this an outstanding read for girls. Highly recommended.

MacDonald, Jake. *Juliana and the Medicine Fish*. 1997. 150 pages. 10 and up.
Juliana has been coping with the separation of her parents and a sudden move to Winnipeg with her mother. She misses her father and her former life in Kenora and at the lodge at the Lake of the Woods. When summer comes, she gets to visit the lodge and her father and learns that he hasn't visited her in Winnipeg because he is barely able to keep his lodge financially viable. He's thrilled to have a big Trophy Hunter fishing competition at his lodge, never thinking that his daughter will enter and try to capture the largest Muskie ever caught on the lake.

MacDonald writes passionately about fishing, and his story of Juliana and her father is both moving and rewarding. Juliana learns about her father, his love for the outdoors, and his lodge, and at the same time comes to understand more about her own beliefs and Ojibwa heritage. This is a satisfying story about a huge fish, a fish of mythic ancestry, and about the nature of Ojibwa knowledge and the need to follow one's own personal beliefs. The story is thought-provoking and original – a good book to discuss with a group.

Marineau, Michèle. *Lean Mean Machines*. Trans. from French. 1998. 127 pages. 10 to 13.
Jeremy's intrigued by Laure, the glamorous new girl in his high school, but it's not long before he realizes that she has a secret, one that makes her vulnerable to sexually predatory Christian. Laure, on the other hand, is amazed by Jeremy's friendly support and his candid acceptance

of his chaotic life with eight brothers and sisters – a far cry from the affluent lifestyle she's been used to. When Jeremy discovers that Laure's wealthy father was convicted of money laundering, drug trafficking, and more before he finally committed suicide, he has to find a way to help Laure accept her new working-class life with pride. At the same time, he risks losing his long-time friendship with Tanya, bicycle-maintenance partner and friend extraordinaire, who thinks Jeremy is sweet on Laure and, in revenge, seems to have taken up with an entomologist.

A quickly paced novel of mystery and friendship, this has a liveliness and warmth that make it stand out among school stories. Jeremy's good-hearted investigations and blundering support make him an endearing male protagonist; his final rueful acknowledgement is charming: "Under certain circumstances, girls are much better than bikes. Bikes, you see, don't get moods."

Matas, Carol. *Lisa*. 1987. 111 pages. 10 to 14.
When the Nazis take over Denmark, fourteen-year-old Lisa and her older brother Stefan are outraged. Before long, Stefan and his friend Jesper have joined the anti-Nazi movement, and Lisa insists on doing her part as well. At first she's helping to hand out leaflets, but as the war continues and Nazi aggression becomes increasingly horrific, she begins to go on more dangerous missions. When Lisa's doctor father gets the message that the Nazis are planning to round up all the Jews and ship them to concentration camps, however, Lisa and Stefan realize that they and their Jewish parents must flee to Sweden with the rest of the Jewish community.

Matas's story is fast-paced, even sketchy – she covers about four years of the war in short order. But while this novel lacks complexity and character development, it does introduce the historical issues of the period in a way that engages less adept and reluctant readers. Short sentences, simple language, and attitudes "typical" of today's adolescents help make Matas's writing accessible and popular.

A sequel, *Jesper*, describes the work of Stefan's friend as he stays on in Denmark until the end of the war. With many suspenseful moments and hair's-breadth escapes, this is an adventure story with the added element of historical veracity.

Matas's subsequent Second World War stories – *In My Enemy's House*, *Greater Than Angels*, and more – have similar strengths and weaknesses.

Matas, Carol. *Daniel's Story*. 1993. 136 pages. 10 and up.
Daniel recounts his increasingly horrific experiences during the Second World War, first in Frankfurt, where the Nazis forced all the Jews out of public schools, and then out of the city altogether; then in Lodz, Poland, where his family was interned with 160,000 other Jews in the ghetto; then in Auschwitz; and finally in Buchenwald. An amateur photographer, Daniel builds his stories around the pictures he looks at in his albums – or in his mind, once he has been sent to Auschwitz. From those of his loving Jewish family in Frankfurt he moves to photos of his sister and his sweetheart at the scene of their forced labour, a sewing factory in Lodz. In Auschwitz and in Buchenwald, he uses his abilities as a photographer to record Nazi crimes.

Matas introduces readers to these traumatic events with sensitivity and respect; at the same time, she doesn't delve deeply into the psychic debilitation inflicted by the Nazis or the despair engendered by this Jewish experience. Her language is fluid and undemanding; the story is useful in drawing children who read with difficulty (or reluctance) into a worthwhile subject. A good first book on the topic.

McKay, Sharon. *Charlie Wilcox*. 2000. 221 pages. 9 to 12.
Thirteen-year-old Charlie longs for the life of a sealer, but knows he can't have it because of his malformed foot. When surgery corrects his foot problem, he finds his parents want to send him to university instead of the "ice," so he stows away on what he thinks is a sealer. To his shock, he wakes up to find himself with a boatload of soldiers heading for the Front; he ends up going to France and volunteering for the Red Cross.

McKay depicts small-town Newfoundland with humour and verve, catching the reader with her straight-speaking characters and their long-standing knowledge of one another ("You got more guts than a punt load of codfish," one character says). Once Charlie departs for France, though, the story takes an abrupt turn in style; gone are the regional cadences and turns of phrase. The novel turns into a story of war and adventure, gripping enough but without the subtleties of the earlier part. However, the chaos and agony of the Big Push, a heroic rescue by Charlie, and an encounter with a nurse and doctor he knows from St. John's make for exciting reading.

McNamee, Graham. *Sparks.* **2002. 119 pages. 7 to 10.**
Last year Todd Foster was in Special Needs; this year he's been "promoted" to the regular grade five class. Last year he was "Sparks," one of the smartest kids; this year he's "Brain-dead," and has a terrible time keeping up. He's afraid to be seen talking to his best friend, Eva, who's still in Special Needs, and he's afraid he's going to be demoted. But with the help of a friendly teacher and an interesting project on Ota Benga (a "Pygmy" who was exhibited in the monkey house of the Bronx Zoo in 1906), Todd finds that imagination and courage bring him success at school and in friendship.

McNamee explores the emotions of this "special needs" student with compassion and humour, and without cloying moralism. Part of the secret is in the interesting characters – family members are all sharply drawn, from the father who insists Todd share his hairstyle (military), to the sister with a deadly aim with Froot Loops and appleseeds. Todd's fears are expressed realistically and intelligently in the first-person narrative; his voice is candid and direct, and never descends to stereotype or predictable slang. An excellent novel for giving insight into struggling learners, indeed, for discussing any child's fear of failure.

In *Nothing Wrong with a Three-Legged Dog*, McNamee once again explores the difficulties of being a misfit, this time describing the experience of a white boy in an all-black school.

McNaughton, Janet. *Make or Break Spring.* **1999. 187 pages. 10 and up.**
It's 1945 and fifteen-year-old Ev, whose father joined up in 1943 and has been missing almost ever since, struggles with the hope that he's still alive. But with the end of the war comes the realization that, indeed, he's not here; to top it off, kindly Doctor Thorne shows signs of courting Ev's mother. Ev is struggling with school exams and changing relationships as well; when a soldier comes to St. John's to tell the family of Ev's father's death, she lashes out in anguish.

Ev is a warm, sympathetic character; her ups and downs are both peculiar to her circumstances and common to adolescence. A brother with a real stuffed bird for a toy (relic of a taxidermist), Ev's first formal dance (in an ill-fitting satin dress of her mother's) – these details give the story the distinctive flavour of place and time. An engaging story, this also gives readers a glimpse of the historical events of postwar St. John's. A sequel to the partly fantastical *Catch Me Once, Catch Me Twice*.

McNaughton, Janet. *The Secret Under My Skin.* **2000. 238 pages. 10 and up.**
The year is 2365, and Blay Raytee is one of the foundling children housed by the governing Commission in a children's work camp in Newfoundland. Her job is to forage in the landfill under the eye of the Warder, who teaches children about the "techno-cost" and environmental hazards – disasters brought about by technology. When Blay is taken from camp to become assistant to the new "bio-indicator" – a girl whose sensitivities to the environment give her special status – her world suddenly becomes larger. The Commission's authority is crumbling; environmental dangers are minimal; the Weavers' Guild is the voice of reason and driving political change. Blay's name, age, parentage, her whole identity, is completely transformed by her new life of learning and her place in a hospitable household.

Scrawny, plain, and fearful, Blay is at the same time loyal, tough, and intellectually curious. NcNaughton blends the warmth of her emotional growth and new love with the excitement of learning, so that her most potent moments of fulfilment come in her perceptions of the Burgess shale, aeolian plankton, and photosynthesis. Natural history and poetry go hand in hand in this engaging critique of environmental degradation, a tale of surprising twists and turns and, ultimately, hope. Part-romance, part-adventure, part-science.

McNicoll, Sylvia. *Bringing Up Beauty.* **1996. 204 pages. 10 to 12.**
Beauty is a black Lab being raised for a year in Elizabeth's house before going to Canine Vision Canada to be trained as a guide dog. At first it's easy for Elizabeth to remain unattached to the pup; it's ugly, and misbehaves. But Elizabeth's mother is caught up in various social projects, her father's obsessed with his computer, and her sister is

caught up with a boyfriend. Although the whole family initially agreed to raise Beauty, Elizabeth finds she's the one who feeds, walks, and trains her. Soon she's deeply devoted to the dog, which proves to be a good thing, as all her friends are now into dating, an interest Elizabeth doesn't share.

McNicoll writes with humour of the tribulations of being twelve – the frustrations of not being allowed to wear makeup, friendships that suddenly turn into dating, and difficult family dynamics. The story is light, but Elizabeth's maturation is believable, and even those who don't love dogs will be moved by her attachment to Beauty.

Medline, Elaine. *That Silent Summer*. 1999. 169 pages. 8 to 12.
Uncle Cliff, author of a hundred-page poem-to-be, grandmother Yanny the pie-maker, and Aunt Anna the silent – these are the ancient relatives eleven-year-old Minnow is sent to visit for the summer. But Minnow grows to love Birch Lake and her relatives in this "Summer of the Purple Paddle." She takes to the water like a fish (hence her nickname), loves The Rock where she goes to think, and even masters the family "pie system." A new resort kills hundreds of birches, burns down a friend's home, and scares off the loons; Minnow swims all the way to Picnic Island, ninety-year-old Aunt Anna gets a first kiss, and Minnow's mother finally returns to the lake after years of absence. It was a sad and lovely summer, Aunt Anna remembers, but "more lovely than sad."

Aunt Anna refuses to speak aloud, but her writing voice governs this cheerful, wistful summer story. The beauties of the natural world and of family affection shine through the doom of development and loss, and human eccentricity is quietly celebrated. This is a thoughtful, sweet summer story, which shows that inner growth can happen even at ninety.

* Montgomery, L. M. *Anne of Green Gables*. 1908. 308 pages. 8 and up.
This "auburn-haired," pig-tailed orphan hardly needs introduction: despite its age, this classic Canadian novel continues to win readers of all ages.

When Marilla and Matthew Cuthbert, an elderly brother and sister, send for an orphan to help them on their Prince Edward Island farm,

Green Gables, they're shocked to find that the orphanage has sent them a girl instead of a boy. But imaginative, garrulous Anne charms Matthew even before he gets her home, and Marilla agrees to keep her so she can "bring her up properly." Anne has an open heart and a penchant for mishaps – she dyes her hair green, intoxicates her best friend, and breaks her ankle on a dare, for instance. Her problems with school, friends, and growing up are still (mostly) relevant, although matters of gender and education are dated.

Girls identify with Anne's strong feelings and moral quandaries; indeed, her honesty and idealism have had measureless influence. Montgomery's romantic rhapsodies about the beauties of nature are balanced by her dry sense of humour and sharp observation of local characters. There are numerous less-satisfying sequels. Highly recommended.

Montgomery, L. M. *Rilla of Ingleside*. 1920. 308 pages. 10 and up.
Of the many sequels to *Anne*, *Rilla of Ingleside* is worthy of note because it's one of the few novels to give children insight into the experiences of Canadian women during the First World War. It is also revealing in its portrayal of Canadian attitudes to patriotism, pacifism, and religion.

At almost fifteen Rilla, Anne's youngest daughter, aims only to be "pretty, popular and delightful," as she heads off to her first dance. Before the night is over, war has been declared; her brothers and the boys who were her dancing partners are heading off to enlist. Rilla rises to new challenges by adopting a "war baby," organizing a Junior Red Cross, and even heading out to the fields, where there are no longer men to bring in the harvest. Most importantly, though, she rises to emotional challenges.

Montgomery describes the heartbreaking toll the war took on the women waiting at home to hear the fate of loved ones – a description that has the intensity of personal experience. Rilla's youth and love-interest engage young readers, but the real heroine here is the elderly housekeeper Susan Baker, whose comic heroism and uneducated, down-to-earth comments reveal the unsung moral fibre of common, unromantic folk.

* Montgomery, L. M. *Emily of New Moon*. **1925. 339 pages. 10 and up.**
When her father dies, orphan Emily Byrd Starr is taken to live with her
spinster aunts, Elizabeth and Laura Murray, and "not quite there"
Cousin Jimmy. Much as she misses her father, she takes to beautiful
New Moon, the Murray farm on Prince Edward Island, and soon feels
she belongs there. But Emily is determined to be a writer, and stern
Aunt Elizabeth won't allow most reading and writing. Amid the conso-
lations of new friendships and the natural beauties of New Moon,
Emily struggles to express herself and to negotiate her terrible clashes
with her aunt.

Emily stands out as the most compelling, passionate child
Montgomery created, and her story reflects the heights and depths
of Montgomery's own experience as a child and a writer. While
readers identify with Emily's feelings of injustice and her clashes with
authority, they are empowered by her personality and unrelenting
commitment to her art. An engrossing coming-of-age story and a vivid
glimpse of rural Prince Edward Island in the 1890s. Highly recommended for girls. Sequels *Emily Climbs* and *Emily's Quest*, alas, don't
have the same punch.

Mowat, Farley. *Lost in the Barrens*. **1956. 244 pages. 10 and up.**
Seventeen-year-old Jamie Macnair has been living with his trapper uncle
for only a year when he's invited to join Awasin on a two-week trip to
search for caribou. The two are to join a hunting party from the starving
band of the Idthen Eldeli – "Eaters of the Deer" – and to help them find
the caribou that will sustain them through the winter. The hunting party
sets out, always fearful of the Inuit (here called "Eskimos"), whose land
they are traversing; when the party splits, Jamie and Awasin find themselves left in the north with winter coming. They struggle to prepare
enough food and fat to get them through the coming months, build a
shelter, and plan a way to cross the Barrens during the winter.

Mowat writes with first-hand experience of the north, and the majestic landscape becomes a character in its own right. The young men are
carefully and respectfully drawn; Awasin's knowledge is critical to their
survival. Readers feel the cold, the darkness of winter, and the thrill of
the caribou run. This is a fast-paced survival story about a soon-to-be-
forgotten way of life. Works by Inuit writer Simon Tookoome (*The*

Shaman's Nephew; *see* Non-Fiction) and Cree writer Tomson Highway (*Caribou Run*; *see* Picture Books) can supplement this.

Mowat, Farley. *The Dog Who Wouldn't Be*. 1957. 238 pages. 10 and up.
See Non-Fiction.

Mowat, Farley. Illustr. Robert Frankenberg. *Owls in the Family*. 1961. 107 pages. 7 to 12.
Mowat's fictional account of his boyhood with two eccentric owls, Wol and Weeps, is still highly entertaining, particularly for children and families who enjoy animal stories. Despite the fact that Billy already has thirty gophers, numerous white rats, a box of garter snakes, ten pigeons, rabbits, and a dog ("but he wasn't a pet; he was one of the family"), his parents allow him to adopt two owls that he rescues out in the prairie near Saskatoon. Both owls come to think they're human: Wol barely learns to fly and Weeps walks everywhere. Mowat's descriptions of the two owls climbing trees, haunting the house (his mother says that until a woman bakes a cake with two horned owls looking over her shoulders, she hasn't really lived), and bringing trophies of dead skunks into the dining room are hilarious. Without being overly slapstick he conveys some of the funnier episodes brought about by these two beloved, peculiar personalities. An excellent read-aloud; Frankenberg's line drawings are very 1950s in style, but show considerable character.

Oppel, Kenneth. *Silverwing*. 1997. 272 pages. 8 to 12.
Runty and insecure, Shade, a silverwing bat, wonders about his father's mysterious disappearance, which may or may not be related to a metal band put on his father by humans. He wonders, too, why bat deity Nocturna agreed to restrict bats to night activity. When Shade defies tradition and watches the sun rise, he brings destruction on the bats' home, Tree Haven. Mortified and disgraced, when the colony migrates south Shade is blown off course. With only a sound map of landmarks in his head, he and a new friend, a brightwing bat named Marina, make the dangerous journey together, all the time tracing news of Shade's father and the mystery of the metal bands. Ice and snow, bat-eating

owls, the evil South American vampire bat Goth, and Shade's own frail ego make for narrow escapes and action-packed adventure.

Oppel combines natural history, various religious traditions, and a Disneyesque mixture of schoolboy vulnerability and bravado in this and its sequels *Sunwing* and *Firewing*. Shade has problems many kids deal with: jockeying for position among the bats and exchanging testy remarks with Marina, he sounds like an eleven-year-old boy. Marina is quick-thinking and brave, able to hold her own in perilous escapes and physical exploits. In a move that is troubling to some readers, Oppel pits the imagery of Christianity (good) against that of indigenous South American religions (bad): in *Sunwing*, Shade and Marina find refuge in a statue of Christ the Redeemer and make allies of rats with conquistador-like names; the consummation of their quest comes with the violent explosion of the locus of all evil, a Mayan pyramid given over to the rites of Zotz, god of the Mayan underworld.

In *Firewing*, Shade's son, Griffin, a psychological copy of his father in his need to prove himself, sets fire to Tree Haven, kills his best friend Luna, and then searches for her in Zotz's kingdom of the dead. Redemption comes when Shade gives up his life to save his son, and when both Luna and Griffin travel back to the land of the living when, in an echo of Christian imagery, they travel by a fiery tree of life, which is Nocturna herself transformed into an avenue of rebirth after her destruction by Zotz. Evil Goth, devotee of Zotz, is also redeemed from the underworld, ensuring that further exploits are in the offing.

Oppel's imagery is interesting and often original, although the implications of his theology are problematic. With their action-packed, one-thing-after-another plots, these stories have the pace, characters, and visual quick-changes of an animated movie. Popular with boys and girls, both eager and reluctant readers.

Pearson, Kit. *The Daring Game.* **1986. 225 pages. 10 to 13.**
Everything is new, exciting, and more than a little scary for Eliza, who is about to start grade seven in a Vancouver boarding school. It doesn't take long for her to gain the respect of teachers and monitors; she's a good, trustworthy student, because she enjoys her studies and respects the rules. But the students in her Yellow Dorm start a series of dares, which escalate over the course of the year, until Helen, a girl Eliza has

tried to befriend, faces expulsion over a final dare. Eliza then must make some very difficult decisions.

Pearson writes this school story in the style of the British schoolgirl novels, but this one reflects a much tamer life at the school. Eliza is amazed at how easy it is for "the jolly school girls in her books to escape for midnight feasts on the cliffs, or forays into town." The story is quite subdued; its focus is Eliza's maturation as she comes to grips with becoming a teenager and makes friends with girls in her dorm. A rather old-fashioned story for girls interested in a realistic look at boarding school.

Pearson, Kit. *A Handful of Time*. 1987. 186 pages. 8 to 12.
Patricia doesn't want to spend the summer with cousins at a cottage out west: she doesn't know them, she doesn't like camping, and she knows that, in her absence, her parents will divorce. Sure enough, Patricia doesn't fit in, but one day when she's left alone, she finds a pocket watch that sends her back in time. There she meets a troubled girl for whom she has immediate sympathy, who turns out to be her own mother, aged twelve. Patricia makes repeated visits to the past and gains a new understanding of her mother and her extended family. By giving up the watch at the end of the summer, Patricia helps her mother repair the relationship with Patricia's grandmother.

Pearson alternates between Patricia's visits to the past and her current rocky relationships with her cousins, giving readers the satisfaction of learning of past pain and troubles while enjoying Patricia's growth and burgeoning friendships. The cousins' contempt for Patricia and their subsequent guilt at their behaviour is realistic and convincing. Pearson writes with compassion for the lonely, chubby child and, delightfully, the child remains overweight at the end of the busy and active summer.

* Pearson, Kit. *The Sky Is Falling*. 1989. 248 pages. 9 to 13.
Ten-year-old Norah loves collecting shrapnel and watching for German fighter planes from her village home in England in the summer of 1940. When her parents decide to evacuate her and her five-year-old brother, Gavin, to Canada, she's furious. She doesn't want to be responsible for her "babyish" brother, and she thinks it's cowardly to leave the war. But

Norah finds that travelling to Canada, getting used to her new school, and, especially, adapting to elderly, magisterial "Aunt" Florence Ogilvie and her timid, grown-up daughter Mary – her new family in the affluent Rosedale area of Toronto – takes a different kind of courage.

Norah's adventures are of historic interest, but, more importantly, she's a character in whom readers can recognize themselves. Often sullen and selfish, she's also independent-minded and kind – and she, like all children, has to endure the decisions adults make for her. Pearson writes with warmth and directness of the messier feelings and behaviours of childhood. This and her capable, undemanding prose have garnered her thousands of readers internationally. An excellent choice for children who usually shun reading. Highly recommended. Sequels *Looking at the Moon* and *The Lights Go On Again* (sometimes published in a single volume, *The Guests of War*) are equally satisfying.

Pearson, Kit. *Awake and Dreaming*. **1997. 228 pages. 9 to 13.**
Pearson combines emotional warmth, complex ideas, and an unusual plot in this story. Deprived nine-year-old Theo, at the mercy of her skittish, indigent mother, Rae, thirsts to be part of a large, stable family like the ones she reads about in books. And when Rae ships Theo off to live with an aunt in Victoria, something magical happens: she suddenly finds herself an adopted member of a large, perfect family she sees on the ferry, the Kaldors. Kindness, stability, acceptance – it's like living in heaven. But eventually Theo fades, literally, from her new life; the Kaldors can't see her clearly any more and she wakes up to find herself back in her "real" life, trying to get used to living with her aunt. Was her time with the Kaldors a dream? she wonders. When she meets the Kaldor children and they don't seem to know her, the mystery intensifies and Theo vows to solve it.

Pearson writes with emotional honesty and a convincing child's-eye view; Theo's palpable loneliness and longing are the engaging heart of *Awake and Dreaming*. And although some aspects of Theo's difficult life are resolved, Pearson doesn't pretend there's a "happily ever after." The story is rich with ideas about the relationship of imagination and dreams, art and yearning – abstract concepts successfully embedded in an original plot, a mixture of realism and ghost story.

Also by Kit Pearson, *Whispers of War* (*see* **Dear Canada series**).

Richardson, Bill. *After Hamelin*. **2000. 227 pages. 8 to 12.**
When the Pied Piper spirited away the children of Hamelin, eleven-year-old Penelope, stricken deaf the morning of the Piper's visit, was left behind. Now, at 101, she tells what happened after – how her gift of Deep Dreaming allowed her to travel to the Piper's world and recover the lost children. A "singing Trolavian" from a land of militaristic winged trolls, a skipping dragon named Quentin, and Penelope's cat Scallywaggle are stalwart companions in her quest. Courage, ingenuity, harp-building techniques, and great skipping all come into play in this adventure.

Richardson's dream country is expansive, with squeeze-tight tunnels, bottomless cliffs, snowy vistas, and thick woods. Numerous narrow escapes and unexpected encounters keep the narrative bowling along. But it's Richardson's voice that keeps kids glued to the tale; his natural, poetic prose intensifies the story's fairy-tale quality. His wistful lyrics and catchy skipping rhymes ring in the ear, and so does his unforgettable fairy-tale turn of phrase: "For yes is all you ever need to say to begin a journey." Good for girls and boys who like adventure and fairy tales.

Roberts, Ken. *Pop Bottles*. **1987. 87 pages. 7 to 10.**
It's the Depression, and money is scarce. When Will McCleary's family's new house in Vancouver turns out to have a path to the back door made of buried pop bottles, twelve-year-old Will sees the possibility of riches for himself and his friend Ray Fanthorpe. When Marty, a local bully, starts digging up the bottles himself, Ray and Will have to challenge him if they're going to safeguard their treasure – so Marty and Will compete against one another in a city-wide bolo-bat contest. Will beats out Marty, but he doesn't beat his mother, who has also calculated the value of the backyard treasure.

This has a quick pace, much dialogue, and suspense enough to appeal to reluctant readers. At the same time, Roberts's imagination is inventive and nicely surprising. Will's mother, daughter of missionaries, has an endearing nomadic personality that fits into the plot perfectly, and Ray's parents, who insist that the now-bankrupt Fanthorpes were born to rule, turn out to have pleasant alternate careers at the movie theatre. With its convincing, colourful portrayal of Depression Vancouver, this also reads as an historical novel without heavy-handed pedagogic overtones.

Roberts, Ken. *Past Tense.* **1994. 110 pages. 8 to 11.**
Thirteen-year-old Maxwell, fatherless since the age of one, lives with very creative people – his Mom; his Aunt Lois, who writes sensational stories for the tabloids from her wheelchair; his brother Denny, a teenaged chef, who writes a cooking column under a female alias; and especially his Uncle Chuck, an independent talk-show-segment pro- ducer, who's always thinking of eccentric ideas for talk shows. Only the family knows that Uncle Chuck is also "Elspeth," a strange woman who appears every Hallowe'en and does magic tricks before trick-or- treating at the home of the Cluffs, long-time neighbours. When Mr. Cluff is terminally ill, "Elspeth" pays him an unseasonal visit and, although Maxwell at first thinks this a bad idea, he comes to see that, even at the point of death, new things can become part of a dying person's life.

The distinctive characters with their off-kilter take on life (Uncle Chuck is a master of "indirection") give this novel an outlandish but quiet humour, a perfect medium for the wisdom and feeling that lie at its heart. A study of family love and the painful lessons of mourning, it has a nicely lighthearted momentum, and Roberts's clever turns of phrase reveal the amusing possibilities of language.

Roberts, Ken. Illustr. Leanne Franson. *The Thumb in the Box.* **2001. 95 pages. 6 to 10.**
When a fire breaks out in the isolated fishing village of New Auckland, near Prince Rupert, British Columbia, the inhabitants decide it's time to get a good salt-water pump for the town. When they appeal to their local MP, however, he wants to show his generosity by donating an entire fire truck, and a road, and a garage to put it in. New Auckland prides itself on the absence of cars, so the inhabitants get together and plot to use the truck the way that suits them best. The truck's arrival is made even more exotic by the presence of "Little Charlie" and his thumb trick.

Told in the voice of Leon, who loves Little Charlie's pretence of removing his thumb, this has the exaggerations and highly coloured "little guys trick the big guys" plot of a tall tale. With its short chapters, strong momentum, and occasional pictures, it makes a good choice for readers just starting to enjoy novels.

Scrimger, Richard. *The Nose from Jupiter.* **156 pages. 1998. 7 to 11.**
When thirteen-year-old Alan Dingwall wakes up in a hospital bed, clad
only in his underpants, he can't remember how he got there. But as he
recalls the events that have transpired since he first noticed an alien
voice issuing from his nose, he remembers that much of what happened
was brought about by Norbert – a Martian who has taken up residence
in Alan's olfactory organ. Norbert is responsible for Alan scoring a
winning goal, making friends with Miranda, and shaming the school's
bullying squad. And even though Norbert can't transform the personalities of Alan's disaffected parents, he does make life easier to bear.

Scrimger's humour works off the eccentricity of the situation –
underpants, a Martian in the nose, a whole school that mistakenly
expects Shania Twain for assembly. Scrimger points out the bizarre
ways the human mind works, making kids hoot with laughter. At the
same time, he encourages child underdogs: thinly veiled beneath the
fun is the moral lesson that, with a guardian angel like Norbert, even
the weakest can learn to be brave and upright. With its clear message
and straightforward personalities, not to mention its accessible
humour, this is particularly entertaining to reluctant readers.

A sequel, *A Nose for Adventure*, sees Alan and Norbert travelling to
Manhattan, where they befriend a paraplegic girl and, through a series
of slapstick situations, rather unconvincingly repair the estrangement
between the girl and her family.

Scrimger, Richard. Illustr. Linda Hendry. *The Way to Schenectady.*
1999. 162 pages. 7 to 11.
Jane Peeler and her family are heading from their home near Toronto
to meet their mother in the Berkshires in Massachusetts. Before
they've even started, however, the trip's gone off the rails – Jane's
grouchy, obscenity-muttering, chain-smoking grandma is on board,
along with Jane, her father, and her younger brothers. Not only that, at
a gas-station stop, Jane meets an elderly, penniless man, who says
he needs a ride to a funeral in Schenectady, and she decides she'll
have to smuggle him along – and ensure that her father drives to the
Berkshires via Schenectady, New York.

The silly plot is enlivened by Scrimger's authentic re-creation of
humorous domestic chaos, from the very first moments in the novel,

when the well-meaning father, who refuses to waste food, is frying up chicken for breakfast on the morning of departure. Tough old Grandma, funny mainly because she's the antithesis of a stereotype, turns out to have a human side after all; she and Jane end up with a new partnership, not to mention new mutual respect, when Grandma gets in on the smuggling act. With occasional funny illustrations by Linda Hendry, this is a quick, light read. Sequel *Of Mice and Nutcrackers* has similar qualities.

Slipperjack, Ruby. *Little Voice.* **2001. 246 pages. 10 to 12.**
Ray, an Ojibwa girl (aged 10 to 14 in the story), longs to leave small-town Northern Ontario and live with her grandmother in the bush. But the welfare cheques Ray's mother needs require that Ray attend school, and she has to make do with seeing Grandma only in summer. Yearly, Grandma and Ray canoe into the wilderness, harvest berries, fish, fend off bears when necessary, and, in Grandma's case, attend to those who need a medicine woman. As Ray's familiarity with Grandma's ways and Ojibwa language increases, so does her understanding of her own mixed town-and-bush upbringing, and her sense of purpose in using it.

This novel is a rare commodity: a coming-of-age story with an appealing heroine, without moping or preaching, and a tale that's distinctly, honestly reflective of the Ojibwa culture of the author. Ray's voice, which seems almost flat, conveys something essential to the mode of communication she describes – a language of key words, gestures, and facial expressions. Slipperjack illuminates but never simplifies the tensions between white and Aboriginal cultures. Her glimpses of the flora and fauna, and especially of the feelings, of this place and culture are valuable and engaging.

Smucker, Barbara. *Underground to Canada.* **1977. 144 pages. 10 to 12.**
"There's a place the slaves been whisperin' around called Canada. The law don't allow no slavery there. They say you travel north and follow the North Star, and when you step onto this land you are free." This message is given to twelve-year-old Julilly by her mother when Julilly is sold to a slave trader from the Deep South. Work on the new plantation is gruelling, and the overseer is cruel, but Julilly befriends Liza, and the two escape with the help of white abolitionist Mr. Ross. Their flight to Canada with fellow slaves Lester and Adam is fraught with

danger, as slave-catchers are in close pursuit. Help from conductors on the Underground Railroad ensures them a safe arrival in Canada, where Julilly is reunited with her mother.

Here Smucker explores the horrors of slavery and the role Quakers and abolitionists played in the Underground Railroad. The story is tense with the girls' fear as they hide on rooftops or in piles of hay whenever the slave-catchers approach. This account isn't brutal (as it could well be), but it doesn't gloss over hard realities entirely; Adam dies of blood poisoning from his shackle wounds. Smucker includes a powerful message from Martin Luther King, Jr., explaining the historical relationship between African-Americans and Canada.

Staunton, Ted. *The Kids from Monkey Mountain* **series. 2000– . 60 pages. 7 to 10.**
See Books for Beginning Readers.

Sterling, Shirley. *My Name Is Seepeetza.* **1992. 126 pages. 8 to 12.**
In 1952, aged six, Seepeetza is taken from her Salish family on Joyaska ranch in British Columbia's interior and forced by law to attend the Indian residential school in Kalamak. Tootie, McSpoot, or Seepeetza she was called by her family; at school she's told by the nuns that she's now Martha Stone, and she must suppress her Indian ways. When her grade seven teacher shows Seepeetza how to keep a journal, she records not just the happenings of the day (endless laundry, scrubbing, and enforced Irish dancing), but also all the things she remembers from Joyaska and longs for – her family, her flighty horse, the sweet space, her very language.

In this time of commodified fictional diaries, Sterling's fictionalized account of a real and painful time at residential school stands out as an honest, necessary remembrance – a declaration by a voice that was previously silenced. Her understatement, her matter-of-fact tone, avoids sensationalism; the humiliations and deprivation, both physical and emotional, startle but don't traumatize readers. Seepeetza's anecdotes about her family – summer berry-picking, making hay, even her older sister's great comments about Seepeetza's looks ("you have the most beautiful nostrils") – reveal a way of life and a world of affection that can only enrich young readers.

Stewart, Sharon. *The Minstrel Boy*. **1997. 204 pages. 11 to 14.**
Angry with his father, David Baird borrows a motorbike and takes off through Wales. After a bizarre accident, he wakes up in a strange town called Prydain; soon he realizes that he's gone back in time to post-Roman Britain. A young man named "Bear" helps David and introduces him into the community. David's skill at music leads him to train as a minstrel; at the same time, Bear trains David in defence techniques. David's anxious to return to his own time until he falls deeply for Meri, who is smitten with him and his singing. Readers familiar with Arthurian legends will realize that Bear is none other than Arthur.

Stewart combines Arthurian material very successfully with a modern tale of a young man coming of age. The ending of the story is a little tidy, with everything resolved quickly in the last chapters, but the story of a modern teen in Arthur's time is told with passion, and David's rock-music background provides an interesting contrast to his life as a minstrel.

Stewart, Sharon. *My Anastasia*. **1999. 249 pages. 10 to 14.**
Escaping her hard life in a village in Siberia, Dunia falls in with an unusual peasant – Grigory Efimovich Rasputin. Rasputin knows at once that God has ordained this meeting; he transports Dunia to St. Petersburg and sets her up as companion to his go-between, Ania, friend of Russia's Tsar and Tsarina. Dunia faithfully transmits Rasputin's messages, but as her friendship with the four princesses and the tsar-to-be develops, she begins to understand how devious and dangerous Rasputin is to the royal family. By the time the Tsar and his family are imprisoned by the Red Army, Dunia won't be separated from her dear friend, the princess Anastasia; she accompanies her up until the moment of her death.

Stewart's tale fairly races along. Dunia has a sharp, confident voice and is full of pithy remarks and down-to-earth folk wisdom ("well, make yourself a sheep and the wolf is ready"). Lively Anastasia is irreverent and mischievous; underneath the entertaining vignettes of royal education and sibling friction, Stewart delineates a deep, enduring friendship between two unlikely girls at a time of great upheaval. Excellent for its very readable portrayal of Russia at the time of the Revolution.

Stinson, Kathy. *One Year Commencing.* **1997. 147 pages. 10 to 14.**
Twelve-year-old Al has been living in Alberta with her mother for most of her life, but the court orders that she spend a year living with her father in Toronto before Al decides which parent she will live with permanently. Al has always enjoyed spending time with her father, and said that she wished her vacations with him wouldn't end, but living with him for a year is another matter. She makes various plots to return to Alberta, but ultimately finds it impossible to disappoint her father, who has planned the year so carefully and thoughtfully.

Each chapter deals with one month of Al's "exile": the decision that seemed so certain when she first arrives is shaken as she becomes involved with art school, makes a friend, and discovers that she likes the way her father treats her. She also gains an awareness of the tragic life of Toronto's many homeless people. Her personal growth and her acceptance and understanding of her situation are the focus of the story; Stinson respects her audience and doesn't pretend there are easy answers. *Fish House Secrets*, also by Stinson, is another thoughtful look at the teen years.

Takashima, Shizuye. *A Child in Prison Camp.* **1971. 100 pages. 10 and up.**
See Non-Fiction.

Taylor, Cora. *Julie.* **1985. 101 pages. 10 to 14.**
The seventh child of the seventh child, Julie has always told stories about things only she could see. But she soon learns that the "Julie stories" of buffalo and dancers that only she can see make everyone around her squirm, for her family doesn't want to accept that she has the ability to see both past and future. Old Granny Goderich, however, also has the ability to see into the future. She warns Julie about her gift and tells her that it can be both "wonderful and terrible"; she must learn "to be strong." Julie's family pass off the visions of Julie's second-sight as coincidence, until a near-tragedy forces them to acknowledge it.

Taylor gives readers a glimpse of what seeing into the future might really be like: what appears to be a wonderful gift is both frightening and isolating for Julie. Taylor builds tension in the story in small ways:

the smell of flowers, the touch of a tree trunk, and the vision of fire off in the distance keep the reader, like Julie's family, fascinated in what lies ahead. This memorable story is deeply satisfying.

Taylor, Cora. *On Wings of a Dragon*. 2001. 251 pages. 10 to 14.
In a doorless tower room, Kour'el awakes from a traumatic accident. In a village near by, a young woman named Maighdlin finds a piece of gossamer fabric. These two events spark the beginning of the end of Queen Mariah, who has drugged the king and oppressed the people of this fantasy world. Maighdlin is conscripted to become a maid at the palace; Kour'el's beloved dragon friend, Api'Naga, is reborn and rescues the winged Kour'el from the tower. With the help of Maighdlin's faithful grandfather and a soldier loyal to the king, the three of them overcome Queen Mariah's evil plots, and Maighdlin, who discovers she is really a queen, takes up her own regal inheritance.

Taylor's prose is deft; her fantasy world, a blend of science fiction and fairy tale, is focused and convincing. Some readers will have difficulty managing the numerous points of view in this story, but the characters of Maighdlin, a resourceful, intelligent protagonist, and the ethereal Kour'el are appealing, particularly for girls. The motifs of the wicked queen/stepmother, and the poor girl growing into her regal destiny, give this a strong fairy-tale structure.

Tennant, Veronica. Illustr. Rita Briansky. *On Stage, Please*. 1977. 176 pages. 7 to 10.
Tennant, a former principal dancer of the National Ballet of Canada, depicts the education of a child dancer in this tale that is likely to appeal only to child balletomanes and budding dancers. Nine-year-old Jennifer starts off her lessons with a fearsome teacher, but at ten applies to the Professional School of Ballet in Toronto. Once she's accepted, she has to deal with the hard work and discipline demanded by the school regime; at the same time, she struggles with homesickness and the complications of friendship in an atmosphere of intense competition. Her crowning moment comes when she dances the part of a fairy attendant in a National Ballet production.

Although Tennant doesn't explore Jennifer's inner growth very deeply, she gives a good sketch of the physical and emotional difficulties and joys of training as a child dancer. Her inside account of life in the ballet school gives readers a view of the practical aspects of the school's organization and training.

Tibo, Gilles. Illustr. Louise-Andrée Laliberté. *Naomi and Mrs. Lumbago*. 2001. 86 pages. 6 to 9.
Every day after school, Mrs. Lumbago looks after Naomi until her parents get home. The two are best friends, and when Mrs. Lumbago reports that her husband always says there is a treasure hidden in the apartment, Naomi can't rest until she finds it. As the story unfolds, Tibo reveals how Mr. Lumbago's troubled past in the war affected his mind and heart. When Mr. Lumbago dies, Naomi helps her best friend through her grief, but keeps up her search for the treasure – with surprising success.

Tibo's story combines themes that are more challenging for young readers than those of most books for the age. Death, a funeral, memories of the war, and frustrations with a thwarted life are balanced with Naomi's excitement as she searches for treasure. Laliberté's pencil sketches capture both the humour and the sadness within the story. A memorable, moving depiction of a friendship between youth and age.

Tingle, Rebecca. *The Edge on the Sword*. 2001. 277 pages. 10 and up.
It's the 890s, A.D., and fifteen-year-old Æthelflæd loves the lessons in reading and writing her father, King Alfred, insists upon. But when she learns that she's to be betrothed to Ethelred of Mercia and must accept the protection of a gruff new bodyguard named Red, Flæd rebels. A foolish escape has serious results, and she realizes that Red has something of value to teach her: the skills of battle and self-defence. And when Flæd's entourage is ambushed en route to Ethelred's court, it's her careful study of history and war strategy, as well as her courage and fighting skills, that bring the company through in triumph.

King Alfred's eldest daughter, Æthelflæd, became the renowned "Lady of the Mercians," a woman who took over her husband's kingdom at the age of forty and went on to drive back various invaders for years, unifying a large part of England. Tingle imagines the kind of childhood and adolescence that might have prepared this remarkable woman for such feats in such a time. It is a spirited introduction to the period, and a dramatic, entertaining story.

Toten, Teresa. *The Onlyhouse*. **1995. 112 pages. 10 to 12.**
Lucy Vakovik desperately wants to fit into her new neighbourhood with "real Canadians," so she tries to dress and act like everyone else. The task is made difficult by her Croatian mother, who works in a cafeteria, cleans offices nights and weekends, and rents out the upstairs to keep up the payments on their newly acquired detached "onlyhouse" in the good Canadian neighbourhood. In hilarious scenes, Lucy discovers that her embarrassingly proud and enthusiastic "You be 'scusing my sometime English is broking" mother is a hit with her friends and their families. Lucy makes it in with the popular kids, realizes that they have problems too, and discovers that sometimes being true to yourself is more important than fitting in.

Toten's very funny first novel has crisp dialogue that sweeps the reader right into the irresistible world of the Vakoviks. The depiction of an immigrant child desperately wanting to fit in with the blond Canadians rings true, and Lucy's rich immigrant life is lovingly portrayed against the backdrop of Toronto's "real Canadians," who shop at the supermarket where everything is wrapped in plastic.

Truss, Jan. *Jasmin*. **1982. 196 pages. 10 to 12.**
Afraid she's failing sixth grade and fed up with her chaotic, boisterous family, twelve-year-old Jasmin takes matters into her own hands and runs away into the nearby woods and hills of western Alberta. There she finds a little cave for herself, and spends her days looking after her needs and modelling animals out of clay from a nearby creek. A huge storm literally flushes her out of her hiding place; when she's rescued by a couple of "hippie" artists (known as "THEM PEOPLE" to the conservative locals), they help her see that she must return to her family. At the same time, they show her that she has an unusual talent for sculpting, a knowledge that gives her the courage to face school again.

Jasmin's a sympathetic character, and her uneducated, demanding family spills out over the pages of the story, from her well-meaning, voluminous mother to her dear mentally disabled brother Leroy. Jasmin shows courage and resourcefulness in executing her escape, and her return is prompted not by incompetence, but by love. The story alternates between Jasmin's escape and her family's efforts to find her; a subplot has Leroy follow her out into the woods, only to become "lost" himself. An engaging read for girls.

Valgardson, W. D. *Frances*. 2000. 190 pages. 10 to 14.
The past haunts twelve-year-old Frances Sigurdsson, mainly because her career-woman mother refuses to talk about it. But Frances has always wanted to know about her Icelandic ancestors, and about her father who disappeared when she was very young. When she finds a handwritten Icelandic diary in a family trunk, she pedals straight to the local "old folks' home" and finds a translator. "You might not like what you find," her Gran warns her; but Frances's introduction to the ravens of Odin, the "Yule boys," runes, and the hardships of early Icelandic settlers in Manitoba helps unlock both the past and her mother's emotions.

Intergenerational relationships and the discontents and uncertainty of adolescence are at the heart of this novel. Although Frances's uptight mother is something of a stereotype, Frances's penchant for long words, and her determined exploring spirit, make her a sympathetic, interesting protagonist. The novel is also notable for its poignant evocation of the dreamy, time-stopped feelings of adolescence, and its portrayal of the Icelandic community and natural beauty of southern Lake Winnipeg.

Vande Griek, Susan. Illustr. Mary Jane Gerber. *A Gift for Ampato*. 1999. 109 pages. 8 to 11.
Eleven-year-old Timta is one of the "chosen" girls in her Inca community in the Andes. Although she knows she'll never become a good weaver like her friends, she enjoys life in this special community beneath the mountain Ampato. But when ash and dust issue forth from Ampato and neighbouring peaks, and Inti, the sun god, refuses to shine and nurture the crops, the priests choose a special sacrifice to appease and honour Inti – and that sacrifice is Timta. Timta doesn't want to become a human sacrifice, but how can she avoid it?

Vande Griek's story is inspired by the discovery of a mummy uncovered in the Andes in 1995, that of a young girl who was obviously offered as a human sacrifice. Between each chapter, Vande Griek inserts a paragraph on what archaeologists discovered about this mummy: the story is her imaginative reconstruction of the event that led to the sacrifice.

Vande Griek establishes the logic of ancient Inca beliefs with respect. At the same time, she allows Timta a modern liberty – the ability to think outside her Inca upbringing, making her a girl readers can identify with. This very short tale introduces children to what will be a new culture for most of them; it's one of the only pieces of fiction set in this period and place. This is short and its vocabulary is limited, but its content is fairly mature, making it a good candidate for older readers (10 and up) who are just beginning to tackle "chapter books."

Walters, Eric. *Trapped in Ice.* **1997. 205 pp. 10 to 12.**
Helen is only thirteen when she, her nine-year-old brother, and their mother, hired as a seamstress for an Arctic expedition, board Captain Bartlett's *Karluk* in Vancouver in 1913. The expedition is unlike the many that Helen has read about, although its leader, Vilhjalmur Stefansson, is as romantic as she can imagine. However, the expedition turns into a nightmare, when an early freeze-over traps the *Karluk* in the Arctic Ocean and shifting ice carries it further and further from land. Captain Bartlett's heroic, careful plans lead family and crew to the safety of land, but not before they've encountered hungry polar bears and horrific blizzards.

Written in part as Helen's fictional diary (although this is based on a real expedition), this story gives a child's-eye view of the enormity of the venture. Helen's inner growth and her increasing respect for Captain Bartlett are a strong element in the story; the image of the music of Mozart issuing from the doomed *Karluk* as she sinks through the ice is unforgettable. Walters provides a plot-driven, exciting tale, but readers who really want to feel the bite of winter and the fear of the ice and snow should try Mowat's *Lost in the Barrens* (see above).

Walters, Eric. *War of the Eagles.* **1998. 224 pages. 10 and up.**
Set in Prince Rupert, British Columbia, during the Second World War, this story explores the friendship between Jed, part-Tsimshian, part-white, and his friend Tadashi, a Japanese Canadian, at a time when the

Canadian government is rounding up Japanese Canadians and con-
fiscating their fishing boats. Jed's English father is in service, and Jed
is living with his Tsimshian grandmother and his mother, one of the
cooks at the nearby Forces base. Jed and Tad are invited to hunt for
game to feed the soldiers, and in so doing get a glimpse of life, both
good and bad, at the base. When a soldier wounds a bald eagle and it's
brought to the base, Jed cares for it. The eagle takes on a political and
emotional significance for Jed, and the imprisonment of the majestic
bird foreshadows the impending internment of Tadashi and his family.

Walters has established himself as one of Canada's foremost
writers for boys who are not interested in reading; his stories usually
function on plot rather than character or style. This one includes
hunting sprees, moonlit jaunts in British Columbia's rain forest, fist
fights, and even a standoff with thieves who break into the deserted
homes of the Japanese. At the same time, Walters alerts readers to
issues of prejudice, liberty, and friendship. Boys who enjoy fast-
paced, undemanding stories will find this satisfies, but it also helps
them think beyond their own parameters.

The story of Tadashi Fukushima and his family's internment is continued in *Caged Eagles*. Multiple titles by this author are currently
available (*Camp X*, *Northern Exposures*, *Visions*, and more).

Waterton, Betty. *Quincy Rumpel.* **1984. 137 pages. 6 to 10.**
Quincy Rumpel, aged ten-and-three-quarters, has lots of good ideas,
but they don't always work out quite the way she plans. Efforts to make
her hair frizzy like lovely cousin Gwen's, to explore the attic in the
family's new old house, and even to enjoy the benefit of her new
rose-tinted glasses result in strange and silly situations involving ambu-
lances, horrible smells, and sitting on the roof nearly naked. Quincy
and her haphazard family muddle their way through a move from
Ontario to Vancouver with good cheer and high spirits, even though
inventor Dad isn't always as successful as he might be.

This is good, light fare for younger readers, who will recognize
the perils and enjoy the humour in Quincy's hare-brained schemes.
Many sequels (*Starring Quincy Rumpel*, *Quincy Rumpel and the
Woolly Chaps*, and so on) show the Rumpels' continued capacity for

misadventure. Some deliciously loony lines creep into the slapstick situations: "I faint quite often when I'm wearing these boots," Aunt Fan claims.

Watts, Irene. *Good-bye Marianne*. **1998. 106 pages. 9 to 12.**
Marianne can't believe it when she's turned away from her school in Berlin in 1938. At first it seems a stroke of luck, since she doesn't have to write her math test; but when her bookseller father is forced to go into hiding and life becomes increasingly restricted, Marianne's feeling turns to fear. Even her new friend, a fellow admirer of *Emil and the Detectives*, reveals himself a traitor when he shows up in the uniform of the Hitler Youth. By the time Marianne's mother arranges for Marianne to be sent to England on a *Kindertransport* – a special train that allowed Jewish children to leave Germany at a time when their parents could not – Marianne knows she must go in order to survive.

In this short novel, Watts evokes the soothing and frightening daily realities of 1938 Berlin – not only the fear of the police, but also the happy sound of the market, warm baking, and life in a pokey apartment. The warmth and affection between Marianne and her mother underscore the trauma of their separation when Marianne is sent to England for safety. This is an excellent novel for introducing children gently to the fate of the Jews in Hitler's Germany. A subsequent volume, *Remember Me*, describes Marianne's experiences in England. *Finding Sophie*, another novel by Watts, explores the emotions of a *Kindertransport* evacuee when the war is over and she fears she will have to return to a country she hardly knows.

Woods, Shirley. Illustr. Celia Godkin. *Black Nell: The Adventures of a Coyote*. **1998. 89 pages. 6 to 10.**
This unsentimental nature story follows the life of a rare black coyote from the time of her birth until she's a year old. Woods describes the growth of the infant coyotes, then follows Nell and her brother, Thor, as they leave their parents and make their way in the woods of southern Ontario, fending for themselves and learning the dangers and tricks of the wilderness. Hunted by a couple of rifle-toting boys even before their eyes are open, the coyote pups find that human threat – from Starboot the trapper to cars on the highway – proves to be the hardest

to avoid (and Thor doesn't succeed). This is solid, factual fiction, a good read (or read-aloud) for children who are interested in animals. Godkin's occasional black-and-white illustrations have both atmosphere and accuracy. Two further animal stories by Woods, *Kit: The Adventures of a Raccoon* and *Jack: The Story of a Beaver*, both illustrated by Godkin, have similar strengths.

Wynne-Jones, Tim. *The Maestro*. 1995. 223 pages. 11 to 14.
See Novels, 12 and Up.

Wynne-Jones, Tim. *Stephen Fair*. 1998. 218 pages. 10 to 14.
See Novels, 12 and Up.

* Wynne-Jones, Tim. *The Boy in the Burning House*. 2000. 231 pages. 10 to 14.
See Novels, 12 and Up.

Yee, Paul. *Breakaway*. 1994. 144 pages. 10 to 14.
Kwok-ken Wong wants to change his first name to Clark so he'll appear more Canadian on his scholarship applications for university. Life as a Chinese farmer in Vancouver during the Depression is hard, and Kwok and his mother know that the only way out of farming is through education. Kwok's an excellent student and a great soccer player, so he ought to get a scholarship. But racism is rampant on the streets and in the higher institutions of learning, and Kwok is Chinese. In addition, Kwok's father wants him to work the family's market farm, which will flounder without Kwok's labour. Eventually Kwok takes pride in his Chinese heritage, gives up his plans for education, and throws his lot in with his father.

This tale of a Chinese Canadian family with a market garden in Vancouver is perhaps the only one of its kind for a juvenile audience. The frustrations of meeting continuous racism are played out against the excitement of various soccer matches; Kwok's losing battle to forge ahead in a way that will use his intelligence is heartbreaking. Although all the themes in the story don't quite come together, it's a powerful tool to show just how hard Chinese Canadians had to struggle to gain a place in Canada.

Young, Scott. *A Boy at the Leafs' Camp*. 1963. 244 pages. 10 to 14.
Bill Spunska has the chance to go to a professional hockey training
camp and to try out to become a player on a national team. Eighteen
years old and fresh from high school, Spunska's chances of being
picked are slim, and he has two weeks to prove that he has what it takes
to be a pro. A thoughtless comment makes an enemy of a fellow player,
and that enmity is played out on the ice and in the media. When
Spunska checks his rival and knocks him unconscious during a game,
he has to question his own motives and his passion for hockey, as well
as the game and its brutality.

Young writes with authority about the game and its passions, jeal-
ousies, and camaraderie. He includes a wealth of information about the
process for choosing players, the effects of the media, and the mania of
the fans. Written in the sixties, this story reflects the sensibilities of its
time: Gord Howe's comment, "Sure, it's sometimes tough, but why
not? It's a man's game," is repeated as "the definitive comment about
professional hockey"! The story stands on its own, but it's the final
volume in a trilogy that includes *Scrubs on Skates* and *Boy on
Defence*. Most useful as a way to interest hockey fans in reading.

Short Story Collections and Anthologies, 7 to 12

L ike poetry, short stories can be one of the most effective literary genres to share with children. Many of these stories can be read aloud in just a few minutes or in a period that's too short for anything more substantial; they allow a child the satisfying experience of narrative closure almost at once. They can be excellent for children who find it difficult to follow the thread of a novel, or who don't have the patience to wait for a punchline. And, like poetry, short stories often challenge us to look at the world anew – a certain character, an enigmatic moment, can unsettle us, or startle us into seeing things differently.

Anthologies which include excerpts from novels can be frustrating (what happened next?), but they are also enticing. Excerpts included in the anthologies listed below are almost all from novels that are currently available.

Archbold, Rick. *Canada, Our History: An Album through Time.* **2000. 160 pages. 8 to 11.**
See Non-Fiction.

* Ellis, Sarah. *Back of Beyond: Stories.* **1996. 159 pages. 11 and up.**
Ellis quotes from Barbara Reiti's *Strange Terrain* at the beginning of this collection of stories: "Most 'fairy' experiences are unspectacular, private affairs, unaccountable little slippages in space or time . . ." These tales recount a variety of strange encounters that happen to seemingly ordinary teens. Kenton almost loses his babysitting charge,

Elizabeth, when she hears voices in the tunnel under the road. Ellen and Katie meet two beautiful visitors, who soon have them dancing by candlelight – a hand's-breadth away from a crumbling cliff edge. A new kid in his class gives Curt a knife he threw into the ocean six years ago. Each story has a small, inexplicable, shudder-producing moment.

Ellis depicts believable teens caught unaware by the unexplained in these eerie, sometimes laughter-provoking, and often awe-inspiring stories. Written in the first person, each story communicates a strong sense of character and place; readers feel the moody atmosphere thicken as reality comes into question. Highly recommended.

Ellis, Sarah, ed. *Girls' Own: An Anthology of Canadian Fiction for Young Readers*. 2001. 348 pages. 9 to 13.
"What is it that women want most?" Ellis writes in her introduction here, quoting an old Arthurian story. The answer? "What a woman wants most is to be in charge of her own destiny." The twenty entries Ellis includes showcase girls grasping their future and taking charge of their own destiny as they grow. These Canadian stories include excerpts from well-known novels (many of which of are reviewed elsewhere in this book) and one original story. Settings are as diverse as North America at the time of Columbus's arrival, ancient China, contemporary Toronto, and a Blackfoot camp in Alberta. The young women have vastly differently lives and concerns, but each one charts her own course.

Reading these excerpts will entice readers to search for the novels from which they were taken. Some children will be reminded of an old favourite and will savour the tales in this new context. Among others, Jean Little, Kit Pearson, Teresa Toten, and Linda Holeman are represented; so too are Tim Wynne-Jones, Thomas King, and Paul Yee.

Hughes, Monica, ed. *What If . . . ? Amazing Stories*. 1998. 199 pages. 11 to 14.
Some of Canada's finest writers for children answer the question "What if?" in this anthology. "What if a being from another planet were marooned on Earth?" "What if something still lurks in the culvert?" "What if the animals grew huge and took over?" Well-known science-fiction and fantasy writers Monica Hughes, Charles DeLint, and James

Alan Gardner are joined by Sarah Ellis, Tim Wynne-Jones, and Joan Clark in answering these and other questions in stories that are imaginative, fantastical, and frightening. Alice Major's poem "Star-Seeing Night" opens the collection, and Robert Priest's powerful "The Water Traders' Dream" ends it.

Hughes has done an admirable job of pulling together stories that intrigue and amaze. Her collection gives new life to some wonderful stories that will lead readers to pursue the contributors' additional writings. A good introduction to speculative fiction for those unfamiliar with the genre.

Lunn, Janet, ed. *The Unseen: Scary Stories.* **1994. 171 pages. 10 and up.**
This anthology of stories and poetry, some of them written specifically for the collection, includes poetry by Archibald Lampman, Dennis Lee, and Michael Bedard, and eerie stories by a diverse group of well-known authors, including Monica Hughes, L. M. Montgomery, Tim Wynne-Jones, Kit Pearson, and Ken Roberts. Set anywhere from a backyard in Scarborough, Ontario, to Sable Island in Nova Scotia, each story focuses on something unseen, but felt, heard, or otherwise sensed.

Each writer provides his or her own trademark voice and style: Brian Doyle has a wonderfully funny story of baking a carrot cake during the hour that never was – the hour we lose when the clocks are turned back; Paul Yee writes passionately of a young man finding the ghost of his father in a mine shaft; and Jean Little weaves a tale of mysterious twins. The stories are memorable, not overly gruesome, but unnerving enough to provide chills.

Mackay, Claire, ed. *Laughs: Funny Stories.* **1997. 199 pages. 10 and up.**
"Laughter may be the best medicine in the world," asserts Mackay in her introduction. Over twenty contributors, with a wide range of styles and sense of humour, guarantee that every reader will find something to amuse her or him. Variations of "Mary Had a Little Lamb" come from David Booth; Loris Lesynski shares "I Hate Poetry." Roch Carrier's *The Hockey Sweater* (*see* Picture Books) is included; so too is "The Day of the Raisin," Martin Godfrey's true story about a boy

who tries to gross out his fellow students by shoving a raisin up his nose, only to have it get stuck there. "Introducing Norbert" is the story that gave rise to Richard Scrimger's popular novel *The Nose from Jupiter* (*see* Novels, 7 to 12). Mackay includes notes that direct children to additional titles by the contributors.

Pearson, Kit, ed. *This Land: A Cross-Country Anthology of Canadian Fiction for Young Readers.* **1999. 317 pages. 9 and up.**
Pearson brings together twenty-two short stories and excerpts from novels, representing settings and characters from all across Canada. Arranged by province from west to east and concluding with "the North," these stories give readers a colourful, invigorating view of some of Canada's most memorable fiction. Excellent for getting readers or listeners hooked on some of Canada's finest writers for children – Paul Yee, Janet McNaughton, Brian Doyle, Budge Wilson, Michael Kusugak, and more are represented. Good for boys and girls.

Sadiq, Nazneen. *Camels Can Make You Homesick, and Other Stories.* **1985. 89 pages. 10 and up.**
Five short stories explore what it's like to be a Canadian child with South Asian heritage and were inspired by the experiences of Sadiq's own children as they tried to come to terms with their Pakistani heritage as well as their desire to fit into "Canadian" society. In "Shonar Arches," Amit is irritated by a visit from his grandmother from Calcutta. He hates her spicy cooking; later he takes great delight when he introduces her to the glories of fast food – and she likes it. Jaya learns to take pride in her heritage when she dances the classical Indian peacock dance at school, in "Peacocks and Bandaids." In the story "Figs for Everyone," Shanaz has her hands painted with henna to celebrate Eid-ul Fitr, and is embarrassed when she realizes that the patterns will remain for the next month.

Sadiq writes with understanding of the challenges faced by children trying to fit into a new culture while their families are anxious for them to retain their heritage. The cast of characters, from Amit's grandmother in her purple sari to Mrs. Amjad, creator of the lacy henna patterns, reflects the diverse South Asian community in Canada.

Valgardson, W. D. *Garbage Creek, and Other Stories.* **1997. 132 pages. 8 to 12.**

In eight humorous short stories Valgardson explores the unexpected ways that children can make the world a better place, even when they don't have conventional power or resources. In "The Chicken Lady," Erin shows her father the reason he shouldn't sell their forty acres of land. In the title story, two children clean up a creek in the hope that salmon will once again spawn there.

Each character is sharply realized, from Rainbow, who lives on a Vancouver Island beach with her mother (a woman at one with the universe), to Richard, who hates living in Victoria, separated from his friends in Port Alberni, and who has to babysit a young Chinese girl who speaks no English. The stories deal with issues of concern to children – the need to earn money, the place of family and friends. Valgardson ends each tale with a zinger line, often making the reader laugh out loud, but also forcing the reader to take note of the changes within the protagonist. These stories will make every child think about his or her life and surroundings.

Valgardson, W. D. *The Divorced Kids Club and Other Stories.* **1999. 184 pages. 10 to 14.**

These six stories, some eerie, some funny, show kids managing their way through a variety of circumstances brought on by – and causing – changes in their lives. "Adults found it so hard to adapt sometimes," says one boy, faced with a move to a new town. The protagonists here have to adapt to such situations as divorce, a weekend stranded in a cabin, and unreliable friends. Several want to find ways to earn money, whether via sidewalk entertaining, selling drinks, digging gardens for old-age pensioners, or scouring the beach with a metal detector. "When you're little you think the giants know everything. Then you get older and the world gets real scary because you realize they may be bigger but they aren't always using a compass that works," one character comments, reflecting that significant moment of growth that happens when children become aware of the limitations of adults.

Settings range from Vancouver Island to the Icelandic community on the Prairies. This strong anthology shows how kids, sometimes completely different from every other member of the family, can manage change with ingenuity and resilience.

* Wynne-Jones, Tim. *Some of the Kinder Planets*. 1993. 136 pages. 9 and up.

Wisecracking Harriet hasn't put nearly enough obvious effort into her project on the solar system; her planets are made of rolled-up balls of newspaper, some held together with grape chewing gum. But Harriet's the only student who can give a first-hand report on sighting Mars the night before.

Wynne-Jones's awe-inspiring collection of nine stories is full of surprises and humour, but most of all it's full of the kindness of friends and strangers. In "Save the Moon for Kerdy Dickus," a drunk teen stumbles on a house that looks like a glass igloo in the woods; although he's fed and sheltered by the family there, he is obviously unnerved by their unconventionality. Months later his picture appears in a tabloid; he reports on the night he was abducted by Martians – much to the amusement of the family who looked after him.

Here's a strange but winning group of characters, including Kent, who pastes the names of exotic places to his body so that he can plan his future travels, and Quin, who stays with sleeptalking Nanny Vi, who unwittingly gives Quin an image that helps her through a starring role in a major theatrical production. An outstanding collection. Highly recommended.

Wynne-Jones, Tim. *The Book of Changes: Stories*. 1994. 143 pages. 10 to 14.

Wynne-Jones includes a wide cast of characters in this collection of stories that showcase family, school, and everyday life. Dwight learns how to conquer a bully using his excellent Donald Duck impression in "The Clark Beans Man"; Tobias discovers a few secrets in "The Book of Changes"; and Tyler Taylor, the great hockey goalie, is haunted by his winning streak in "The Ghost of Eddy Longo." In one tale, a boy on a seven-hour bus ride is put off by his weird, black-clad seat-mate, with her bizarre music, nine earrings, various nose rings, and two-tone Mohawk hair. But at the end of the ride, when the boy's life is shattered, he discovers that his seat-mate has bequeathed him a tape – her weird, but wonderfully comforting, music. Each story has a character who must embrace change. Wynne-Jones writes in his typically wry, wise, and engaging manner.

Wynne-Jones, Tim. *Lord of the Fries*. 1999. 198 pages. 9 to 12.
Seven not-so-short stories make up this collection, which range from the tale of a vanload of French-Canadians stuck in a snowstorm with their newly adopted Chinese babies, to the title story of a surly chip-wagon cook who has a hidden, heroic past. In each story children discover hidden talents, double lives, and strange pasts in others, which leads them to re-evaluate their assumptions, even their place in the world. In "Ick," classmates band together to assist a girl made uncomfortable by the unwanted attentions of a teacher. In "Lord of the Fries," two girls research a man's past in the hope of selling his story to a tabloid, but realize that there are things more important than quick money. Wynne-Jones's respectful portrayal of his young protagonists shows them to be understanding, resourceful, and caring.

Wynne-Jones, Tim, ed. *Boys' Own: An Anthology of Canadian Fiction for Young Readers*. 2001. 297 pages. 10 to 14.
Twenty recent stories and excerpts make up this anthology "*especially*, not *exclusively*" for boys, each one chosen, as the editor says, because it hums and crackles. In an excerpt from Joan Clark's *The Dream Carvers* (*see* Novels, 7 to 12), Greenlander Thrand awakes to find he's been kidnapped by the Osweet. In "Eat, Sleep, Jump High for Smarties," by R. P. MacIntyre, an enterprising young man finds it doesn't pay to become a poet. Nazneen Sadiq's story "Shonar Arches" tells how a boy introduces his grandmother from Calcutta to the joys of North American fast food. Suspense, heartbreak, ambition, and poignant moments of growth come together in this strong anthology, an excellent collection for reading aloud, at home or at school.

Part of the joy here lies in Wynne-Jones's open, almost confiding, introductions to each story, some of them small masterpieces in literary analysis. Sarah Ellis "trusts her reader; she knows you're going to get the joke, so she doesn't explain it," he points out. Of R. P. MacIntyre, Wynne-Jones writes, "He is always original and not a little twisted. And he wields a metaphor like a finely honed sword. . . . As well, [he] is an intrepid explorer of emotional territories just off the edge of the map."

* **Yee, Paul. Illustr. Simon Ng.** *Tales from Gold Mountain: Stories of the Chinese in the New World.* **1989. 64 pages. 7 and up.**
These eight original stories, each alluding to a different aspect of the experience of Chinese immigrants in Canada, combine the elements of Chinese folktale with an eerie, New Worldly edge. Miners, railway labourers, cannery workers are remembered; the traditional values of Chinese culture come up against those of the New World in stories of mixed marriages, forbidden marriages, and futile efforts to preserve the family name. In "Spirits of the Railway," a man comes to the Fraser Canyon to appease the ghosts of unburied railway workers. In "Forbidden Fruit," a legacy of exotic tomatoes is all that remains when a father won't let his daughter marry a man of another race.

Yee's prose conjures visions – piles of rock, the raw enclosing walls of unfinished tunnels, the "blue as sky, green as pine" flashes of a gambler's eyes. Readers learn the facts and scandal of Canadian policies towards the Chinese; at the same time, these powerful stories take on an almost mystical dimension in showing the human response to unmanageable feeling, to the uncontrollable nature of life. "Must we forever follow the old ways?" one daughter asks plaintively, a question that will connect with immigrant experience everywhere. Highly recommended.

Yee, Paul. Illustr. Harvey Chan. *Dead Man's Gold and Other Stories.* **2002. 112 pages. 10 and up.**
In ten memorable ghost stories, Yee alludes to moments during 140 years of Chinese presence in Canada, from the poor men who sought out "Gold Mountain" in the gold rush of the 1850s to those who fled Communist China via Hong Kong. Murder, trickery, and loneliness are followed inexorably by curses, hauntings, and eerie disappearances. Both informative and moving, Yee's tales touch on the experiences of those who came to the Promised Land, only to find themselves penni-less after the Gold Rush, working a saw in the precipitous fjords of British Columbia's Inside Passage, or irremediably separated from

wives and lovers by exclusionary immigration policies. Here are market gardeners, peddlers, launderers, and cooks; here is the squeal of machinery, the stench of a mine, the warm beauty of jade. Gruesome, haunting, but full of human wisdom, these stories make a terrific read-aloud for the whole family.

Series Books

S eries books don't have to be literary junk food although they often are. Here we review some of both – popular mystery series, whose only virtue is the information they convey about Canadian settings, and more enriching stories that will appeal to the desire for adventure and, at the same time, push the imagination that little bit farther. If you have a child who is hooked on one series or another, we recommend that you use the subject index to find titles that will pick up on the topics or genre of that series. Often, stories written to fill a publisher's formula can become a stepping stone leading readers to stories with more complex plots and characters, and with more colourful and textured language.

Bailey, Linda. *Stevie Diamond Mysteries.* **1992– . ca. 175 pages. 8 to 11.**
Twelve-year-old Stephanie sets herself up as detective Stevie Diamond when her mother's funds for "Garbage Busters," an environmental group in Vancouver, are stolen. In the first case, *How Come the Best Clues Are Always in the Garbage?* which involves some disgusting dumpster work, Stevie acquires a partner in her neighbour Jesse. Despite jumping to conclusions and sometimes making fools of themselves, the two go on to solve a number of mysteries of greater and lesser difficulty. Stevie is spirited and persevering, and Bailey's prose is colloquial and quick throughout the series. The school-aged protagonists and down-to-earth mysteries make these stories very approachable.

Bailey, Linda. Illustr. Bill Slavin. *Good Times Travel Agency.* **2000– . 48 pages. 8 to 10.**
Josh and Emma Blinkerton, and sometimes their little sister Libby, travel back in time using the magic books found at the Good Times Travel Agency. They quickly discover that the reality of the past is different than they imagined, and they have to work their way through some challenges before returning to the present.

These books are in comic-book format, but filled with information. Each spread covers a different topic, for example, "A Castle Meal" or "A Peasant's Furniture." Factual information is incorporated into the children's adventures and mishaps. Slavin's illustrations convey much of both adventure and information, and the speech balloons from Josh and Emma will appeal to readers. There is a wealth of material here, provided in illustrations and text, with plenty of laughs to ensure the books will be read from beginning to end. Titles include *Adventures in the Middle Ages*, *Adventures in Ancient Egypt*, *Adventures in Ancient Greece,* and *Adventures with the Vikings*.

Dear Canada. **2001– . ca. 200 pages. 10 to 12.**
This series of fictionalized diaries by twelve-year-old girl protagonists was inspired by the success of a similar series published in the United States, *Dear America*. Some of Canada's strongest and most acclaimed children's writers have contributed volumes to the series, including Jean Little, Sarah Ellis, and Kit Pearson. Set in various places and periods of Canada's past, in each "diary" a girl relates the happenings of one eventful year, from Jean Little's Victoria of 1897, who tells of the year a Barnardo child came to live with her family (reviewed in Novels, 7 to 12), to Carol Matas's Isobel of 1815, who recounts the events of a long year travelling from Churchill, Manitoba, down the Red River, only to find that conflicts between Canada's two fur-trading companies won't allow her family to settle. Generally these stories are engaging, the characters fully realized and the conditions described with clarity and vivacity. Despite the unlikelihood of a child making effusive diary entries under some of the circumstances described – such as in a tent at 40 below Fahrenheit in northern Manitoba – these give readers a good introduction to the different periods. Thick, creamy paper and a marker ribbon make the books attractive.

Bradford, Karleen. *With Nothing But Our Courage: The Loyalist Diary of Mary MacDonald, Johnstown, Québec, 1783*.

Ellis, Sarah. *A Prairie as Wide as the Sea: The Immigrant Diary of Ivy Weatherall, Milorie, Saskatchewan, 1926*. *See* Novels, 7 to 12.

Lawson, Julie. *A Ribbon of Shining Steel: The Railway Diary of Kate Cameron, Yale, British Columbia, 1882*.

Little, Jean. *Orphan at My Door: The Home Child Diary of Victoria Cope, Guelph, Ontario, 1897*. *See* Novels, 7 to 12.

Matas, Carol. *Footsteps in the Snow: The Red River Diary of Isobel Scott, Rupert's Land, 1815*.

Pearson, Kit. *Whispers of War: The War of 1812 Diary of Susanna Merritt, Niagara, Upper Canada, 1812*.

Korman, Gordon. *Bruno and Boots* **series. 1979– . 160 to 180 pages. 8 to 12.**

What began as a novelette for a grade-seven writing assignment turned into a phenomenally successful children's novel – *This Can't Be Happening at Macdonald Hall!* – and launched the writing career of teenager Gordon Korman. His original story was called *Bruno and Boots*, named after the two main characters, schoolboys whose names became the series title for Korman's first books. The series, featuring the antics of Bruno and Boots at the school Macdonald Hall, includes *Go Jump in the Pool*, *Beware the Fish*, *The War with Mr. Wizzle*, and *The Zucchini Warriors*. Slapstick humour, outrageous situations, and amusing characters are made more hilarious by the constraints of the school setting and the strict principal. Korman's inventive situations, dilemmas, and catastrophes, along with his characters' creative solutions and goofy personalities, keep his stories from being totally formulaic. Popular with boys and girls.

Korman, Gordon. *Slapshots*. **2000– . ca. 150 pages. 9 to 13.**

Korman's lunatic imagination makes this a hockey series with a difference. These stories are told in the voice of self-appointed class sports reporter, Chipmunk Adelman, a boy who has no known skill on the ice, but who covers games played by the Mars Health Food Stars, or Martians. With their well-meaning but hapless coach Bolitsky (a retired NHL player who never got to play) and his dishy wife, the Martians get themselves into one predicament after another, always with bizarrely triumphant results. Korman's writing is fast-paced and undemanding; his humour is goofy and obvious (sometimes playing off gender as well as other stereotypes). But his imagination is innovative and unpredictable.

Korman has also written series on football and on aliens.

Labatt, Mary. *Sam: Dog Detective.* **1999– . ca. 115 pages. 6 to 9.**
Old English sheepdog Sam has an overactive appetite and an overactive imagination, and his neighbour, ten-year-old Jennie Levinsky, somehow has access to his thoughts. In this series Sam leads Jennie and her friend Beth into investigations of hauntings, spooks, and ghouls in various locations: after their often suspenseful sleuthing, the girls and Sam usually discover that there's no mystery at all. With its safe small-town settings and fairly bland or non-existent mysteries, this is likely to appeal mainly to younger children. Large print and a limited vocabulary make it appropriate for newly confident readers. First volume: *Spying on Dracula.*

MacGregor, Roy. *The Screech Owls Series.* **1995– . ca. 120 pages. 9 to 13.**
This series of formula mysteries has particular appeal for readers interested in hockey. Earnest, upstanding Travis and his outrageous friend Wayne Nishikawa, or "Nish," are implicated in a series of mysteries which begin, in volume one, *Mystery at Lake Placid*, with the crimes of a destructively ambitious hockey parent, and in subsequent volumes crank up to incidents which involve major theft and murder. Settings range from Lake Placid to Nagano. Although the Screech Owls are considered a veritable "United Nations" of a team, with representatives from various racial and ethnic groups – including girls – most of them are virtually indistinguishable from one another. Exciting game sequences, moments of suspense, and predictable culprits make these rewarding for many reluctant readers. MacGregor's prose is quick and deft.

McClintock, Norah. *Chloe and Levesque Mysteries.* **2000– .**
ca. 200 pages. 11 and up.
Sixteen-year-old Chloe is disgusted that her mom has remarried and
relocated the family to a small nickel-mining town in northern Ontario.
And she's not sure what she thinks of Levesque, her new stepfather and
a local "Officer-of-the-Law, cop-on-duty, the guy with the quickest,
sharpest eyes in town." In *Over the Edge*, a local high-school student
disappears and Chloe decides she'll do a little sleuthing on her own:
she almost ends up at the bottom of a cliff.

Told in the voice of quick-thinking Chloe, McClintock's mysteries
are clever and involving. Both Chloe and her stepfather are interesting
characters in their own right (no mere formulaic ciphers); their relationship of mutual respect and testy exchange gives texture to the
emotional backdrop of the story. Unlike some mysteries for teens,
the answers to these aren't obvious from page one: they keep the brain
puzzling and the heart pounding by turns. Chloe and Levesque reappear in sequels *Double Cross*, *Scared to Death*, and *Break and
Enter*. Readers who enjoy these may also enjoy McClintock's independent mysteries, *Mistaken Identity*, *The Body in the Basement*,
and *The Sins of the Fathers*.

Our Canadian Girl. **2001– . 60 to 90 pages. 6 to 10.**
This series was designed to give younger readers access to Canadian
history via ten-year-old girl protagonists. In some ways it's reminiscent
of the popular American series *The American Girls Collection*, but this
series is less formulaic in structure. Various authors, including Anne
Laurel Carter, Julie Lawson, Budge Wilson, and Sharon McKay, among
others, locate their young protagonists in various periods and places in
Canada. *Marie Claire: Dark Spring* takes place during Montreal's
smallpox epidemic of 1885; *Rachel: A Mighty Big Imagining* tells of
conditions awaiting an ex-slave and her family when they arrive to
"freedom" in Nova Scotia in 1783. Because of their limited length and
occasional illustrations – as well as their attractive series-style cover
designs – these books are visually appealing to children first heading
into "chapter books." Occasional historical inaccuracies and thin characters mar some of the stories, but this series is useful nevertheless.
Enforced brevity makes some of these stories frustratingly sketchy.

The series is useful in drawing attention to diverse events and conditions in Canada's chequered past.

Carter, Anne Laurel. *Elizabeth: Bless This House*. Nova Scotia, 1762.

Kositsky, Lynne. *Rachel: A Mighty Big Imagining* and *Rachel: The Maybe House*. Nova Scotia, 1783.

Taylor, Cora. *Angelique: Buffalo Hunt*. Batoche, Saskatchewan, 1865.

Stinson, Kathy. *Marie Claire: Dark Spring* and *Marie Claire: A Season of Sorrow*. Montreal, 1885.

Lawson, Julie. *Emily: Across the James Bay Bridge* and *Emily: Disaster at the Bridge*. Victoria, 1896.

McKay, Sharon. *Penelope: Terror in the Harbour* and *Penelope: The Glass Castle*. Halifax, 1917.

Harris, Dorothy Joan. *Ellen: Hobo Jungle*. Vancouver, 1939.

Wilson, Budge. *Izzie: The Christmas That Almost Wasn't*. Halifax, 1941.

Peacock, Shane. *Dylan Maples Adventures*. 1999– . ca. 200 pages. 10 to 13.
Dylan Maples, about twelve years old and an only child, finds himself embroiled in a series of quasi-supernatural mystery/adventure stories in this series. Like Eric Wilson, discussed below, Peacock uses his series to educate children about the places and history of Canada; in a recent volume, *Bone Beds of the Badlands*, Dylan and his friends are in the process of enjoying an educational week at Alberta's Royal Tyrrell Museum in Drumheller, when they become prey to an escaped criminal. The location becomes the occasion for communicating a great deal of information about dinosaurs, archaeology, and the geology of the area; all this is wrapped up in the excitement and suspense of the chase.

Wilson fans would do well to turn to these as a slightly more substantial alternative to the *Tom and Liz Austen Mysteries* (see below). Although Peacock's language has the tone of one trying rather hard to be "cool," it's more enriching than Wilson's. Previous titles include *The Mystery of Ireland's Eye* and *The Secret of the Silver Mines*.

Slade, Arthur. *Northern Frights*. **1997–99. ca. 170 pages. 12 and up.**
See Novels, 12 and Up.

Staunton, Ted. *The Kids from Monkey Mountain*. **2000– . ca. 60 pages. 7 to 10.**
See Books for Beginning Readers.

Trembath, Don. *Black Belt Series*. **2000– . 158 pages. 9 to 12.**
In the first title, *Frog Face and the Three Boys*, the principal, known as Frog Face, sends three troublesome seventh-grade boys off for karate lessons instead of detentions. Talkative Charlie has never exercised; Jeffrey has never been good at fighting; and Sidney fights so much that he has no friends. Karate begins as a great trial, but soon the boys enjoy it, and begin to learn more about themselves and their families' inter-woven histories than they could have imagined.

Each boy has a different family situation. Jeffrey lives with his mother and grandparents; Sidney with his waitress mother; and Charlie with his parents, who are fed up with his constant lying. A small-town setting allows the humour of deep familiarity; Grandpa Anderson recalls the principal as a "sissy boy," who cried all the time, and he doesn't want him to tell his grandson what to do. The story doesn't make many demands, but offers an often hilarious story that will appeal to boys who need fast-paced easy-to-read material. Subsequent titles are *One Finger Missing* and *The Bachelors*.

Wilson, Eric. *Tom and Liz Austen Mysteries*. **1983– . ca. 150 pages. 9 to 12.**
This pair of mystery-prone amateur sleuths have cavorted across Canada solving crimes in every province, from Prince Edward Island to the Edmonton Mall to the Strait of Juan de Fuca in British Columbia. In one of her more recent adventures, *The Emily Carr Mystery*, seven-teen-year-old Liz travels to Victoria, British Columbia, to celebrate a friend's wedding to Paris, the son of one of Victoria's old, wealthy fam-ilies. When a precious painting by Emily Carr is stolen from the house and Liz starts delving into the crime, not only does she walk into danger, but she also reveals that wealthy Paris is deeply in debt. After the twists and turns of her sleuthing (which involve doing just about every tourist

activity in Victoria), she's held at gunpoint; a little quick thinking enables her to nab the thief.

The unlikely plots and inane characters in these books are well matched by Wilson's stunningly unambitious language. "The stained glass windows glowed with the glory of love," we read. "The blues were so blue, the greens so green." Or, "The ferry was so cute . . ." Although the sheer act of reading may be good for the brain, these stories won't develop anyone's abilities with language. However, they're popular and their one benefit is that they introduce readers to the sights of Canada's tourist spots. Eric Walters and Shane Peacock are good alternative authors for Wilson fans.

Novels, 12 and Up

These books for teen and some readers' preteen years deal with more mature themes, and some are written specifically for an older audience. Many deal with issues crucial to adolescents (such as sexual fears and first experiences, acceptance, and gender relations). A good foundation of exploring these issues in fiction can prepare a young adult to meet the challenges of growth with greater confidence and self-awareness. Some of the most soaring and empowering literature in this guide is included in these titles. For the most part, the novels listed here will appeal to both young men and young women; some titles are cross-listed from "Novels, 7 to 12" because their appeal is not limited to the younger group. Please note that some works in the chapter on non-fiction (such as *The Sex Book*) also address the particular interests and concerns of adolescents.

Bastedo, Jamie. *Tracking Triple Seven.* **2001. 215 pages. 10 to 14.**
See Novels, 7 to 12.

Bedard, Michael. *A Darker Magic.* **1987. 183 pages. 12 and up.**
Teacher Miss Potts finds a handbill for a magic show hidden in one of the school desks: "Professor Mephisto presents *The Children's Show* – an evening of magic and mystery. . . . Among the features will be found the following wondrous acts . . . the celebrated *Decollation of John the Baptist* unanimously proclaimed to be the most amazing wonder ever

witnessed." The handbill is from a show Miss Potts saw as a child on August 8, 1936, when she witnessed an illusion of a boy having his head cut off and then reattached. Miss Potts recalls that later that year the boy, never quite having recovered from the "decollation," died in an accident. Once again, August 8 is a Saturday: Miss Potts and her student Emily must work to save a classmate from the threatening "darker magic" of Professor Mephisto.

This is an eerie, well-paced novel, with three separate plot lines leading to the climax of the much-feared magic show. Dread pervades the story; with its moody atmosphere, difficult family, and eccentric cast, it's both rich and frightening.

In a sequel, *The Painted Devil*, the now-adult Emily helps her niece fight the darker magic when it reappears. The story is once again tense and well crafted.

Bedard, Michael. *Redwork*. 1992. 12 and up.

Teenaged Cass and his single, graduate-student mother move into a flat in a wealthy area of Toronto; their landlord, ancient Mr. Magnus, is the bogeyman for all the local children. At first Mr. Magnus does seem frightening: when Cass and his friend Maddy spy on him, they discover that he's involved in alchemical experiments. Closer acquaintance shows that Mr. Magnus is a lonely man immured in the objects of the past and caught up in an alchemical quest he first began after his stint in the First World War. Maddy and Cass help him bring his quest for the Philosopher's Stone to almost disastrous completion, despite threats by local bullies.

Imagery from William Blake's poetry, old films (Cass has a job in a decrepit movie theatre), the First World War trenches, and alchemical treatises combine in this thought-laden, leisurely paced story; the narrative has the crowded feel of Mr. Magnus's artifact-filled house. Momentum builds slowly; although local bullies pose a threat, this doesn't reach any real pitch until the end of the story. Highly wrought – even overwrought – and with little dialogue, this book's main appeal is the struggling character of Cass, who tries to manage the family finances and deal with uncertainties about his own identity and security at the same time.

Bell, William. *Forbidden City: A Novel of Modern China.* **1990. 278 pages. 12 and up.**

In April 1989, when Alex's father announces the two of them will go to Beijing to report on Gorbachev's visit there, Alex is thrilled. But Gorbachev's visit is upstaged by student demonstrations in Tian An Men Square; before long, Alex is caught up in the bloody injustices of China's repressive regime. With videocam and tape recorder in tow, he does his best to record and bring back the true story of the students' reasonable demands and peaceful demonstrations, and the searing horror of the violence with which they were crushed.

Character isn't Bell's strong point, but here, the action and political situation are enough to compel readers. With clarity and fluidity, Bell outlines the nature and practicalities of Chinese policies, thus setting the stage for the events of Tian An Men Square. Alex's first-hand account of the soldiers marching in on the demonstrators is tense and suspenseful; it demands that readers consider this very real situation – and others in which opinion is suppressed by military force – seriously. Alex's friendship with his Chinese interpreter, and, later, with a student who saves his life, helps make real and personal the deaths of the demonstrators. This is one of the only works to present the events of Tian An Men Square to readers in this age group.

Bell, William. *Zack.* **1998. 214 pages. 12 and up.**

Son of a black singer and a Jewish professor, seventeen-year-old Zack's full of resentment when he has to move to Fergus, a small Ontario town. Not only must he deal with racism in his new school, but he's failing his history course. When the history teacher allows him to redeem his grade by doing a project, he chooses to investigate some artifacts he dug up in his backyard, and discovers that his house was originally built by Richard Pierpoint, an ex-slave who fought for the British in the War of 1812 and ended up eking out a living in Fergus. Zack's project sparks his interest in his mother's estranged family; he borrows the family car and heads down to Mississippi, where he meets his grandfather and begins to understand why his mother can't go back.

Bell's novel is notable in treating an issue that is otherwise virtually ignored in Canadian children's fiction, the fate of ex-slaves who chose to make their life in Canada. Pierpoint's story (based on real historical records) is thus useful and enlightening. Zack's quest for his family brings up issues of racism and identity; this novel should spark good discussion on these matters. Bell's prose is quick and undemanding; secondary characters are barely developed, but Zack himself is realistic enough. A good choice for reluctant teen boys.

A subsequent novel, *Stones*, pursues some of the same issues in an account of two teens who put to rest the ghost of a persecuted ex-slave who once had a farm near Orillia.

Bradford, Karleen. *There Will Be Wolves: The First Book of the Crusades*. **1992. 214 pages. 10 to 13.**
See Novels, 7 to 12.

Bradford, Karleen. *Shadows on a Sword: The Second Book of the Crusades*. **1996. 195 pages. 10 to 14.**
See Novels, 7 to 12.

Bradford, Karleen. *Lionheart's Scribe: The Third Book of the Crusades*. **1999. 175 pages. 10 to 14.**
See Novels, 7 to 12.

* **Brooks, Martha.** *Two Moons in August*. **1991. 157 pages. 12 and up.**
"Saturday, August the fifteenth. Today is my sixteenth birthday. Will this be my lucky year? Last year, on this very day, my mother died." The summer of Sidonie's sixteenth birthday is filled with memories and repressed grief. Her father works day and night at the nearby tuberculosis hospital; her sister Roberta cooks and cleans; Sidonie spends sleepless nights and plays cards with her cat. "We all get a little despondent from time to time. Around here it's practically normal," she says. When handsome Kieran moves in across the street, he and Sidonie are instantly attracted to one another; slowly, the emotions in the bereaved household begin to thaw.

Summer heat, adolescent boredom, loving, longing, and pain resonate in the pages of this poignant novel, a potent love story and a beautiful evocation of grief and healing. With the appeal of a summer romance, this offers too the remarkable literary qualities of Brooks's lyrical prose; the story's intense emotional impact has made it a favourite with teenaged girls. Highly recommended.

* Brooks, Martha. *Bone Dance*. 1997. 179 pages. 12 and up.
In the last months of high school in Winnipeg, Alex has dream-visions of her beloved grandfather and the mysterious shaman, "Old Raven Man." Far away, out on the land of southern Manitoba, eighteen-year-old Lonny is haunted by something he can't identify – his mother, who died years ago? the people of a burial mound he disturbed as a boy? or the land itself, sold by his stepfather so Lonny can go to university? When Alex receives a legacy of land from the father she has never met, she and Lonny begin their slow, inexorable movement towards one another – and towards giving up grief and accepting a place in a land peopled by the spirits of their Dene ancestors.

The heady, sensual beauty of the natural world is given moral and mystical significance in this unusual, compelling love story. The smell of skin, of grass over water, the unexpected light on trees – Brooks writes deeply of the concrete connection between our very beings, heart and soul, and the land we live on. Images and wisdom from Aboriginal cultures underlie the characters' maturing, and Brooks's writing has a poetic force which will lead adolescent readers into literary writing for adults. Particularly satisfying for girls. Highly recommended.

Brooks, Martha. *Being with Henry*. 1999. 173 pages. 12 and up.
Laker Wyatt's underage, a runaway, and haunted by memories he knows he "can't possibly have." When he fetches up in Bemidji, Minnesota, and eighty-three-year-old widower Henry Olsen offers him a job doing yard work, Laker has a chance to catch his breath and make a few plans. "You can stay for as long as it takes to get yourself together," Henry promises. Laker returns to school, finds a (paying) part-time job, and falls into a different family dynamic – one that includes Henry's bossy daughter, who doesn't think Laker should be around, and also his temperamental granddaughter, Charlene, who eventually finds Laker rather intriguing. With the help of Henry, Charlene, chance, and his own memory, Henry finally gains a little self-knowledge.

Flavoured with compassion, bittersweet humour, and Brooks's characteristically restrained poetic prose, the story moves towards a final, brilliant revelation. Slowly, subtly, Laker moves from blame to recognition; we begin to understand those memories "he can't possibly have" and the reasons he can never move back home. Based on characters who first appeared in the short story "The Kindness of Strangers" in *Traveling On into the Light* (*see* Short Story Collections and Anthologies, 12 and Up), *Being with Henry* is a story to read more than once, a psychological novel of increasing depths. Brooks deals here with emotions rarely treated, in a story with appeal for teenaged boys as well as girls.

* **Brooks, Martha.** *True Confessions of a Heartless Girl.* **2002. 210 pages. 13 and up.**
One thunderous July night, a stranger rides into the small southern Manitoba town of Pembina Lake. About to close up her café for the night – maybe for good – Lynda Bradley hesitates, then lets the stranger in. It's seventeen-year-old Noreen – friendless, familyless, and pregnant. Years of living in a dysfunctional family have developed in her a bottomless obstinacy and a pig-headed neglect for tomorrow. "I don't love anybody. Period," she says. But as the people of Pembina Lake rally around her, Noreen finds that, even though every single thing she does turns out wrong, she can still bring healing out of disaster.

Brooks's joyous, poetic celebration of sorrow and healing lies on the verge of adult novel-hood. For as much as love-starved, pregnant Noreen is the centre of the story, so too are thirty-seven-year-old Lynda, fifty-two-year-old Delbert, and seventy-six-year-old Dolores ("OLDEST FIRST NATIONS WAITRESS IN MANITOBA" reads her sweatshirt). Noreen's story draws adolescent readers in; the thwarted older characters show just where dumb decisions and heartbreak can get you. Suffused with a spirituality born of a place where earth and sky command full attention, this novel is one of Brooks's finest – bracing, lyrical, prayerful, and funny. Highly recommended.

Buffie, Margaret. *Who Is Frances Rain?* **1987. 192 pages. 10 to 14.**
See Novels, 7 to 12.

Chan, Gillian. *Golden Girl and Other Stories.* **1994. 119 pages. 12 and up.**
Five separate voices tell their stories of life in Elmwood High School, and their interconnected stories deal with issues common to teen life. The characters include Bob, the school bully, who makes bullying an art form; Dennis, who is safe as long as there's another victim for the bully; Anna, the "golden girl," and Donna, her best friend, full of jealousy and spite; Elly, the victim of a suffocating mother; and Andy, who struggles with the demands of a father driven by the culture of his homeland. Each story stands on its own, but characters reappear in other stories, making the book read like a novel; for example, the school bully is first introduced in a story told by a potential victim; he plays a secondary role in a subsequent story; and finally he tells his own story at the end of the book.

First-person narrators give the stories immediacy, and the issues Chan treats are realistic and timely. Foibles of parents and friends, foolish mistakes, crushes, passionate teachers, lousy teachers, and ultimately adolescent hopes and dreams are thoughtfully drawn. Chan's companion book *Glory Days and Other Stories* continues the exploration of life at Elmwood High.

Chan, Gillian. *A Foreign Field.* **2002. 184 pages. 11 and up.**
See Novels, 7 to 12.

Clark, Joan. *The Dream Carvers.* **1995. 226 pages. 10 to 13.**
See Novels, 7 to 12.

* Curtis, Christopher Paul. *The Watsons Go to Birmingham – 1963.* **1998. 210 pages. 10 and up.**
See Novels, 7 to 12.

Dale, Mitzi. *The Sky's the Limit.* **1990. 153 pages. 10 to 13.**
When Kim Taylor's friends decide they're going to "get" boyfriends in order to make their transition into high school easier, Kim decides that, instead, she'll make friends with the most popular girl in school. Amazingly, Kim's tactic of helping in a local drama production works, and soon she and wealthy, beautiful Skye are hanging out regularly in

Skye's elegant home. They even take drama classes together, and join a local improvisation competition. But at times Skye is moody and unavailable, and when Kim finds out why, it changes her perspective of Skye's "easy" life entirely.

Kim's irreverent account, and especially her fine comic sense, give breathless dash to this story, which engages the serious issue of sexual abuse along with more benign aspects of growing up. Kim's loving, supportive working-class family contrasts with Skye's high-powered professional mother and creepy, sexually predatory stepfather; Kim's growth in wisdom and coming into her own as a comedian make an engaging coming-of-age story. Dale's knowledge of drama and improv give this added interest. Sequel *On My Own* also available.

Doyle, Brian. *Easy Avenue*. **1988. 180 pages. 10 and up.**
See Novels, 7 to 12.

* Doyle, Brian. *Uncle Ronald*. **1996. 138 pages. 10 and up.**
See Novels, 7 to 12.

Doyle, Brian. *The Low Life: Five Great Tales from Up and Down the River*. **1999. 397 pages. 9 and up.**
See Novels, 7 to 12.

* Doyle, Brian. *Mary Ann Alice*. **2001. 160 pages. 9 to 13.**
See Novels, 7 to 12.

Doyle, Brian. *Spud in Winter*. **1995. 140 pages. 8 to 13.**
See Novels, 7 to 12.

* Ellis, Deborah. *The Breadwinner*. **2000. 176 pages. 10 and up.**
See Novels, 7 to 12.

Ellis, Deborah. *Parvana's Journey*. **2002. 197 pages. 10 and up.**
See Novels, 7 to 12.

Ellis, Sarah. *Out of the Blue*. **1994. 120 pages. 10 to 14.**
See Novels, 7 to 12.

* **Foggo, Cheryl.** *One Thing That's True*. **1997. 128 pages. 10 to 14.**
See Novels, 7 to 12.

Goobie, Beth. *Mission Impossible*. **1994. 160 pages. 12 and up.**
The football team's Lovely Legs Competition doesn't get much of a
reaction from most students in Jill's high school, but Jill herself thinks
the event degrading. Her football-player brother doesn't want her to
enter the competition, because she'll be labelled a slut, but Jill grows
the hair on her legs and enters as an act of protest. She doesn't intend
to make enemies, but her act of protest makes everyone feel uncomfortable and angry. She's labelled a "Les," and in no time is ostracized
by everyone but her brother.

Jill has a seemingly tough exterior and a wicked sense of humour;
underneath, though, we see how confused and torn she really is. The
story's lightened by Goobie's candid humour: "Leg hair, penises, the
cheerleading squad, she didn't have to figure it all out now." The movie
The Mission is a recurring image in the novel, but readers unfamiliar
with it will nevertheless find the story rivetting. Jill comes across as a
heroine who makes her whole school re-evaluate its traditions.

* **Goobie, Beth.** *Before Wings*. **2000. 203 pages. 12 and up.**
Fifteen-year-old Adrien Wood thinks it's natural to see spirits over the
lake when she arrives to spend a summer working at her aunt's summer
camp. After all, since suffering a brain aneurysm two years before, she
hasn't been too sure whether she's on the verge of the spirit world or in
the land of the living. When brooding Paul, a fellow staffworker, tells
her that he dreams of her presence at his death almost nightly, she
knows that her spirits and his dream are related. Could they be
connected, too, to her aunt's moodiness and preoccupation with five
former campers?

This is an utterly engrossing love story/ghost story: the sexual elec-
tricity between Adrien and Paul fairly crackles and hums "in the skin,"
as Goobie might say. Even grass, leaves, and trees thrum with sensual
and spiritual meaning. The mystery of the haunting and the threat of
death whisk the plot along, a backdrop to something even more valuable – the honest, joyous celebration of bodily life. Colloquial edge

("kick ass spirits") and lyric intensity make this a cut above most young adult novels. Highly recommended.

Goobie, Beth. *The Lottery*. 2002. 264 pp. 12 and up.
Reminiscent of the quiet, horrifying short story of the same title by Shirley Jackson, this is the tale of a similarly sinister lottery in Saskatoon Collegiate. Each September, students fear receiving the black-ribboned scroll from the Shadow Council, announcing that they are the "Lottery Winner: Shadow Council's Dud for the Year." Sal, in grade ten, at first doesn't believe she's the "winner" when a scroll arrives, but when she's summoned to the council, the realization that she'll be the school's ultimate loser turns her life into a hellish nightmare. Friends avoid her, no one talks to her, and she finds herself as the messenger (always with bad results) for the all-powerful Shadow Council.

Goobie writes with terrifying realism. Readers identify not only with Sal, but also with her friends who have to struggle with their acquiescence through the year. Students' actions are both understated and understandable as the students bend to the power of the Shadow Council. Council members are portrayed as multi-dimensional, but as Sal says, "there are no *nice* jerks." Goobie shows the strength one needs to take a stand against an entire student body and retain one's identity. This story will have a powerful resonance with students everywhere.

Goobie, Beth. *Sticks and Stones*. 2002. 89 pages. 12 and up.
The cover photograph of a high-school locker with the word SLUT written on it sets the tone and topic for this book. After a date with good-looking Brent (also known as "Mr. Warp Speed"), Trudy discovers that, even though she didn't do anything with him in the back seat of his car, her reputation is in tatters. Trudy and a male friend form the Slut Club and challenge the other students to examine the ease with which they label each other.

Goobie tackles the issue of reputation and name-calling in this short, gritty novel, which is a quick, engaging read. Although this is intended for reluctant teen readers, the issue makes the book relevant for a wide audience.

Haig-Brown, Roderick. *Starbuck Valley Winter*. **1944. 272 pages. 11 to 14.**

Despite its age, this novel still has appeal as a boys' outdoor-adventure story. Sixteen-year-old Don Morgan convinces his guardians that he's old enough to work a trapline in the mountainous interior of Vancouver Island. He and his friend Tubby set themselves up in a refurbished trapper's cabin, but they're disappointed with their modest results. They're suspicious, too, of competitor Lee Jetson, who's been snooping around and clearly wants to scare them off. Tubby hurts himself, and Don has to bring him out of the wilderness on his own. Perseverance and fortitude, a few revised opinions, and a willingness to learn allow Don finally to triumph.

This novel starts slowly, but the excitement of the rescue gives it a momentum that carries through to the end. Haig-Brown's prose is clean and practical; his knowledge and interest in the ways of the wilderness is everywhere apparent. Don's wholesome expressions may seem a tad old-fashioned, but his desire for independence, "to get out without a bunch of older folks under foot all the time," will never be outmoded. This will raise questions about current and former hunting and trapping practices.

The sequel, *Saltwater Summer*, explores Don's coming to manhood as the skipper of his own salmon troller, fishing the waters from the mouth of the Fraser River north to Prince Rupert.

Harrison, Troon. *A Bushel of Light*. **2000. 244 pages. 10 to 13.**
See Novels, 7 to 12.

Haworth-Attard, Barbara. *Love-Lies-Bleeding*. **1999. 140 pages. 10 to 14.**
See Novels, 7 to 12.

* **Heneghan, James.** *Wish Me Luck*. **1997. 197 pages. 10 to 14.**
See Novels, 7 to 12.

Hewitt, Marsha and Claire Mackay. *One Proud Summer.* **1981. 159 pages. 11 and up.**

When thirteen-year-old Lucie's father is killed in a labour accident in 1946, she has to quit school and start work in Valleyfield's local textile mill, owned by Montreal Cottons. The hours are long and hard, hot and dusty, and made more oppressive by her leering overseer. When Lucie's friend Annette tells Lucie that the workers are forming a union, Lucie goes along to find out about it. And when authorities at the mill refuse to negotiate with the union, the workers vote for a general strike – one that stretches into weeks, then months. Despite everything the mill does – bring in scab labour, police, Catholic priests, armed personnel – the workers, with their strong will and indomitable spirit, win out in the end for better wages (a raise of seven cents per hour), better hours, and one week's paid holiday a year.

Hewitt and Mackay's fictionalized story of this historic Canadian strike is clear and moving; their account both honours the participants and makes for an absorbing read – sometimes touching, sometimes heart-stopping. Deft, lively prose, fully imagined characters (including generations of mill labourers), and a courageous, energetic protagonist characterize this empowering story. An excellent supplement to any study of Canadian labour history, and a successful novel in its own right.

Holeman, Linda. *Mercy's Birds.* **1998. 198 pages. 12 and up.**

Mercy, fifteen, lives with her alcoholic, fortune-telling Aunt Moo and her mother, Pearl, who is clinically depressed and eventually hospitalized after an overdose. Mercy fears the return of Moo's boyfriend, "B," with his threat of sexual predation. As Mercy works at a florist's every day after school to support the family, she struggles to find a way to evade B. Only Mercy's Italian boss and his mother offer a warm haven.

Mercy, in her severe dress, with her ugly, black-dyed hair, her love of words, and her tentative desire for friendship, is complex and appealing; Holeman avoids the preachiness and posturing that often come with a "problem" novel. The strength of the story lies in feelings and incidents any reader can share – the embarrassment of a birthday put on by an aunt who doesn't know the people she invites aren't your friends, for example. Also satisfying is Holeman's novel *Promise Song*.

Holeman, Linda. *Raspberry House Blues*. **2000. 238 pages. 12 and up.**
Sixteen-year-old Poppy is looking for her birth mother. Fed up with her
adoptive mother, she flies to Winnipeg to spend the summer with
her adoptive father and new (very pregnant) stepmother and toddler
half-brother. Life at their house is messy and squalid, and finding her
birth mother isn't as easy as Poppy thought it would be. But when she
befriends aging actress Becca Jell and begins to hear her life story,
she suspects she's found her mother at last. "That's movie material,"
her stepmother says sceptically – and she's right, Becca isn't Poppy's
mother, but learning this puts real family love in perspective.

Poppy's frustrations, her frail sense of identity, and her self-
consciousness ring true to adolescent concerns. Her first-person
narrative is tight and convincing, going beyond its initial posturing to
become more multi-layered. Holeman's knack for detail makes places
come alive; even the initial caricature of the health-nut stepmother is
mitigated by the end, leaving the reader not with cheap laughs but with
a sense of the likeable person behind the behaviour, and the message
that misplaced "attitude" can prevent true knowledge. A good read for
adolescent girls.

Holeman, Linda. *Search of the Moon King's Daughter*. **2002.
308 pages. 10 to 14.**
Emmeline Roke knows a happy, literate life in an English village, until
the day her father succumbs to fever. Then she, her mother, "Cat," and
her deaf brother, Tommy, are forced out of the shop they kept;
Emmeline begins to work for a seamstress and her mother to labour in
the cotton mills. When Cat, now addicted to laudanum, sells Tommy
off as a chimney sweep, Emmeline heads alone to London to retrieve
him. She finds employment below stairs in an ailing lawyer's house,
makes friends with the hired help (Sukey and Thomas), and in the end,
manages to steal Tommy away from his master sweep. When her
employer dies, he bequeaths her two valuable books, which she's able
to sell in order to set up business for herself, Tommy, and her two
friends (Sukey is now pregnant by the lawyer's ne'er-do-well son).

With a plot worthy of a period soap opera, this tale travels from pastoral village life of the 1830s to the hardships of factory work and utter
indigence, and to the protocols and social boundaries of Victorian

London's urbane middle class. Amidst all the period detail, Emmeline is a strong, persistent protagonist; her struggles and difficulties make an engaging read.

* **Holubitsky, Katherine.** *Alone at Ninety Foot.* **1999. 179 pages. 10 to 14.**

Pam Collins can't help haunting North Vancouver's spectacular, savage Lynn Canyon. Maybe it's because her mother used to take her hiking there; maybe it's because her mother threw herself off the canyon suspension bridge. In the last month before graduating from junior high, Pam struggles with her enduring sadness: "It's like this mean little animal deep inside me," she says, feeling she can't move on without her mother to share the changes. As her friends, her dad and his girlfriend, and even a puppy rally around her, Pam makes her peace with Lynn Canyon and wins some confidence for the future.

This story is written in the first person, and a snappy sarcasm makes it fairly sparkle along; Pam's comments about classmates and her dad's girlfriend (who uses ridiculously outmoded slang) are ironic, funny, and self-aware. Mixed in with high-school concerns (classmates, love life, and dress) is the deeper issue of bereavement, lyrically expressed. "In silence, life keeps raging on," Pam reads in a journal by Emily Carr – and indeed, that's the central issue of the novel. Person and place are beautifully wedded: "It is the smells and tastes and feel of a place that makes it part of you," Pam claims. Holubitsky allows us to smell and taste and feel the coastal rain forest. Highly recommended.

Holubitsky, Katherine. *Last Summer in Agatha.* **2001. 185 pages. 11 to 14.**

Rachel's happy to leave Vancouver and spend her summer helping her aunt and uncle, veterinarians in Agatha, southern Alberta. She's even happier when she strikes up a romance with Michael, a local boy struggling with the tragic drunk-driving death of his older brother. When the seemingly innocent pranks of Michael and his high-school rivals start getting out of hand – especially when those pranks tap deeply into Michael's conflicted grief – Rachel doesn't know whether to bring adults into it or not.

Holubitsky explores the knotty issue of trust and responsibility, touching also on some of the complexities of sibling bereavement. Firm friendships and interesting, believable characters make this an appealing high-school story, but more distinctive is Holubitsky's sharp evocation of place, "the flat yellow land [that] stretches hundreds of miles into the distance, to the Sweet Grass Hills of Montana." The story has the smells and sounds of prairie summer – fireweed, bees, and tumultuous downpours – and glories in the skills and local knowledge of small-town prairie teens. It is also notable for showing a girl well able to fight off the unwanted advances of the boy she's in love with.

Hrdlitschka, Shelley. *Dancing Naked.* **249 pages. 2001. 12 and up.**
Finding herself pregnant at sixteen, Kia faces the future with confusion, frustration, and fear. Her thug of a boyfriend insists that abortion is the only answer; when Kia refuses, he vanishes from her life. Kia turns to her youth-group advisor, Justin, for support; he accompanies her to prenatal classes, encourages her, and shows great interest in the baby. Predictably, Kia falls for him; but Justin is gay, a fact he's been hiding even from himself. Eventually Kia realizes that it wouldn't be right for her to try to bring up this baby, and she gives it up for adoption to parents she has chosen through an agency. An elderly woman Kia's been helping tells Kia that she admires her courageous decisions: Kia is "dancing naked," "exposed completely, moving to an internal rhythm all [her] own."

Hrdlitschka structures the book in forty chapters, one for each week of Kia's pregnancy: each chapter begins with a record of the baby's size and development. Kia's parents are barely characters and even Kia and Justin are mysteriously hollow and simplistic; nevertheless, the teen pregnancy and gay themes, combined with the thoughtful consideration of pregnancy options, make this an appealing and useful title for discussion. This will be a tear-jerker for many.

Hudson, Jan. *Sweetgrass.* **1984. 138 pages. 12 and up.**
Fifteen-year-old Sweetgrass hopes that her parents will choose Eagle Sun for her husband, and not some older man with many horses to offer her father. But the concerns of the young Blackfoot girl change dramatically when her father goes on a hunting trip and she and her

brother, Otter, are left behind with the family. The whole family succumbs to smallpox; Sweetgrass is their only hope for survival as she
tends to each of them. "In the few hours I had been away, Little
Brother's blisters had broken," she says. "They ran blood. His cheeks
and his forehead were now one bloody scab." Sickness and starvation
threaten as Sweetgrass tends to the sick and dying, proving that,
indeed, she is no longer a child.

Hudson's gut-wrenching novel is set in the period of the Blackfoot
confederacy of 1830s Alberta. The first-person narration gives
Sweetgrass's account of the worry and fear of smallpox and starvation
an horrific edge. The story is based on written records of the winter of
1837–38, and a bibliography is included, but the real emotion of the
tale lives in Sweetgrass's powerful, articulate voice. Unforgettable.

**Hughes, Monica. *The Keeper of the Isis Light*. 1980. 191 pages.
10 to 13.**
See Novels, 7 to 12.

Huser, Glen. *Touch of the Clown*. 1999. 223 pages. 11 to 14.
Barbara (full name Barbara Stanwyck Kobleimer) cares for her sister
Livvy (short for Olivia de Havilland), as well as her grandmother (who
thinks she used to look like Claudette Colbert) and indigent father –
inveterate drunks whose idea of serious communication is to put the
VCR on "pause." Their days are spent waiting for the next cheque and
watching old movies. "Livvy's clothes submerged in smelly water in the
soaking sink . . . the pot of Kraft dinner getting gluey on the stove . . .
the sound of Daddy being sick when he's drunk too much . . ." – all this
is Barbara's reality until she meets the young man Cosmo and, for the
first time since their mother died, she and Livvy do more than watch
old movies. "The touch of the clown . . . a little smudge of Clown
White. It enters our pores and we are changed forever," Cosmo says as
he wipes a white paint off his cheek and marks Barbara, showing her
how to find and use a "clown life preserver" – a sense of wonder that
will help her endure. And even when Cosmo ends up dying of AIDS,
that life preserver stays with her.

Huser's dialogue, from the grandmother's continual reminders to
"get a Claudette Colbert movie" to Barbara's memories of the best

moments in her life, is both crisp and emotional. Despite its portrayal of grim reality, this is a readable, forward-looking story, without pat solutions but with an honest promise of hope. Barbara's strength, Cosmo's love and grace, and their shared passion for reading comes through clearly.

* **Johnston, Julie.** *Hero of Lesser Causes*. **1992. 178 pages. 11 and up.**
Johnston's dry humour and vivifying originality make this coming-of-age novel a work of genius. Twelve-year-old Keely sees herself as a screwball-hero, riding a silver steed and fighting for great causes. But the only steed available is an ornery breadwagon horse, and Keely's bravado usually ends in disaster – a shower of skunk spray or a dunk in a leech-ridden pond. These disasters pale, however, when Keely's teenaged brother Patrick is suddenly paralyzed by polio in the summer of 1946, and Keely feels responsible for rescuing him from despair. She fears that her triumphs in causes of "lesser magnitude" – moving Patrick's bed, making him laugh, finding him a friend – may not be enough to pull him through.

The Ottawa Valley setting and the late 1940s come alive in Johnston's telling. But even more impressive is the intelligent humour and compassion with which she writes of Keely's difficult passage into adolescence and her deep, bantering affection for her brother. Keely's new romantic interests and her efforts to become "mature" all at once lead to some of the funniest moments in fiction for this age group; on the other hand, Patrick's slow emergence from grief provides some of the most moving. Johnston's deceptively sophisticated writing is nevertheless very accessible. Highly recommended.

* **Johnston, Julie.** *Adam and Eve and Pinch-Me*. **1994. 180 pages. 12 and up.**
Soon to be sixteen, Sara Moone plans to set off on her own and leave foster-home life behind her. Although she knows her birth mother is trying to contact her, she's decided that it is "too late." Placed on a sheep farm run by a taciturn farmer and his garrulous wife, Sara now has to tolerate the situation, and the company of two additional foster children, one young and demanding and the other deeply troubled.

Sara adopts a policy of no involvement – with her foster family, her classmates, and especially her birth mother.

"The only thing in this world I'm attached to is my computer," Sara claims as she expresses her feelings on a printerless computer. But kindness breaks down her guard eventually – "My keyboard's getting all crusted up. Tears have a lot of salt in them," she says – and when her sixteenth birthday looms, she finds the emotional strength to stay with the people who desperately need her. With incisive prose and a complete lack of sentimentality, Johnston allows us insight into a girl who struggles to open herself to love and loving. Highly recommended.

Johnston, Julie. *The Only Outcast.* **1998. 221 pages. 12 and up.**
Constantly humiliated by his father, Fred Dickinson's confidence is further eroded by his terrible stammer. When he heads off for his grandparents' summer home on Rideau Lake in June of 1904, he hopes he'll manage to do something to make his father proud. But embarrassment plagues him – he's caught in a skinny-dipping dive by a lovely girl; he drinks birch beer and amazes passengers on the local boats with his rendition of "Good Night Ladies"; and he and his cousin almost crash the family boat. But only Fred has the courage to solve the mystery of an old murder, and in that moment, he begins to see his father, and himself, in a different light.

Fred's frustration getting his words out, as well as the relentless family dynamics he endures, invite the reader's sympathy; at the same time, there's spark and humour in the arguments and tart exchanges between the relatives, and Fred's comments about women are often amusingly wry or guileless ("Talking about emotional things with women is not for the faint-hearted," he opines). It's a moment of understated triumph when Fred's father is thrown into the water and has to be rescued by Fred. Johnston uses the actual diaries of the real Fred Dickinson as a base and makes the Rideau Canal and Lanark County in 1904 come to life in this tale of self-discovery.

* Johnston, Julie. *In Spite of Killer Bees.* **2001. 253 pages. 11 and up.**
When parentless Aggie and her sisters arrive in Port Desire to claim a legacy from their grandfather, Aggie's sure it's the beginning of her

dream – a big house, money, and her mother come back. But the house is a mausoleum/museum, with all its artifacts, seventy-year-old jars of preserves, and dead plants. And the girls can't inherit it unless forgetful Aunt Lily agrees to leave her beloved island and move in with them. Neighbours and relatives don't trust them because of their formerly thieving father; and Aggie's "Scottish Highlander off duty" look on the first day of school doesn't succeed quite the way she'd hoped. Just when it looks as though the sisters will pull their lives together, their mother shows up and threatens their carefully earned stability.

Johnston's understated, ironic humour gives a delightful edge to this story of the triumph of sisterhood in the absence of parents. Underneath the flamboyant dressing (Helen in black, Jeannie in see-through, and Aggie in vintage) and dry turns of phrase, Johnston depicts the dynamics of the sisters with authenticity and even an air of rakish camaraderie. Aggie's deep yearning for "home" gives the story a vibrant emotional core, and her problems with school, friends, and a possible romance bring it into the realm of common adolescent concerns. Johnston brings all to a satisfyingly triumphant, eccentric ending, never bending to moralism or mawkishness. Highly recommended.

Katz, Welwyn Wilton. *Witchery Hill*. 1984. 244 pages. 10 to 14.
See Novels, 7 to 12.

Katz, Welwyn Wilton. *False Face*. 1987. 155 pages. 10 to 14.
See Novels, 7 to 12.

Khan, Rukhsana. *Dahling, If You Luv Me, Would You Please, Please Smile*. 1999. 206 pages. 12 and up.
Zainab's sister Layla keeps an alphabetized list of Zainab's faults, complete with "time, date and exact circumstances in which the fault was demonstrated." But Zainab's gruelling "self-improvement" sessions with her pious, domineering sister are no worse than her problems at school, where she's the only Muslim and one of two "Indians" in her class. Zainab stoops to stealing to acquire trendy clothes; her only friend stoops to posing for nudie pictures in order to attract a popular boy. Finally Zainab finds the wisdom and courage to stand up for her friend, herself, and her own cultural tradition.

Khan's depiction of Zainab's class, and her friend Jenny, is forced and superficial; but her portrayal of Zainab's family relations is interesting – especially as Zainab begins to argue back with her sister, text by religious text. Zainab's feelings of marginalization and the difficulties of her friendship with a Hindu girl bring up issues of culture and assimilation. This is one of the only novels for this age that portrays a Muslim family.

Lawrence, Iain. *Ghost Boy*. 2000. 328 pages. 11 and up.
See Novels, 7 to 12.

Lawrence, Iain. *The Lightkeeper's Daughter*. 2002. 246 pages. 13 and up.
A non-linear narrative and mature subject matter make this an almost-adult novel. With her three-year-old daughter in tow, seventeen-year-old "Squid" returns to her childhood home – Lizzie Island, a tiny place off British Columbia's north coast, an island on which the only inhabitants are her parents, Hannah and lightkeeper Murray McCrae. Returning home evokes Squid's memories of an idyllic childhood, with her father's entertaining lectures on marine life and the freedom of having a whole island at her command. But she remembers, too, the despair of her brother Alistair, who found insular life and his father's authority stifling. Alistair drowned one night while recording the songs of humpback whales: Squid's return awakens all the questions, blame, and grief of his death.

Shifting from Squid's point of view to Hannah's, from the readjustments of the present to recollections of the past, Lawrence delineates the psyches and complex emotions of a family isolated in a remarkable locale. The abundant diversity and peculiar habits of marine life seem to infuse the family, from the "wonderful, thunderous rush" of sea lions to the sex life of barnacles. The story has loose ends that flutter like streamers of kelp at the change of the tide; but its unanswered questions are evocative and thought-provoking rather than frustrating. For thoughtful readers.

Leavitt, Martine. *The Dollmage.* **2001. 159 pages. 12 and up.**
Every doll in Seekvalley represents the life force of one person in the community. The Dollmage is the wise woman who creates the dolls, ensuring a good life and safety in the valley. It's her responsibility, too, to predict the day on which the future Dollmage will be born, for when she is old she must pass her skills and knowledge on to a young woman. But this Dollmage has a dilemma, for two girls, Anna and Renoa, were born on the appointed day, and both have powers. They have grown up together; they have contested with one another, and tragedy has been the result. As the story begins, the Dollmage goes back to the beginning of their lives in an effort to stop the community from stoning the woman who should inherit her role.

Leavitt writes with vigour and imagination. Anna, the beleaguered heroine, frustrated in her creative art, is an appealing, strong protagonist. While this is a rich fantasy and a spellbinding story, Anna's heartrending rape by a boorish villager introduces a painfully realistic element into the imaginary world. Leavitt also writes under the name Martine Bates.

* **Lemieux, Michèle.** *Stormy Night.* **Trans. from German. 1999. 240 pages. 9 and up.**
See Novels, 7 to 12.

* **Lunn, Janet.** *The Hollow Tree.* **1997. 260 pages. 10 to 14.**
See Novels, 7 to 12.

Major, Kevin. *Hold Fast.* **1978. 170 pages. 12 to 16.**
"There's still that time after every day when, no matter how much I've done, everything gets quiet and I'm all alone with all that's happened and I feels like bawling," confesses Michael. Michael's parents have been killed in a crash, and his life in a small Newfoundland outport community is changed forever. Sent to live with relatives in a city hundreds of miles away, Michael's emotional journey is tough; he argues with his tyrannical uncle and rebels against the changes that have been forced upon him. Finally, he and his cousin Curtis escape and make their way back to Michael's outport town.

Major's forthright language, strong characters, and the uncompromising reality of the Newfoundland landscape and community make this a forceful account of an adolescent's struggle against unfair, domineering authority. *Hold Fast* established Major in the international world of young adult literature when the book was first released in 1978. Written in Michael's strong Newfoundland voice, this story of his struggles with events he can't control, his love for family, and his pride still resonates.

Marineau, Michèle. *The Road to Chlifa*. Trans. from French. 1992. 142 pages. 12 and up.
A new immigrant to Montreal, sixteen-year-old Karim can't connect with anyone in his new school; however, when he rescues My-Lin, who is being sexually threatened, it unlocks a series of memories. Back in war-torn Beirut, he had been besotted with sensuous Nada. When Nada was killed, Karim befriended her independent-minded sister, twelve-year-old Maha, who vowed to take her baby brother to the village of Chlifa for safety. As Karim, Maha, and the baby hike the dangerous wilderness and mountain passes to the village, Karim learns that rebellious, imaginative Maha has much to teach him. When Maha is raped and killed, Karim is heartbroken and crippled by guilt. Through the rescue of My-Lin, he is able to resolve some of his anguish.

Recounted in multiple voices – via Karim's "journal" and by students from his Montreal high school – the first and last parts of this story are fast-paced and colloquial, perhaps too full of adolescent attitude and posturing. But the middle section, the part that happens in Lebanon, is told by an omniscient narrator, and it's poignant and involving. We see Karim slowly mature and deepen under the influence of Maha, an irresistible mixture of vulnerability and fierceness. Marineau's picture of Lebanon – both half-destroyed Beirut and the beautiful landscape – is engrossing. While the voices of the story don't jibe entirely, nevertheless this is a good choice for reluctant adolescent readers and a useful avenue for discussing immigrant experience.

Martel, Suzanne. *The King's Daughter*. 1980. 211 pages. 12 and up.
At eighteen, Jeanne Chatel knows "her prison door is opening and that the great adventure is beginning" when she's chosen to go to New France as a "Fille du Roi," a prospective bride, in 1672. Always brave and spirited, she's thrilled to go to a glorious future – but when she

arrives in New France, she's required to become the wife/housekeeper of an older man, recently widowed in a massacre. Jeanne accepts her new role and quickly asserts herself, proving to her husband that she's well able to build a life in the wilderness with his children. Although she learns to love him, the memory of his first wife haunts the marriage.

Canadian history leaps to life in this rivetting story of a feisty young woman establishing herself in a new country, fighting off Iroquois attacks, learning to dance in the wilderness, and ultimately falling in love with her husband. Martel's Jeanne is a memorable heroine, headstrong, demanding, skilled with the frying pan as both cooking implement and weapon. Historical figure Marguerite Bourgeoys supplies Jeanne with medical supplies and knowledge, encouraging her to learn from both Indians and settlers. An ideal story for the study of New France. Unfortunately, illustrations by Debi Perna are aimed at a young audience and may deter older readers.

Matas, Carol. *Lisa*. 1987. 111 pages. 10 to 14.
See Novels, 7 to 12.

Matas, Carol. *Daniel's Story*. 1993. 136 pages. 10 and up.
See Novels, 7 to 12.

McNamee, Graham. *Hate You*. 119 pages. 1999. 12 and up.
Alice Silvers's voice was shattered by her father when he choked her years ago. Left with what she calls her "Frankenstein" voice, Alice finds it impossible to sing the songs that she loves to write. At seventeen, she has a strong relationship with her boyfriend and she gets along with her mother, but her hatred towards her father is still going strong – it has been smouldering since he was forced out of the house the night he choked her. When Alice discovers her father is dying and wants to see her again, she must confront that hatred at last.

In her own edgy, ironic "voice," Alice shares her frustrations with her mother, her amusement at her constantly aroused boyfriend, and the apprehension and anger she feels about visiting her father. Her comments about life and her mother's plays are both amusing and insightful; she describes the play *Big City Lifeboat* as "the longest half hour of my life. . . . A postmodern, existential nudie show." McNamee balances Alice's pain with her sharp humour in this fast-paced, smart-talking story of the legacy of a father's physical violence. McNamee writes with unusual effectiveness about this issue.

McNaughton, Janet. *To Dance at the Palais Royale.* **1996. 218 pages. 10 and up.**
In 1918, Aggie Maxwell leaves her family and a harsh life in the Scottish mines to join her sister as a domestic servant in Toronto in the hope that the two of them can earn enough to bring the whole family to Canada. Life as a maid in a rich household provides plenty of contrasts for Aggie, but she soon learns that the rumours of Canada's wealth – "the people in Toronto are so rich they heat the streets in winter" – aren't true. She earns only twenty-five dollars a month, has only two afternoons off, and knows her opportunities for anything better are limited, while the young women who visit the household have money and opportunities galore. But by the time her family arrives, determined, diligent Aggie has not only helped a Russian Jew learn English, but has danced in disguise with the wealthy, learned of other cultures, and found a kind, loving suitor.

Aggie's tragedies and common disasters – she is wrongfully accused of stealing and she has a boorish sister – come to vivid life in this captivating story. McNaughton conveys beautifully the immigrant hope of a better life in Canada, introducing readers to the struggles many people of the period had when they first came to Toronto.

McNaughton, Janet. *Make or Break Spring.* **1999. 187 pages. 10 and up.**
See Novels, 7 to 12.

McNaughton, Janet. *The Secret Under My Skin.* **2000. 238 pages. 10 and up.**
See Novels, 7 to 12.

Melling, O. R. *My Blue Country.* **1996. 196 pages. 12 and up.**
Jesse McKinnock is seventeen when she's accepted into a cross-cultural work project in Malaysia. From a small town in Ontario, she joins sixty youths from across Canada for three months of training in

Alberta, where the group must develop some mutual respect and learn communal effort. In her journal, Jesse comments on the differences in religion, status, class, money, and background among the participants, as well as the regional disparities and the difficulties of working in Canada's two official languages. Jesse's experiences in Malaysia change her perspective forever – not only because her group becomes as close as a family, but also because she and a Muslim boy fall in love, a relationship they both know must be short-lived.

Melling's diary format is perfect for this tale of growth. Jesse's forthright questioning of her own values, in contrast with those of the other Canadians, and then with those of the hosts in Malaysia, is unsophisticated but insightful. The Canadian teens are quite believable, with their idealism and self-absorbed behaviour. Jesse's descriptions of the burgeoning relationships among the Canadian volunteers make her doomed love for the Malaysian boy all the more poignant.

* **Pearson, Kit.** *The Sky Is Falling*. **1989. 248 pages. 9 to 13.**
See Novels, 7 to 12.

Pearson, Kit. *Awake and Dreaming*. **1997. 228 pages. 9 to 13.**
See Novels, 7 to 12.

* **Sheppard, Mary.** *Seven for a Secret*. **2002. 189 pages. 13 and up.**
"I'll be an old maid by the time I finish grade eleven!" complains fifteen-year-old Melinda to her cousins, homemaker Rebecca and ambitious city girl Kate. Growing up in the outport of Cook's Cove, Newfoundland, Melinda can only think of when she'll be able to set up house with her fisherman sweetheart. But when a visitor offers Rebecca art lessons in Boston, Melinda, the cleverest of the three clever cousins, starts thinking that maybe nursing school would be a possibility – and it might be the way to persuade Aunt Grace to let Rebecca out of Cook's Cove. But formidable Aunt Grace has opinions and a past of her own, which bold Melinda threatens to disclose.

This empowering, revelatory novel of family secrets and female solidarity is written with a spirited vivacity that makes it immediately engaging. Capable, lively, and sure of herself, Melinda tells her story with a wry humour that comes straight out of the uncompromising hardships of life in a fishing village, and what women have to do to support one another. Sheppard shows Melinda's cheerful, pragmatic wisdom to be both heartbreaking and liberating. With its salty flavour and mixture of tragedy, romance, and humour, this is among Canada's best writing for adolescent girls. Highly recommended.

Slade, Arthur. *Draugr*. Northern Frights series. 1997. 171 pages. 12 and up.
Teenaged cousins Sarah, Michael, and Angie come to Gimli, Manitoba, to spend the summer on Grandpa's farm. Grandpa's an avid storyteller: on their first night, he tells stories from his Icelandic heritage, including one about "the draugr," a man who comes back from the dead. It soon appears that a draugr has come to life close to the farm, for a man long dead is now back to seek vengeance on Grandpa.

Slade quickly sets up the simple plot, then cranks up the tension with the introduction of an unknown horror that visits the cabin on the children's second night. The pace quickens, the pages turn, and Northern Frights, the title of the series this book is part of, shows itself to be appropriate. The Icelandic mythology the story is based on will not be familiar to all, but the tension and fast-paced plot will entice teen readers.

Slade, Arthur. *Dust*. 2001. 168 pages. 10 to 14.
It's the Depression on the Prairies, and when seven-year-old Matthew Steelgate accepts a ride with a stranger, he seems to vanish from the face of the earth. But Robert Steelgate can't forget his brother, or stop feeling responsible for his disappearance. When an ivory-skinned man named Harisch appears in town and promises the people not only rain but their heart's desire as well, Robert is strangely repulsed – and also horrified, as he realizes that his parents' involvement with Harisch has made them forget Matthew. Only Robert continues to search for his brother and the other children who have disappeared since Harisch arrived. Robert's search reveals the creepy, dangerous side of the man, who has bewitched children with beautiful butterflies, and adults with promises of a rainmaking machine.

Slade's evocation of the smells, sounds, and feel of the hot dusty prairie is so intense and realistic, it almost seems odd when this tale takes a turn towards the supernatural. The little prairie town of Horshoe is precisely realized, up to and including its formerly boarded-up theatre, the place where Harisch dazzles the townspeople with his magic mirror. The climax of the story, which involves aliens, stretches credulity; but Harisch's mixture of evil and showmanship is truly sinister, and the story's first chapter is guaranteed to arrest the reader's attention.

Slade, Arthur. *Tribes.* **2002. 134 pages. 12 and up.**
When his anthropologist father disappeared from his life, Percy Montmount, Jr., adopted the pseudo-scientific language and approach to life that he considered suitable to an anthropologist "observer." With the help of these observing tactics, he and his friend Elissa are trying to make it through the last few days of the bizarre rituals of their fellow graduands before they leave high school forever. But as the anniversary of the suicide death of Percy's friend Willard approaches, and as Percy tries to resist his feelings for Elissa, he finds that his policy of detachment – sustained partly through ritual self-mutilation – can't keep him from admitting what he's been avoiding: that his father abandoned Percy and his mother for "another woman."

Percy's immersion in anthropological jargon and "observation" is so profound that it's a mental illness: he's pathologically dissociated. Slade certainly conveys this effectively, but Percy's refusal of emotional engagement may eventually dissociate some readers – as it does his friend Elissa. A final breakdown and revelation at the end of the story seems to happen too quickly and neatly; but this is a bold experiment, intriguing if not entirely satisfying.

Stewart, Sharon. *The Minstrel Boy.* **1997. 204 pages. 11 to 14.**
See Novels, 7 to 12.

Taylor, Cora. *Julie.* **1985. 101 pages. 10 to 14.**
See Novels, 7 to 12.

Taylor, Cora. *On Wings of a Dragon.* **2001. 251 pages. 10 to 14.**
See Novels, 7 to 12.

Tingle, Rebecca. *The Edge on the Sword*. **2001. 277 pages. 10 and up.**
See Novels, 7 to 12.

Toten, Teresa. *The Game*. **2001. 208 pages. 12 and up.**
Danielle Webster awakes to find herself in a clinic, recovering from what she can hardly remember: a drug-and-vodka overdose. Slowly, under the care of a messy, gum-chewing therapist – but even more under the care of her tormented but loving roommate "Scratch" and friend Kevin – Dani remembers how it all started, with her slick father's violent "punishments," her mother's passivity, and the need to protect her little sister. As she moves towards reconciliation with her mother, she helps Scratch and Kevin find ways to negotiate their problems, too.

The "forbidden" subjects of physical abuse, homosexuality, and sexual predation will attract some readers simply because they're forbidden; but there's much more than sensationalism here. Edgy, often funny prose is central to what makes this novel stand out – precise, unexpected turns of phrase and turns of character. Toten writes with depth, understatement (irony conveys worlds), and wisdom. "You got to face it," Kevin tells Dani, speaking of her trauma. "And when you get out, you learn how to wear it." There are no false promises here.

Trembath, Don. *The Tuesday Café*. **1996. 121 pages. 11 to 13.**
Harper Winslow has no friends, his parents are too busy to spend time with him, and he has a "bad attitude" at home and school. After he's caught setting fire to school garbage, a judge sentences him to community service and a two-thousand-word essay entitled "How I plan to turn my life around." His mother signs him up for a writing workshop called "The Tuesday Café," not knowing that it is geared towards adults with special needs, learning disabilities, and poor literacy skills. The class isn't what Harper expected, but his fellow classmates and the demands of weekly writing push Harper to a better understanding of himself.

Harper is quick-witted and amusing; he's also confused, frightened, and angry at his parents and school. Through the short essays he writes for The Tuesday Café, we gain insight into Harper's journey towards understanding. Trembath's adults are multi-dimensional; the reader sees that, although they seem busy, in fact they are responsive to Harper's efforts to communicate.

Harper continues with his writing career in *A Fly Named Alfred* (where he writes an anonymous column for the student paper), *A Beautiful Place on Yonge Street* (in which he finds love), and *The Popsicle Journal* (which places Harper working at a real paper).

Valgardson, W. D. *Frances*. **2000. 190 pages. 10 to 14.**
See Novels, 7 to 12.

Wennick, Elizabeth. *Changing Jareth*. **1999. 278 pages. 12 and up.**
Jareth has to undergo a complete psychiatric evaluation after he pulls a switchblade on a classmate. At seventeen, he hasn't had an easy life: his mother drinks, doesn't remember his father's name, and can't hold down a job; his stepbrother is always on the verge of dying; Jareth gets his spending money by breaking into houses. Now, as much as he dislikes the psychiatrist, the thrice-weekly visits force him to think about his life. But when his mother beats his brother so severely that he dies, Jareth begins a downward spiral. His life finally changes when he asks for help from a friend's father, and he is given the opportunity to find himself.

This is a gritty, tough survival story. From the opening chapter, when Jareth and a friend surprise an old man during a break-in and cause him to have a fatal heart attack, we know Jareth's headed for deep trouble. With realistic dialogue and strong supporting characters, Wennick shows that everyone has choices in his or her life. Some of the plot's surprises seem melodramatic, but they reflect the harsh reality of many teens living on the streets. Wennick reminds readers, "It's up to us whether we want to be heroes or villains."

* **Wieler, Diana.** *Bad Boy*. **1989. 191 pages. 12 and up.**
Canada's passion for hockey is in full force in this powerfully written story of a stormy relationship between teenage boys. Life is going well for sixteen-year-old A. J. Brandiosa when he and his best friend, Tully, make it onto a Triple A hockey team. But A.J.'s world crashes down around him when he discovers that Tully is gay. A.J.'s rage and fear are played out during hockey games, and turn him into the "Bad Boy" of the title.

Wieler's writing is taut, tense, and explosive, much like the game she is writing about. Readers, both male and female, will be drawn into the power of the game and the tension between the two friends, a tension heightened by A.J.'s budding relationship with Tully's sister Summer. This is one of few teen novels with a strong gay character who is not confused or ashamed of himself. Wieler explores teenage sexuality with honesty and compassion, while at the same time exploring aggression and violence in hockey. Highly recommended.

Also by this author is ***Drive***.

Wieler, Diana. *Ran Van: The Defender*. 1993. 170 pages. 12 and up.
Rhan uses the name RanVan to enter his name and score on *Stormers*, his favourite video game at the local Rite Store. Nine years before, Rhan's father killed Rhan's mother, then committed suicide. Now Rhan lives with his loving grandmother, the underpaid caretaker of a small apartment building. At school the principal respects Rhan, whom he sees as a "spark, frustrating, troublesome, and yet so bright you can't keep from looking at it." When Thalie, a fellow student, excites Rhan's interest, he decides she needs his help. Thalie lives in an affluent, comfortable neighbourhood, but she's troubled by the presence of her mother's partner – with whom Thalie herself was once involved. Although Thalie doesn't encourage Rhan, in an heroic, almost superheroic gesture, he stands up to defend her.

Wieler writes for teen boys with an energy and brightness that reflects the speed and action of video games. Using the game *Stormers* as a backdrop, Wieler surprises us with the tight connections between the game and Rhan's and Thalie's story. Rhan's grandmother is a strong, appealing character, and Rhan's difficult past gives a layered complexity to his motives and actions. Here's a boy who's both action hero and man of inner depth.

Wieler continues Rhan's story in two more titles: in ***Ran Van: A Worthy Opponent***, Rhan and his grandmother move to Thunder Bay and Rhan has to battle a competitor known as The Iceman; in ***Ran Van: Magic Nation***, Rhan moves to Calgary to study film and finally finds resolution for his aggression in love and a good cause. Wieler's writing is fast and sharp, satisfying "non-readers" and, at the same time, providing literary depth.

Wynne-Jones, Tim. *The Maestro*. **1995. 223 pages. 11 to 14.**
Thanks to the distracting sight of a helicopter ferrying a grand piano over the woods of Northern Ontario, fourteen-year-old Burl Crow escapes a beating. Months later, fleeing his abusive father, Burl comes across the cabin that houses that piano. Starving and bedraggled, he asks the musician who lives there for refuge. The "Maestro" Nog abandons the camp, its piano, and his latest composition to Burl and heads back to the city. When Burl hears that Nog has died, he has to move out – but he finds he's the only person who knows about the famous musician's *magnum opus*. Trying to retrieve it, he arouses the wrath of his father, with disastrous results.

With its violent confrontations and intense evocation of the beauties and savagery of Ontario's wilderness, this has the appeal of a survival story and the potent psychological kick of a father/son contest. Burl's a rare male protagonist in having both inner depth and outdoor survival skills: he's at home scaring off bears, catching fish, and maintaining the cabin. The "Maestro" bears a close resemblance to eccentric Canadian pianist Glenn Gould, but this is really the story of Burl's metamorphosis into manhood. Ideal for boys.

Wynne-Jones, Tim. *Stephen Fair*. **1998. 218 pages. 10 to 14.**
Night after night, fifteen-year-old Stephen wakes in terror, his mind full of images of fire, treehouses, and babies crying. These are the very same nightmares his brother used to have before he left home abruptly, not long after Stephen's father abandoned the family. Why is he haunted by his brother's dreams? Stephen wonders. Why is his mother increasingly distraught? Is she hiding something from him? When Stephen intrudes on an emotional moment in a friend's family, an important memory comes rushing back – and Stephen knows he has to get to the bottom of this painful mystery.

This is a mystery, but it's also an engaging, compassionate portrayal of a boy's struggle with self-knowledge and forgiveness. Wynne-Jones taps into the tricks of the psyche in a way that makes readers think, and his depiction of Stephen's friendship with flamboyant Dom and would-be movie director Virginia celebrates the joys and strengths of peer relationships. Colourful, quirky details abound: Stephen's home is made of trees, wrecking-yard doors, and an old schooner, "like something Noah would have built without God's help." Like all Wynne-Jones's novels, this is satisfying literary fare.

* **Wynne-Jones, Tim.** *The Boy in the Burning House.* **2000. 231 pages. 10 to 14.**
Jim Hawkins's father disappeared a year ago, and Jim has almost put his grief behind him when sixteen-year-old Ruth Rose comes barrelling into his life with a message he'd rather avoid: "Fisher killed your father." As intense and erratic as she is, there's something plausible in Ruth Rose's claim that her stepfather, Fisher, killed Hub Hawkins. And when Jim starts looking into accounts of his father's youth and his history with "Father" Fisher (now an evangelical minister), an unwelcome story emerges. As Jim and Ruth Rose come closer to unravelling the knots of the past, Father Fisher becomes a deadly threat.

Here's a mystery/thriller with style – a perfect choice for kids ready to be weaned off flaccid formulaic series mysteries. Suspenseful, dramatic, a bit hair-raising, this also explores deeper questions: the motives in human choices, the tension between trust and reason, denial, and self-knowledge. Complex emotions, fascinating characters, and a vivid evocation of the setting (a fictional Perth and environs) underlie the thriller action. Wynne-Jones's precise language and clever imagination make this a mystery of unusual literary richness. Highly recommended.

Short Story Collections and Anthologies, 12 and Up

The short story is a perfect genre for adolescents, particularly because of its modernist acceptance of open-endedness and melancholy. Here you'll find some stories that have the satisfying closure of a conventional tale; but mostly these are stories that invite readers to see the significance of certain moments, to reflect on the melancholy of loss, and to celebrate the potent triumphs of emergent adulthood.

* Book, Rick. *Necking with Louise*. 1999. 151 pages. 12 and up.
In linked short stories, Book homes in on seven significant events in sixteen-year-old Eric's bittersweet entry into adulthood. A neighbour's affair, a close hockey game, a night in a blizzard, a long kiss, a first job, each becomes occasion for revelation and emotional growth. Book writes with precise recollection of adolescent feeling – not just of the amazing new pleasures of a first kiss, but of the strange unfamiliarity of a first job with people outside the sphere of childhood experience, or the feeling of surging into powerful control, into adult capacity, outdoors or on the hockey rink.

Subtle and sensual, the stories evoke the traumas of the mid 1960s and at the same time, recreate the smells and sounds and facts of prairie life – specifically life on a Saskatchewan farm – in ways that can only come from one rooted in an intense familiarity with it.

Outstanding reading, good for adolescent boys and girls. Highly recommended.

Brooks, Martha. *Traveling On into the Light and Other Stories.*
1994. 146 pages. 12 and up.
Brooks best describes these stories: "Each story is a window on the
lives of young people who are trying to reach the light. Each finds
the path lit through various means: the kindness of strangers; the powerful support of friends, family or lovers; the sanctity of a safe place
from which personal dragons can finally be faced." Brooks's beautiful
writing seems to reach a deep, quiet place within each of us. In every
story a character faces a serious issue, from Sam, whose father has just
announced he's gay and moved to Santa Fe with his lover, to Jamie,
who is coming to terms with his father's suicide.

Readers of Brooks's earlier title, *Two Moons in August* (*see* Novels,
12 and Up), will be delighted to discover three stories that continue the
tale of Sidonie and Kieran. The story "The Kindness of Strangers"
introduces Henry Olsen and Laker Wyatt, who become the main characters of Brooks's later novel *Being with Henry* (*see* Novels, 12 and
Up). Brooks's earlier collection of equally beautiful and outstanding
short stories is *Paradise Café and Other Stories*.

De Lint, Charles. *Waifs and Strays.* **2002. 394 pages. 12 and up.**
Sixteen short stories, gleaned from various periods in De Lint's
writing career, are brought together in this collection, which serves as
a useful introduction to De Lint's fantasy and science-fiction works.
From remarkable happenings in the Ottawa Valley to the Faerie realms
at the edge of a futuristic "Bordertown," De Lint represents adolescent
protagonists coming to terms with their pasts, forging new identities,
or finding their way into a world of magic. Although De Lint's writing
is uneven, these stories leave the reader with memorable images – of
streets ruled by gang fights and Celtic music, or of trees and caves that
give way into shimmering Faerie realms. Celtic mythology and folklore provides the backbone of much of De Lint's imaginings.

Many additional titles by De Lint, among them *The Dreaming
Place* and *The Riddle of the Wren*, are available.

* Ellis, Sarah. *Back of Beyond: Stories.* **1996. 159 pages. 11 and up.**
See Short Story Collections and Anthologies, 7 to 12.

Hughes, Monica, ed. *What If . . . ? Amazing Stories.* **1998. 199 pages. 11 to 14.**
See Short Story Collections and Anthologies, 7 to 12.

Lewis, Wendy. *Graveyard Girl – Stories.* **2000. 189 pages. 12 and up.**
In 1982 Miss Twitchett arranged for students at Lee High School to act out the Royal Wedding of Prince Charles and Princess Diana. In 1999, one of the students unearths a photograph of the event, prompting this series of linked stories, told in the voices of the students who participated. Ten stories, five set in 1983 and five in 1993, explore the complicated emotions and pivotal moments in the lives of the teenagers: a popular hockey star doesn't make it with a girl he admires; a teen mom makes peace with her own mother; a resentful adolescent comes to recognize her love for her half-sister – and more.

Engaging, believable characters and rewarding, read-between-the-lines confessions make this a satisfying read. Although the stories are not all equally sharp, this is a strong collection, and it brings to light issues and feelings common to adolescent experience.

Lunn, Janet, ed. *The Unseen: Scary Stories.* **1994. 171 pages. 10 and up.**
See Short Story Collections and Anthologies, 7 to 12.

* Musgrave, Susan, ed. *Nerves Out Loud: Critical Moments in the Lives of Seven Teen Girls.* **2001. 112 pages. 12 and up.**
Seven established women writers write of youthful incidents that have had enduring emotional impact on their identities as writers and women. Melanie Little recalls the moment she quit competitive skating; Marnie Woodrow, her first kiss (with a girl); Karen Rivers, the "white hot anger, a raging hatred" she felt for her own body. Madeleine Thien recalls the moment her father returned to his native Thailand, and Susan Musgrave, 1967, the Summer of Love. Carellin Brooks remembers her feelings of helplessness as she negotiated around the advances of a sexually predatory foster father. In a heartbreakingly funny story, MK Quednau addresses her high-school English teacher, who advised her to telephone Morley Callaghan for advice on what to study in order to become a writer.

The lostness and uncertainty of each of these girls is palpable; the restrained, powerfully articulate stories map the moment of transformation from passivity to agency with candour and openness. These brave voices will comfort and inspire teenaged girls, not only in showing that survival is possible, but in celebrating the saving power of language. Excellent fare. Highly recommended.

A subsequent anthology edited by Musgrave, *You Be Me: Friendship in the Lives of Teen Girls*, doesn't have the same breath-taking punch. However, stories by Gayla Reid and Lydia Kwa are particularly potent, and the embarrassments and confusions of popularity versus friendship in many of the others will strike a chord with early adolescents.

Valgardson, W. D. *The Divorced Kids Club and Other Stories*. 1999. 184 pages. 10 to 14.
See Short Story Collections and Anthologies, 7 to 12.

Wilson, Budge. *The Leaving: Stories*. 1990. 207 pages. 11 and up.
This collection includes nine portraits of young women growing up in Nova Scotia. Taken together, the stories challenge readers to think about life from multiple perspectives. In one story, a girl confides her disturbance over her changing body to her pen pal, only to find he's a boy. In "The Leaving," a twelve-year-old girl is awakened by her mother at 3:00 a.m. and told they must leave the impoverished family farm. Having acquired *The Feminine Mystique* from a Salvation Army box, Ma now wants to "do some thinkin'," so she takes her daughter to Halifax for a respite. Eventually, they return to the farm; Ma, who has been treated like a drudge by her husband and sons, doesn't expect many changes, but insists that her husband now call her by name. Slowly her requests for respect and help are rewarded with minimal gestures from her family. This, and indeed each of the stories here, catches the reader with its arresting honesty.

Wilson writes with power, grace, and humour. The characters in this collection have strong voices, speak out on many different issues, and reveal emotions that will move and touch readers. Subsequent collections by Wilson include *Cordelia Clark* and *Fractures*, both excellent reading.

Wynne-Jones, Tim. *The Book of Changes: Stories.* **1994. 143 pages. 10 to 14.**
See Short Story Collections and Anthologies, 7 to 12.

* **Wynne-Jones, Tim.** *Some of the Kinder Planets.* **1993. 136 pages. 9 and up.**
See Short Story Collections and Anthologies, 7 to 12.

Non-Fiction

C anadian non-fiction for children deserves a guide in itself; here we have listed only a few titles that are particularly well written, or of subject matter so fascinating that they are likely to catch the interest of otherwise-reluctant readers – or to woo avid readers of fiction into the rich and varied world of information.

Anderson, Lil. *Beavers Eh to Bea: Tales from a Wildlife Rehabilitator.* **2000. 178 pages. 10 and up.**
This book isn't just about beavers. It's the true story of a woman who, through referrals from the Ontario Ministry of Natural Resources, vet clinics, and the Humane Society, helps abandoned or injured wildlife in Northern Ontario. Her life as the daughter of a trapper and her job as a fish-and-wildlife technician have given her both the passion and the background for wildlife rehabilitation.

Anderson describes her work with beaver kits, and also with orphaned or abandoned fawns, eagles, hawks, and squirrels. She describes how animals die because of the deadly but well-intentioned kindness of ignorant humans, and teaches readers about the needs of various orphans. The story of beavers Eh and Bea is fascinating and reveals much of beaver life. A few colour photographs in the centre of the book add interest. Directed towards those interested in wildlife, Anderson's account is gripping and convincing.

Archbold, Rick. *Canada, Our History: An Album through Time.*
2000. 160 pages. 8 to 11.
Archbold presents fifteen events that occurred between 1900 and 2000,
describing them through the eyes of fictional children who "were
there." What was it like to be a little Polish girl travelling to Canada in
1905? Or a kid caught up in the great Winnipeg strike? A child on a
school trip to "Quintland" to see the famous quintuplets, or the brother
of an FLQ member in 1970?

A miscellany of photographs old and new supports the fifteen
stories, providing images of the event and supplementary information –
like the brief insert on Wayne and Shuster in the chapter "Off to War."
At about ten pages each, and with fairly large print, these are digestible
by young children and provide a good supplement to some of the series
of historical fiction that are currently popular. Stories range from
"Potlatch Village" on the west coast to the Halifax explosion on the
east, from an immigrant story in 1905 to an e-mail exchange about
millennial celebrations. While he makes no pretence towards exhaus-
tiveness, Archbold offers an engaging view of some of the memorable
events that made and marred Canada's last century.

Archibald, Jo-ann, Val Friesen, Jeff Smith, and Shirley Sterling,
eds. *Courageous Spirits: Aboriginal Heroes of Our Children.* **1993.**
172 pages. 9 and up.
The stories collected here are the winners of the 1992 Aboriginal Heroes
Contest held across Canada for school children of Aboriginal ancestry
(First Nations, Indian, Métis, Inuit, Treaty and Non-treaty). Children
were invited to write stories, poems, or essays on Aboriginal people
who inspired and encouraged them in their own cultural identities; the
winning entries are here laced together with a Trickster theme by
Shirley Sterling.

Sitting Bull, Chief Dan George, and Thayendagea each have a part
here, but pride of place is reserved for mothers, fathers, grandfathers,
and especially grandmothers. From elders who inspire simply by their
love and integrity to those who have gone out into the world to achieve
for the benefit of their Aboriginal community, the children remember
significant lessons taught and learned. "That's what I call a hero," one

girl concludes after telling of her Inuit aunt's repeated relocation by the authorities, "putting up with the government." "All rain is glory," a young woman's Cree great-grandfather is remembered saying. Dogrib, Salish, Cree, Ojibwa, Chippewa, Mi'kmaq – Aboriginal heroes from all across Canada, north and south, come alive in these often-childish accounts. For Aboriginal readers, this is a proud statement of cultural identity; for others, it provides valuable insight into a current, and often invisible, world. Probably most successfully read in conjunction with an adult.

Bailey, Linda. Illustr. Bill Slavin. *Good Times Travel Agency.* **2000– . 48 pages. 8 to 10.**
See Series Books.

Baillie, Marilyn, and Catherine Ripley. *The Anti-Boredom Book.* **2000. 128 pages. 6 to 12.**
The editors of *OWL* and *Chickadee* magazines compile some of the best activities that have been published in these well-known magazines and present them in a lively, fun book. Contents are divided into four sections – Magic, Kitchen, Party, and Outdoor Fun – with fourteen activities in each. Bright, colourful photos of children engaged in the creation or enjoyment of the project make each activity enticing. The tricks, instructions, and necessary tools are carefully explained. Activities include making pizzas, creating a volcano, mind-reading, and even some giggle games. The book is perfect for a child who finds reading boring, for the wealth of activities collected here is certain to include something to pique the interest and encourage reading.

Bannatyne-Cugnet, Jo. Illustr. Son Nan Zhang. *From Far and Wide: A Canadian Citizenship Scrapbook.* **2000. 24 pages. 6 and up.**
Not strictly non-fiction, this work by Bannatyne-Cugnet and Zhang takes a look at the power of Canadian citizenship in the story of Xiao Ling Li, who documents the day she and her family got their citizenship in a scrapbook for her soon-to-be-born sibling. Xiao's family join thirty-six people from thirteen different countries when they receive their Canadian citizenship at Xiao's public school.

Zhang depicts, in photograph-like illustrations, the events of this thrilling day. The scrapbook includes images of the ceremony, snapshots taken at school, the handwritten oath of citizenship in both official languages, and pictures from the celebration afterwards. The book is a tribute to the many new Canadians who choose Canada as their home. The author includes information on the history of Canadian citizenship, the process of application, and the words to the national anthem.

Batten, Jack. *The Man Who Ran Faster Than Everyone: The Story of Tom Longboat*. **2002. 104 pages. 10 and up.**
An Onondaga from the Six Nations reserve near Brantford, Ontario, Longboat distinguished himself by winning numerous prizes in world-class races, including the Boston marathon, from 1907 to 1920. Batten describes Longboat's childhood and early racing – running was something he did for fun – and gives a dynamic account of the suspenseful wins and losses of his career. Longboat's love of running comes through loud and clear; so too does the shameless condescension and hypocrisy with which he was treated by his white managers. With a clever, critical eye, Batten shows that we only know Longboat the "outsider" by judicious reading between the lines. This doesn't just offer up a clear, sensitive, and highly readable sports biography; it also introduces children to the notion that we have to read the media with a certain amount of scepticism and analysis. With numerous photographs.

Bowers, Vivien. Illustr. Martha Newbigging. *Crime Science*. **1997. 64 pages. 10 to 12.**
In direct, lively prose Bowers describes modern techniques of crime investigation, including matching evidence, identifying forgeries and criminals, and tracking computer hackers. Clear explanations of the problems and techniques are accompanied by short accounts of particular crimes in which the techniques proved successful in convicting the criminal. Occasional activities and "Clue In" quizzes are also included. Photographs and comic drawings enliven and elucidate the information. As this has substantial text per page, it's likely to appeal most to a reading child already interested in the material.

Bowers, Vivien. Illustr. Dianne Eastman and Dan Hobbs. *Wow Canada! Exploring This Land from Coast to Coast.* **1999. 160 pages. 8 to 11.**
In this bright, lighthearted fictional and factual travelogue, scrapbook, and guide, twelve-year-old Guy records routes, stops, mishaps, and more on his family's trip across Canada – including visits to the Northwest, Nunavut, and Yukon territories. Guy describes the trip of the day, not failing to mention pillow fights and lame puns made en route. The scrapbook element shows souvenir and family photographs (even of a paper bowl of *poutine*), postcards, stamps, snacks, napkins used as notepaper, necklaces, feathers . . . you name it. E-mails and letters to friends give more information as do repeated "Food I Was Introduced to for My Own Good" napkins and handwritten "Exceedingly Weird" fact memos and survival tips.

This very busy, magazine-like production is chock full of information about every province and territory in Canada. Based on a real family trip, it gives a good sense not only of the ups and downs of cross-country car travel, but of the on-the-ground expanse and variety of the nation.

Bradford, Karleen. *Animal Heroes.* **2000. 160 pages. 8 to 11.**
In five-to-eight-page accounts Bradford tells of pets who have saved lives under extraordinary circumstances. Most of the stories are about dogs – especially German shepherds – but a polar bear, a rabbit, and even a pig show their remarkable alertness and care for other creatures. From the Nimpkish River on northern Vancouver Island, where a three-legged Labrador retriever pulls both owner and boat from the water, to Lethbridge, Newfoundland, where a German shepherd retrieves a boy from a bicycle accident, these stories cover much of the breadth of Canada.

Bradford doesn't dramatize the accounts but reports them in a straightforward, factual voice. This is likely to appeal to children who already like animals, not to win converts. Because of its anecdotal nature, it's a good choice for children who find a novel-length text hard to get through.

Caswell, Maryanne. Illustr. Lindsay Grater. *Pioneer Girl.* **2001. 82 pages. 8 to 11.**

Pioneer Girl comprises the letters of a real pioneer, fourteen-year-old Maryanne, who, between April 1887 and January 1888, wrote diligently to her grandmother as her family journeyed from Palmerston, Ontario, to Clark's Crossing, Saskatchewan – or the North-West Territory as it was at the time. The long train journey, the struggles to make a success of a farm on the prairie, the funny and frightening happenings of homesteader life, are here recorded by an actual nineteenth-century adolescent.

Maryanne writes in an elegant, evenly paced prose, understating emotion so that her few emotional comments are all the more meaningful. "Sometimes we do get lonesome, Grandma," she says simply at the end of an account of a week haying with only her father. Once she concludes a letter, "There's beauty here, Grandma." Technical matters, practical adventures – a broken axle, runaway stock, a turkey who steps in the porridge, and even a lost mother – are as engaging as those recorded in historical fiction. A nice companion-piece for those girls caught up in the popular series of "historical" diaries.

Cooper, John. *Rapid Ray: The Story of Ray Lewis.* **2002. 144 pages. 10 and up.**

Born in Hamilton in 1910, Ray Lewis grew up sprinting in the streets for fun, and went on to become a champion runner for his high school. As a young man, he won a bronze medal in the 4 x 440 relay at the 1932 Olympics, and a silver medal in the mile relay at the 1934 British Empire Games (now the Commonwealth Games). The first African-Canadian ever to compete in either Games, Lewis was awarded the Order of Canada in 2001.

Aside from being an eminently readable tale of victory, this is also a social history of an aspect of Canadian culture that's usually hidden from children but is still painfully relevant. Lewis recalls events no one speaks of – such as the day the Ku Klux Klan paraded through Hamilton, to no public outcry – and describes, with quiet dignity, the racial intolerance he met at every step of his journey. A description of the black community in Hamilton, the humiliating and sometimes funny incidents Lewis encountered working as a porter for the CPR, and anecdotes about more recent encounters with racism, make for rich and rewarding reading.

Drake, Jane, and Ann Love. Illustr. Jocelyne Bouchard. *The Kids Book of the Far North.* **2000. 48 pages. 8 to 11.**
Drake and Love choose a geographical rather than a human boundary for their look at the Far North; here the Arctic tree line becomes the defining feature. Eight countries claim part of the Far North above the tree line, but this book makes clear that the exigencies of shared climate, landscape, and vegetation in the polar region are more decisive and enduring than differences arising from political borders.

Generously illustrated, with short paragraphs and some information in point form, this informative work has the appeal of a picture book and will attract younger children who enjoy non-fiction. The environment, plant, and animal life, the ancient peoples, the natural resources, and current "everyday life" are all part of this global treatment. Descriptions of ancient reindeer herders and early Arctic hunters, as well as information on life in Nenets, Inupiat, and Inuit communities today, present the Far North as a place of ancient and continuing culture and habitation, not just the object of expansion and exploration, as it is often treated. "Ecowatch" inserts alert readers to the ominous effects of southern culture and of industry – Chernobyl, PCBs, pesticides, and global warming.

Ellis, Sarah. *The Young Writer's Companion.* **1999. 128 pages. 8 to 12.**
Anecdotes, quotations, and little facts ("It was not unusual for Lewis Carroll to write thirteen letters a day") abound in this book of advice and inspiration for kids who write. From Islands to Family Stories, Newspaper Clippings to Dreams, Ellis supplies sensible, accessible ideas about how to let your imagination and pencil fly. Blank, lined pages in each chapter are an invitation to write now; comments and information on well-known writers for children (Susan Cooper, R. L. Stevenson, L. M. Montgomery) demonstrate how successful stories can have small beginnings. Each section ends with a list of novels related to the chapter's themes, so this also works as a reader's companion.

Englander, Anrenee. *Dear Diary, I'm Pregnant: Teenagers Talk about Their Pregnancy.* **1997. 160 pages. 13 and up.**
In this frank and important book, Englander interviews ten pregnant teens and records their stories of pregnancy, abortion, adoption, and raising babies. These true stories and honest voices have an immediacy that is gripping. The stories are not limited to discussions of pregnancy and the decisions that surround it, but include relationships with mothers and sisters, families, in-laws, boyfriends, and fathers. The young women consider the future of their newborns. The ease with which these teens got pregnant will surprise readers – just as it surprised a few of the young women who were on the Pill, but didn't understand how it worked. The strength of this book lies in the fact that it doesn't preach, but simply offers the stories of teen pregnancies and discusses options open to each girl.

This is a powerful tool and can be used for guidance and support for all teens, pregnant or not. An excellent final entry is entitled, "You are pregnant – Now what?" It offers further help to pregnant readers facing difficult decisions.

Farris, Katherine, ed. *You Asked? Over 300 Great Questions and Astounding Answers.* **1996. 160 pages. 8 and up.**
Readers of *OWL* sent hundreds of questions into the magazine over the twenty-year period preceding the publication of this book. Farris has compiled three hundred of the most frequently asked questions and their answers in this one compendium, which includes chapters on the working of the human body, on science and technology, and on space and wildlife. Why do we have hair? How do reflectors work? Why do boats have round windows instead of square ones? Each question is answered in a succinct paragraph; information is clear, thorough, and straightforward. Full-colour photographs or cartoon-like illustrations enliven every page. This is a good book for curious minds to dip into; it is also a likely choice for readers who are discouraged by vast quantities of text. Includes material from previously published *I Didn't Know That!* and *Would You Believe It?*

Gorrell, Gena. *Heart and Soul: The Story of Florence Nightingale.* **2000. 146 pages. 11 and up.**
The insipid image of "the lady with the lamp" is put to rest in this comprehensive account of Florence Nightingale and her achievements. "The real Florence was a difficult, demanding woman," the author says, "driven by frustration, by resentment, by outrage at the wrongness she saw around her." Gorrell stresses the agony Florence endured as a girl and a young woman, when her family refused to let her to work and instead insisted that she stay home, wait on her sister, and make conversation. The spirit and determination with which she finally launched into reforming hospital and nursing practices during the Crimean War come through searingly. Quotes from Nightingale's copious letters show how she continued to organize, reform, and write all her life, hoping to improve the treatment of the wounded and the sick, fighting passionately against complacent and ineffectual male authorities.

With background information on Victorian culture and mores, and numerous supporting photographs and engravings, this biography gives readers an unforgettable insight into the restrictions and problems of the time. Gorrell's prose is clear and readable; although this looks like a history book, readers who persevere will be galvanized by the story.

Granfield, Linda. *Cowboy: A Kid's Album.* **1993. 96 pages. 9 and up.**
Everything anyone ever wanted to know and more of the truth and myths about cowboys, cowgirls, their history and future is covered in this fascinating book. Here is information to appeal to all interests: the history, language, and life of cowboys, the famous men and women in the field such as Calamity Jane and Nat Love, or actors Tom Mix and Will Rogers, recommended films, the history of clothing (including Levi's), the Calgary Stampede, and the life of modern cowboys. Granfield explores the often-neglected contributions of women, Native, and African-American cowboys, and discusses the stereotypes that have been perpetuated in films and literature. Sidebars with information about songs, clothes, horses, rifles, food, and Prairie Nymphs (saloon dancers) enhance the appeal of the book.

Granfield's simple text supports her elaborate use of memorabilia and archival photos in sepia, colour, or black and white. Illustrations also include movie stills, famous paintings, advertisements, and original illustrations. Good for drawing in reluctant readers. ***Born to Be a Cowgirl***, by Candace Savage (see below) is a good companion piece to this volume.

Granfield, Linda. Illustr. Janet Wilson. *In Flanders Fields: The Story of the Poem by John McCrae*. 1995. 32 pages. 9 to 12.
Many children know the famous poem "In Flanders Fields"; few have any familiarity with its history or setting. Granfield interweaves information about soldiers' lives in the trenches of the First World War, the causes of the war, and the story of Canadian medical officer and poet John McCrae, with the text of McCrae's famous poem. Wilson interprets the impact of the war in some of her finest work to date. Her impressive paintings show scenes on battlefields, hospitals, and graveyards, as well as those in more intimate settings, such as a bedroom in which we see a woman crying, a letter in her hand. Posters, postcards, photographs, and other artifacts are included throughout the book and enhance its immediacy. An excellent aid for parents and teachers discussing war and its effects.

Granfield, Linda. *Circus*. 1997. 96 pages. 9 and up.
Starting with the birth of the circus, or at least the first documented interest in animal and acrobatic acts, in ancient Egypt, Granfield explores the history, growth, life, and romance of the circus and the people associated with it. Although eminently browseable, the rich, intriguing detail makes this a work that demands to be read from cover to cover. Topics range from circus lore from the Roman writer Juvenalis – who said that people want "bread and circuses" – to controversies about sideshow curiosities and animal treatment, and Granfield explores each with compassion and understanding. She includes discussion of Canada's contributions to the circus, from Andrew King (who became one of the world's leading circus-poster printers) to the phenomenally successful Cirque du Soleil.

Granfield has researched and compiled an amazing array of photographs and archival material to illustrate the book. Old black-and-white photographs, circus posters both North American and international, newspaper clippings, postcards, and art by Tissot enhance the reading throughout. Manifold details – why clowns have red noses, how pink lemonade came to be – captivate readers. Older readers might want to read *Ghost Boy* by Iain Lawrence (*see* Novels, 7 to 12) for a fictional account of circus life.

Granfield, Linda. *Pier 21: Gateway of Hope.* **2000. 32 pages. 8 to 13.**
Halifax's Pier 21 was the main gateway for immigrants to Canada from 1928 until 1971. Granfield has documented its history in this brief but fascinating work – like a museum exhibit in book form. Black-and-white photographs, documents, and other memorabilia illustrate the conditions, and the joy, fear, and consternation immigrants experienced as they arrived in Canada. Pier 21 was not only the entry point for new immigrants, it was the dock where "guest children" (evacuees) arrived from Britain during the Second World War; it was also the departure point for many troops heading overseas. Photographs show joy on the faces of many "war brides," and concern on the faces of the many displaced persons who entered Canada as refugees. Granfield provides historical notes and interesting tidbits of information – such as the fact that Immigration Canada changed its rules after the arrival of *The Walnut* (built to hold 40 passengers) with its 347 refugees. *Pier 21* is a unique work, focusing on the point of entry for over one million immigrants, 100,000 refugees, and 50,000 war brides who immigrated to Canada.

Greenwood, Barbara. Illustr. Heather Collins. *A Pioneer Story: The Daily Life of a Canadian Family in 1840.* **1994. 240 pages. 8 to 12.**
Fiction, non-fiction, and numerous black-and-white illustrations are drawn together in the story of the Robertsons – Ma, Pa, Granny, and six children – a pioneer family in the backwoods of Ontario in 1840. Fictional anecdotes about the features of their daily life and the highlights of their year alternate with pages and sidebars that give factual historical information pertinent to each chapter. Thus Greenwood's story gives narrative flow to what is otherwise a history text. For example, in one chapter, Sarah and Will find a bee tree with their uncle; information about techniques they would have used to calm the bees and retrieve the honey and wax follow the story, along with recipes, remedies, and information about which bees and buzzing insects sting.

The non-fiction element of the text is extensive and thorough. Instructions and clear diagrams for craft activities are also included. Greenwood makes the information sound fascinating; Collins's informative drawings bring each member of the Robertson family realistically to life.

Greenwood, Barbara. Illustr. Heather Collins. *The Last Safe House: A Story of the Underground Railroad*. 1998. 119 pages. 8 to 12.
In this combination of fact and fiction, Greenwood alternates pages of information with the fictional story of the Jacksons, slaves fleeing the southern United States, and the Reids, a family in St. Catharine's, Ontario, a community that sheltered hundreds of escaped slaves. Two young girls, one from each family, are brought together and foil the attempts of an evil slave-catcher. Greenwood makes the reader feel the impact of slavery not only upon the freed slaves, but also on a household that supported them. Pages of information include maps, activities, and biographies of important figures of the time.

Collins's illustrations are in black and white, but the paper is sepia-coloured, giving the book an air of age. Collins brings Greenwood's characters vividly to life; she also provides simple, clear instructions for making the suggested crafts (such as a cornhusk doll).

Harrison, Ted. *Children of the Yukon*. 1977. 5 to 8.
See Picture Books.

Hegedus, Alannah, and Kaitlin Rainey. Illustr. Bill Slavin. *Shooting Hoops and Skating Loops: Great Inventions in Sports*. 1999; *Bleeps and Blips to Rocket Ships: Great Inventions in Communications*. 2001. 88 pages each. 9 and up.
These two books on inventions showcase the work of Canadians and show how Canada managed to play a critical, innovative role in sports and communications. The authors don't limit themselves to Canadian inventions, but demonstrate too that Canadians played pivotal roles in discoveries and inventions developed elsewhere. For example, the chapter on newspapers contains information on Mary Shadd, a free black from Delaware, who moved to Canada and became the first black

newspaper woman in North America. The story of William Samuel Stephenson, born in Manitoba and known as the spy Intrepid, is included not only for his work on the wirephoto, but also because of his research on cryptography, and for his school for secret agents near Oshawa during the Second World War. Both books are full of fascinating, digestible tidbits of information, and they are informative enough to be used as resources for school projects. Colour sketches by Slavin, suggestions for simple activities, and a complete index make the books essential for schools, and for children interested in inventions.

Lang, Audrey. Illustr. Wayne Lynch. *Nature Babies* **series. 2001– . ca. 36 pages. 4 to 8.**
Each of these titles discusses the growth and maturation of a baby animal from birth up until its first steps towards independence. Lang describes in simple language the eating habits, behaviour, and environment of the animal; Lynch illustrates the information with photographs taken in the wild. Lynch's lucid pictures capture moments of interaction and quirky expressions, and the baby creatures (most of them furry or downy) are endearing and sometimes funny. Both entertaining and informative, these are excellent books not just for children interested in animals, but also for those beginning to develop reading fluency.

Titles include *Baby Bear*, *Baby Penguin*, *Baby Fox*, and *Baby Seal*.

* Lemieux, Michèle. *Stormy Night.* **Trans. from German. 1999. 240 pages. 9 and up.**
See Novels, 7 to 12.

Levine, Karen. *Hana's Suitcase.* **2002. 111 pages. 10 and up.**
This unusual story from the Holocaust begins with a persistent curator's quest to find a girl named Hana Brady, whose name is painted on a suitcase donated by the Auschwitz Museum to the Holocaust Centre in Tokyo. Driven by the interest of children, curator Fumiko Ishioka pursued the clues on the suitcase until she eventually discovered all she could about Hana's short life, from her deportation from Moravia, at age eleven, to Terezin and thence to Auschwitz, where she was murdered. But even as she learned of Hana's tragic death, Ishioka found

that Hana had had a brother, George, who had survived, and is now living in Toronto.

The story of George's open-hearted response to Ishioka's inquiries is deeply moving; reminiscences and family photographs that he supplied make Hana poignantly real for readers. The story alternates between the account of Hana's life before and after deportation, and Ishioka's quest to learn about her, so that children know, even while they read of Hana's pleasures, that she did not survive the camps. George Brady's still-current grief is palpable. This is one of the more useful and honest contributions to material for children about the Holocaust – without the mandatory happy ending of fiction, and with the reminder of an ongoing heritage of bereavement.

* **Little, Jean.** *Little by Little*. **1987. 233 pages;** *Stars Come Out Within*. **1990. 263 pages. 10 and up.**
Canadian children's writer Little is honest, funny, and moving in these books about her remarkable life. Visually impaired from birth, Little describes the ridicule and difficulties of her childhood growing up in Taiwan, as well as the love and joy she found within her family. She recounts passionately the world of her imagination and the beginnings of her own writing in *Little by Little*. Little's sight deteriorates as she ages in *Stars Come Out Within*: she tells how she is looking at the night sky with friends when she discovers that she can no longer see the stars. It is literature that allows her to see them again, "Inside my head, the stars had pricked out one by one . . . the Talking Book Library had given me back my lost stars."

Little's passion for literature and writing is felt throughout both books. She shares her thrill at being published, the joy at introducing literature to children while teaching, the delight at being recognized as an author, and then her fear that she will be unable to write as she loses her vision. Those familiar with her many books will be pleased to read the background to her stories; those who don't know her fiction and poetry will be inspired to look for it after reading this moving auto-biography. Little's frank and often funny stories provide an opportunity for her readers to understand her. Now we wait for the next instalment. Highly recommended.

Lunn, Janet, and Christopher Moore. Illustr. Alan Daniel. *The Story of Canada.* **1992; rev. 2000. 325 pages. 10 to 15.**
Lunn and Moore's highly readable history of Canada begins with life in the Ice Age and concludes with celebrations for the Millennium. In ten chapters, the authors give a clear, fluent account of Canada's first peoples, early European incursions, European settlement, conflict, and the eventual emergence of the nation. Several chapters deal with changes brought about in the nineteenth and twentieth centuries, from the building of the railway to the signing of the North American Free Trade Agreement. The book is liberally illustrated with photographs and ephemera, as well as Daniel's full-colour and often dramatic paintings – exciting, and excited, images of conflict and action. Interesting anecdotes, as well as a breezy, confident style, make this one of those rare history texts that a child will actually read through on her or his own. Material on the late twentieth century is, perhaps predictably, rather scattered, but the authors are careful to point out some of the more significant areas of uncertainty (such as environmental degradation) that are our legacy.

Lynch, Wayne. *The Scoop on Poop! The Fascinating Science of How Animals Use Poop.* **2001. 32 pages. 8 to 12.**
Poop is fascinating stuff, according to Lynch, and no doubt readers of this light science book will quickly agree. Lynch's language will be of instant appeal to some children: his chapter headings include "Poop Tarts" and "The Power of Poop," with sub-headings "Turd Tricks" and "Looking like a Turd." While the language is colloquial, the science is sound, and Lynch's photographs are excellent. Apart from its shock value, the information here will have children considering the amazing complexities of the biological world and should pique their interest. Lynch's lively, amusing text and photography show that animals and humans use poop in quite surprising ways.

Mackay, Claire. Illustr. Bill Dickson. *First Folks and Vile Voyagers: Horrible Canadian Histories.* **2001. 172 pages. 9 and up.**
"Once there were brave, foolish, heroic, cowardly, adventurous, cruel, greedy, romantic, determined, nutty and magnificent people – and they

did unbelievable, terrible, splendid and awesome stuff," states Mackay, and she proves her point in this lighthearted look at Canada's early history. "Crabby Chronology I" begins with the Last Ice Age and quickly moves to the "First Folks" (native peoples) and some of their stories, including The Legend of Dekanahwideh and the origin of the expression "bury the hatchet." The "Vile Voyageurs" include the Norse, English, and French; the book concludes at the end of the 1600s.

Mackay provides an excellent mix of authentic Canadian history with amusing, and often hilarious, asides. Timelines and even quizzes challenge and delight readers throughout. Everything is fodder for amusement here: when Mackay provides the "Skinny on Scalping," she traces scalping history back to the Persian times, pointing out that not all North American tribes practised it and that, in time, even white preachers encouraged it. Instead of an illustration, we see the caption "TOO GRUESOME TO CARTOON!" Dickson's cartoons add to the humour. While the book is wacky and silly, the core of the text is the very real Canadian history that children often think is boring.

MacKinnon, Christy. *Silent Observer***. 1993. 42 pages. 6 to 9.**
Born in 1889, Christy MacKinnon lost her hearing because of a serious illness when she was two. In adulthood, she became a successful illustrator, and after her death, a relative found this written and visual account of her childhood on Cape Breton Island. MacKinnon describes growing up on a farm with her seven brothers and sisters, living with her grandparents after her mother died, the pleasures of getting a stepmother, and, finally, the difficulty of leaving at age eleven for the residential school for the deaf in Halifax.

Speaking frankly of the difficulties and grief her deafness caused her, MacKinnon tells also of funny situations and family love. Here too is an appreciation for sign language and for the people who made a particular effort to communicate well. This book conveys a great deal about deaf experience, sign language, and the limits of speech; it reveals just as much about life at the time. MacKinnon writes with gentle humour and warmth, and this unique, charming account of growing up deaf negotiates the highly charged issues of deaf education with grace.

Maybarduk, Linda. *The Dancer Who Flew: A Memoir of Rudolf Nureyev.* **1999. 180 pages. 10 and up.**
A personal friend of Nureyev, Maybarduk writes with affection about this brilliant dancer, who for three decades dominated the world of ballet. Beginning with Nureyev's poverty-stricken childhood, she follows his study of ballet, rise to stardom, then super-stardom, his defection, and, ultimately, his death in 1993. Maybarduk writes from the inner circle of dancers who were encouraged and inspired by Nureyev, but she doesn't shy away from describing the difficult aspects of his personality. She shows him to be a remarkable dancer, but also a caring, troubled man – one who "would never leave the spotlight of his own free will." "His legendary curtain calls were like an additional last act of the ballet – sometimes a very long last act," she writes wryly. She handles his death from AIDS gracefully, sharing her own memories of his last days.

Nureyev comes across as both superstar and flawed human. This biography is useful not just in showing balletomanes another side of their hero, but in giving children a clear introduction to the concept of citizenship, artistic freedom, and the conditions in the U.S.S.R. at the time of Nureyev's youth.

Meikle, Margaret. Illustr. Tina Holdcroft. *Funny You Should Ask.* **1998. 156 pages. 9 and up.**
Meikle, formerly "The Answer Lady" of the "Gabereau" show on CBC, answers 115 (and a half) questions, including queries about animals, our bodies, food, science, sports, time, and more. Why can't you tickle yourself? Do slugs have any purpose? What did we use before toilet paper? The questions are wide-ranging and varied; Meikle's answers are clear, succinct, and to the point. These bits of information cater to short attention spans, various curiosities, and easy digestion. A good bathroom book.

Merritt, Susan E. *Her Story: Women From Canada's Past. I, II,* **and** *III.* **1993. ca. 171 pages. 11 and up.**
Brief biographies of sixteen strong women from Canada's past make up each of the three volumes in this series. Paragraph headings help

make the information visually accessible; numerous photographs illustrate each of the entries. The women represented span the period from the mid 1600s to the 1980s, and they are of either First Nations, African, or European heritage. Thanadelthur, Molly Brant, and Shawnadithit are featured in the first volume, along with reformers Emily Stowe, Emily Murphy, Nellie McClung, and others. The second and third volumes feature less familiar but equally enterprising figures.

Merritt's mini-biographies are clear and readable; backgrounds on the social issues, historical circumstances, and cultural restrictions of the times are succinct and useful. Photographs of women who represent the various First Nations accompany Merritt's accounts of famous Aboriginal women, giving a sense of a whole population, rather than just a token few. Chapters on Murphy and McClung show photographs of women working in fields and factories ("too delicate to vote" reads the caption), demonstrating the realities of female labour. Introductions contrast European attitudes towards women with the high regard First Nations societies had for them, preparing readers for the huge-spirited, stalwart, and resourceful women they'll meet in the pages. An empowering and eminently useful collection; good for reading aloud.

Moore, Christopher. Illustr. Bill Slavin. *The BIG Book of Canada: Exploring the Provinces and Territories*. 2002. 243 pages. 8 to adult.
Moore begins with Newfoundland and works his way westward across Canada, introducing readers to the land, history, stories, and peoples of each province and territory. In thirteen chapters he describes each province or territory, including a timeline, brief biographies of famous inhabitants, regional culinary specialties, and the languages spoken (including many First Nations languages). Moore includes tidbits of information that give the book extra interest, for example, he lets us know that the name of Flin Flon, Manitoba, was inspired by a fictional character. This combination of anecdotes and concrete facts makes the book of general interest, as well as a useful reference work. Each chapter concludes with a page that shows: Date the province joined Confederation, Motto, Flower, Area, Highest Point, Population, Growth Rate, Capital, Industries, Main Cities, and where to find government information on the Internet.

Moore writes well, sustaining interest in the information. He has a flair for including details that will appeal to young and older readers alike. Archival photos and Slavin's illustrations appear on every page.

Morck, Irene. *Five Pennies.* **1999. 163 pages. 10 and up.**

These biographical stories of the author's father, Archie Morck, have humour, drama, and lilt. From 1915, when Archie is five years old and sees his first "falling cow," to the moment he finishes high school and enters college at the age of twenty-seven, we see what life was like for this pioneering family of the central Alberta woodlands. An ornery lamp that dims when you need it, nights alive with bed bugs – these details create a vivid picture of homesteading life. But the memoirs are delightful too, because plot and momentum drive each episode; in one, cows keep falling through the roof as they climb the snowdrifts to eat the hay that's kept up there. In another, Archie kills a skunk in the hen-house with a lucky shot, then has to get rid of the reeking corpse.

Morck's unsentimental style conveys the child's sense of discovery and puzzlement at the adult world; little by little she reveals Archie's earnest, sensitive nature and allows readers insight into his Danish father's repressive authority. A good family read-aloud, and an excellent way to give children a glimpse into a past way of life.

Mowat, Farley. *The Dog Who Wouldn't Be.* **1957. 238 pages. 10 and up.**

Mutt comes to the Mowats in a roundabout manner, but soon gains a place at the centre of the family. He proves himself skilled at retrieving birds (even if it means diving for them), walking fences (to the frustration of local dog bullies), and even climbing trees and ladders (to the astonishment of a local house painter). Mowat describes the eccentric antics of his beloved dog with tongue-in-cheek hilarity, from the moment Mrs. Mowat adopts him in Saskatoon until Mutt's final fatal amble through spring fields in Ontario. En route, anecdotes about Mowat's two pet owls and his father's abortive nautical career bring additional levity.

This wasn't written for children, and it has the journalistic fluency of its period – balanced, articulate prose and a vocabulary that is fairly complex. Sometimes, too, Mowat's jokes are clearly for adults. Despite, or perhaps because of this, it makes an excellent, funny family read-aloud for people who like animal and family stories.

* Musgrave, Susan, ed. *Nerves Out Loud: Critical Moments in the Lives of Seven Teen Girls.* **2001. 112 pages. 12 and up.**
See Short Story Collections and Anthologies, 12 and Up.

Nichol, Barbara. Illustr. Barry Moser. *One Small Garden.* **2001. 56 pages. 8 and up.**
Disappearing raccoons, disappearing ants, even the sinister disappearance of a gardener poisoned by his own pesticides is food for thought in this unusual series of mysteries, thoughts, anecdotes, and botanical facts about a small garden in Cabbagetown, Toronto. Nichol has used her own garden to tell stories, even to reconsider the interface of nature and culture. An ant's nest is like a city, she writes; but no, one could as well say that a city is like an ant's nest. "A lawn is a human invention made of grass in the same way that a lightbulb's an invention made of glass and wire," she suggests.

Tied together thematically, these brief pieces grow organically one out of the other, revealing bits and pieces of how people have related to plants, the secret life of urban creatures, and the nature of human life itself. Nichol's narrative voice commands attention: it's intriguing, forthright – somehow full of the mystery of an older person offering wisdom. Moser's watercolour illustrations show hollyhocks, sunflowers, trilliums, shining with reflected light. This is a thought-provoking work full of unexpected pleasures, and may be most effective read aloud among the family – especially a garden- or nature-loving family.

Orenstein, Ronald. *New Animal Discoveries.* **2001. 64 pages. 9 to 14.**
While many books deal with endangered animals, it's a rare volume that deals with recently discovered species. But zoologist, lawyer, and wildlife conservationist Orenstein here introduces children to fourteen previously unknown creatures – a turtle, a tree kangaroo, several primates, and some Icelandic micro-organisms (including one whose name means "the strange little girdle") – that belong in two entirely new phyla (the largest groups into which living things are classified).

Orenstein explains what constitutes a new species, discusses scientific naming and the moral ambiguities of collecting, then goes on to tell the interesting and often suspenseful stories behind the discovery of the animals. Much of the information he provides is inherently intriguing (the habits of a creature that looks like "a badly stuffed sock with a sucker at one end," for example), and he writes with excitement, humour, and lucidity. Beautifully illustrated with photographs and maps, this is an excellent book for older children fascinated by animals or biology.

Ouriou, Katie. Julie Johnston, ed. *Love Ya Like a Sister: A Story of Friendship*. **1999. 200 pages. 12 and up.**
When sixteen-year-old Katie Ouriou was about to move to Paris with her family for a year, she made sure her best friends would all stay in touch. "True friends are the ones that visit you in prison and write you when you move," she claimed. This book comprises Katie's correspondence with her best friends during this brief time – brief, because, after three months in France, Katie died of a rare, fast-moving leukemia. Katie's journal-like e-mails and letters appear here, introduced and edited by Julie Johnston.

Katie's letters are earnest, open, sincere, questing – sometimes serious with reflection, sometimes caught up in trivialities. "You know what, I love God!" she exults to a friend, and two paragraphs later proclaims, "Today was monumental in my life, I completely cut off all my nails." In her lively remarks are the questions and irritations of an adolescent world, and the warmth of a good friend. This is thoughtful, heartbreaking, and sometimes funny.

Pavanel, Jane. *The Sex Book: An Alphabet of Smarter Love*. **2001. 200 pages. 12 and up.**
Arranged alphabetically from "Aah!" (sexual satisfaction) to "Yeast infections," the short, informative entries here are written in a non-judgemental, chatty tone, and in a format eminently usable for adolescents. Facts about oral and anal sex, all methods of birth control, legal issues (such as the age of consent) are all here; so is encouraging advice on communication in sexual relationships and on sexual readiness. All

the questions adolescents might be too embarrassed – or even too ignorant – to ask are answered fully, accurately, and authoritatively.

Pavanel's use of slang and colloquial terms helps those who have been mystified in the schoolyard; for those more sexually knowing, the facts of risk and prevention are clear but not alarmist. A topic-a-page format means the information comes in digestible quantities. An index and cross-references add to the work's accessibility, and so does its manageable size. A list of resources, including Canadian and American phone numbers and Web sites, concludes the book. This is a sensible, frank, and empowering guide for today's teens.

Pearson, Debora. Illustr. Chum McLeod. *Load 'Em Up Trucks.* Mighty Wheels Series. 1999. 2 to 4.
See Picture Books.

Ripley, Catherine. Illustr. Scot Ritchie. *Why? The Best Ever Question and Answer Book about Nature, Science and the World around You.* 2001. 192 pages. 4 to 7.
Ripley answers miscellaneous questions that might arise from a very young child's involvement in six common family activities: using the bathroom, grocery shopping, going to bed, playing outdoors, cooking, and visiting a petting farm. Why do my hands get wrinkled? What's behind the staff doors in the supermarket? Where do puddles go? These questions receive short, simple answers. A little science comes in here, and will prompt curious children to ask further questions; those who aren't already insatiably curious will find their brains stimulated to wonder how things work and why. Ritchie's fresh, light illustrations show a multi-racial, diversely abled cast.

Each chapter is also available as an individual volume: *Why Is Soap So Slippery?*, *Do the Doors Open by Magic?*, *Why Do Stars Twinkle?*, *Why Is the Sky Blue?*, *Why Does Popcorn Pop?*, and *Why Do Cows Moo?*

Savage, Candace. *Born to Be a Cowgirl: A Spirited Ride through the Old West.* 2001. 64 pages. 10 and up.
Spunky girls who love horses will take to this account of their spirited predecessors. "Let any normally healthy woman who is ordinarily

strong screw up her courage and tackle a bucking bronc, and she will find the most fascinating pastime in the field of feminine athletic endeavour," one cowgirl claims enthusiastically in the early 1900s. Starting with the 1870s, Savage describes the environment and lifestyle that inspired some women to break the gender barriers of ranching to work as cowhands, own and run their own ranches, and find a place to compete within the Calgary Stampede and other established rodeos.

Liberally illustrated with tinted photographs and with not too much text per page, this is approachable and child-friendly. What makes it highly entertaining, though, is Savage's focus on anecdotes and individual stories. Fanny Sperry, the bronc rider; "Willie" Matthews, who disguised herself as a boy so she could go on a cattle-drive (the cattle didn't care); Lizzie Johnson Williams, who earned enough money to buy her own ranch by teaching school, bookkeeping, and writing sensational romances – the stories of these women show the human, and humorous, side of cowgirl life.

Smith, David. Illustr. Shelagh Armstrong. *If the World Were a Village.* **2002. 32 pages. 7 to 14.**
Using current statistics for world population, Smith invites children to imagine the world as a village with a population of 100, where each villager represents 62 million people. By learning about the villagers, children learn about the people in the real world and about the makeup of our global population. Relying on a variety of sources, Smith translates the cold numbers of statistics into understandable language. Percentages take on human meaning as he gives information about the representation of languages, race, age, and quality of life. For example, "60 people are always hungry, and 26 of these are severely undernourished. 16 other people go to bed hungry at least some of the time. Only 24 people always have enough to eat." Information about the trajectory we're on for population growth is clear and startling. This is an important, timely book; happily, it's also one that's inherently interesting and very accessible to children, without the intervention of adults.

Springer, Jane. *Listen to Us: The World's Working Children.* **1997. 96 pages. 10 and up.**
In this important work, Springer presents in clear, readable language and layout the situation of the world's working children. What is child labour? Why do children work? Where? What work do they do? These questions are answered chapter by chapter, with photographs of labouring children from all over the world, and with personal stories by children who worked in various trades – migrant farming, carpet weaving, the sex trade, an African army, an American fast-food joint. Springer concludes with a chapter on children's rights and, finally, on child activists who have fought against child labour around the world, including Canada's Craig Kielburger.

Anyone discussing trade with children will find this account both helpful and moving. Springer avoids emotional language and the information has all the more potency because of that.

Swanson, Diane. Illustr. Terry Smith. *Animals Eat the Weirdest Things.* **1998. 64 pages. 9 and up.**
With menus ranging from "blood, skin, and cast off parts" to "rotting flesh and bones, ooze, vomit, and dung" and so on, to paper and glue, this covers almost everything awful one can imagine a creature ingesting. It's full of disgusting notions ("Some animals steal vomit from others"), but Swanson's point is that these horrible gustatory choices make for nutritious, easy-to-find meals and the survival of some species. Without all this eating from the insect and animal world, our planet would be a smellier, messier place.

With its extensive text, this book demands reading persistence, but the appeal of the grotesque will entice readers. Full-colour, scientifically accurate drawings and occasional sidebars add to the visual appeal.

Takashima, Shizuye. *A Child in Prison Camp.* **1971. 100 pages. 10 and up.**
In September 1942, Shichan and her family, Canadians of Japanese origin who have lived in Vancouver for years, are relocated and interned in a small "camp" in British Columbia's mountainous interior. Forced by the Canadian government to live in shacks without electric-

ity or running water, even without oil lamps, Shichan and her sister, Yuki, and their devout mother and outspoken father live through the final years of the Second World War. Despite the injustices (Japanese Canadians were told that they had no rights at all) and the hardships – which include carrying their water a mile – Shichan and Yuki take pleasure in one another, and even draw strength from the impassive but awe-inspiring beauty of their environment.

Shichan's reconstructed, slightly fictionalized diary of her experiences as a child in a Canadian internment camp is a vital testament to Canada's "most disgracefully racist episode." And in this world of commodified, fictionalized diaries, this account is readable and engaging (even humbling), all the more so for being authentic. Concrete details – the pearly beauty of new corn, the pleasure of a surprise shipment of soy sauce – help construct a full, vivid picture for the reader. Takashima's watercolours, inserted in the middle of the book, give a visual account of the surroundings. An essential read.

Tanaka, Shelley. Illustr. Greg Ruhl. *The Buried City of Pompeii.* I Was There Series. 1997. 48 pages. 8 to 11.
Combining historical fact, dramatic illustrations, photos, and a story of a family caught in the eruption, Tanaka has produced a book that lives up to its arresting cover art: a painting of Vesuvius erupting, the inhabitants of Pompeii fleeing in terror. The lost world of the buried city is brought back to life through the story of Eros and his daughter Silvia. Eros, a freedman, is the steward of a wealthy household and the only parent of his daughter. Tanaka describes their life on August 24, 79 CE, moments before Vesuvius erupted. Thus she reveals how the ancient city operated and how its people lived.

The story itself provides much information; supplementary sidebars, photos, and illustrations expand on various points. For example, Eros goes to the baths in the morning, and a sidebar provides information about the baths, a layout of the baths, photos of the baths, and an evocative, full-page illustration by Ruhl. Tanaka's writing is direct and draws the reader right into Eros's story; but the photos and illustrations are the great enticement of this book, in which even the placement of the illustrations is very effective. This is a gripping account, and one that will be attractive to reluctant readers.

Additional titles in the I Was There series include the equally fascinating *On Board the Titanic* and *Discovering the Iceman*.

Tookoome, Simon, with Sheldon Oberman. *The Shaman's Nephew: A Life in the Far North*. 1999. 55 pages. 9 to 13.
"I remember being born . . . I remember coming out of my mother's body," claims Tookoome in this memoir, letting readers know that some of what they'll read will be startling. Forced in 1968 to abandon the traditional life of following the caribou and seal, Tookoome, an Inuit artist and hunter, was afraid all knowledge of the old ways would be lost. Oberman has distilled hours of Tookoome's stories and accounts from tapes in the original Inuktitut, and put them together in a text that ranges from personal memories to precise accounts of hunting techniques, naming practices, and more.

Although it doesn't offer much momentum as a story, this book is invaluable for sharing a history, a world view, that most children know nothing of. "I saw Teenaq, a shaman," Tookoome recalls. "He was flying right over my head the height of a low-flying airplane. He circled over the tent twice and made sure I saw him." This kind of anecdote – and others, such as the story of the day Tookoome returned to find a social worker and a Mountie had taken his son away to residential school without telling anyone – offer children material that's both readable and enlightening.

Turnbull, Andy, with Debora Pearson. *By Truck to the North*. Adventure Travel Series. 1998. 88 pages. 8 to 12.
The journey of a truckload of fruits and vegetables travelling north hardly seems like a tale that would make for compelling reading, but Turnbull and Pearson have turned it into a good adventure story. The truck, on its trip of about 5,000 miles, carries enough food to last 500 people for a month. Bill Robinson, the driver, travels with a small dog, T.D., for company: their journey from Vancouver to Tuktoyaktuk is by its very nature remarkable.

The tale of the journey is interspersed with information about the region, wildlife, and points of interest as they travel: from truckstops to timberwolves, from CB radios to caribou. Maps and glorious photos of

the landscape chart the journey as T.D. and Robinson proceed north-
ward. By the time the truck arrives in Tuktoyaktuk, the reader has
some knowledge of the life of long-distance truckers, the route north,
and the landscape en route. The opening of Bill's truck at a store in the
north, with the customer's positive reactions to his fruits and vegetables, is amusing: "I thought cauliflower was supposed to have black
spots on it – but it's not!"

Additional titles in this travel series include *Jungle Islands:
My South Sea Adventure* by Maria Coffey and Debora Pearson, and
52 Days by Camel: My Sahara Adventure by Lawrie Raskin
and Debora Pearson.

Verstraete, Larry. *Mysteries of Time.* **1992. 171 pages. 10 and up.**
Verstraete describes the methods used to uncover various stories and
truths from the past. He examines fourteen different mysteries, from
that of the ancient minotaur and the labyrinth to King Arthur to more
recent mysteries such as fate of the Franklin expedition and the
sinking of the *Titanic*. For each case Verstraete describes the methods
of detection that archaeologists and scientists used under the heading
"The Detective Case," followed by notes in a "Detective File," and a
"Detective Challenge." Each case closes with a "Time Probe" telling
that some cases are still unsolved. Verstraete includes a number of
activities for young detectives – in the case on the Franklin expedition,
for example, the challenge is to calculate body ratios, including
height, using the length of a person's arm.

This book provides challenges for the reader while also giving fascinating stories from all over the world. A comprehensive bibliography
is included for readers who really want to get involved with the mysteries of time. Excellent for reading in small bits.

Verstraete, Larry. *Accidental Discoveries: From Laughing Gas to
Dynamite.* **1999. 134 pages. 9 to 12.**
"Ideas surface in the strangest ways, often when they are least expected.
Sometimes they seem to pop up almost by accident," explains Verstraete
in his introduction to the many errors, accidents, coincidences, and odd
circumstances that have resulted in significant discoveries. Readers will

be fascinated by the many discoveries that came from simple experiences – such as Velcro, which was invented by a man inspired by the discovery of burrs on his clothes in 1948. Popsicles, Post-Its, the Slinky, and even Ivory, "the soap that floats," were discovered by accident or simple error. Verstraete provides supplementary information for some stories under the heading "Did You Know" – for example, that the name Popsicles came from Pop's Cycles. Each invention is described in a page or two. *Accidental Discoveries* contains stories so strange that it's likely to appeal to reluctant readers: its short, well-spaced entries make it attractive for those daunted by lengthy texts. Verstraete includes a bibliography and an index. The book was originally published as *The Serendipity Effect*.

Verstraete's follow-up title, **Extreme Science**, is laid out in the same child-friendly manner; however, it doesn't have the same element of peculiarity and surprise.

Wyatt, Valerie. Illustr. Pat Cupples. *The Math Book for Girls and Other Beings Who Count*. 2000. 64 pages. 9 and up.
About six inches tall and a cross between a fairy godmother and a math/science whiz, Nora (short for Natural Observation Research Activator) shows a young character in the story how math is essential to many aspects of daily experience. Probability, scales, graphs, coordinates, dimension, proportion, and even topology are here presented in a lively manner; readers are encouraged to work through various activities that will help develop a better understanding of some math fundamentals.

Wyatt created this book for girls, and includes projects of particular appeal to girls in an effort to encourage girls to continue with math or science as they go on in their school careers. Children can complete most activities without adult help, but Wyatt also suggests a number of projects for adults to share with girls. Included in the text are snapshots of women in a variety of careers in which math is critical, including illustrator, biologist, and chef. Cupples's lighthearted illustrations add to the humorous tone of the book. Wyatt and Cupples also produced the equally engaging ***The Science Book for Girls and Other Intelligent Beings***.

Highly Recommended Books

Title Index

Bold page numbers indicate main entry.

Author/Illustrator/ Editor Index

Bold page numbers indicate main entry.

Subject Index

Settings in Canada

Geographic regions are listed first, Atlantic Canada, Far North, Mountains, and Prairies. Provinces and territories follow with specific locations identified after the general listing.

By Geographic Region

By Province and Territory

Authors', Editors', and Illustrators' Locations

Authors, editors, and illustrators living outside of Canada, and those whose hometowns were unavailable, are not listed.

Alberta

Calgary	Bailey, Debbie
	Brownridge, William
	Czernecki, Stefan
	Foggo, Cheryl
	Kimber, Murray
	Lynch, Wayne
	Rhodes, Timothy
Edmonton	
	Holubitsky, Katherine
	Hughes, Monica
	Huser, Glen
	Hutchins, Hazel
	Reynolds, Marilynn
	Ripley, Catherine
	Taylor, Cora
	Trembath, Don
High River	Leavitt, Martine
Innisfail	Morck, Irene
Lacombe	Graham, Georgia
Sherwood Park	Bellingham, Brenda

British Columbia

Armstrong	Kiss, Andrew
Burnaby	Lucas, Bernice
Campbell River	Neel, David
Delta	McNeil, Florence
Gabriola	Lawrence, Iain
Metchosin	Horvath, Polly
Nelson	Bowers, Vivien
Prince George	Spicer, Maggee

Manitoba
  Brandon   Denton, Kady MacDonald

  Winnipeg   Brooks, Martha
                             Buffie, Margaret
                             Holeman, Linda
                             Matas, Carol
                             Oberman, Sheldon
                             Verstraete, Larry
                             Wieler, Diana

New Brunswick
  Fredericton   Fitch, Sherry

Newfoundland
  English Bay   Davidge, Bud
  St. John's   Clark, Joan
                             Major, Kevin
                             McNaughton, Janet

Northwest Territories
  Fort Smith   Van Camp, Richard
  Yellowknife   Bastedo, Jamie

Nova Scotia
  Granville Ferry   Butler, Geoff
                             Springer, Jane
  Halifax   Barkhouse, Joyce
                             McKibbon, Hugh
                             Tooke, Susan
  Hubbards   Wilson, Budge
  Kentville   Lightburn, Ron
  Lunenberg County   Richards, Nancy Wilcox
  Mahone Bay   Woods, Shirley
  Portuguese Cove   Wolfe, Frances

Nunavut
  Baker Lake   Tookoome, Simon
  Rankin Inlet   Kusugak, Michael Arvaarluk

Ontario

Acton	Reczuch, Karen
Belleville	Crook, Connie Brummel
Burlington	McKay, Sharon
	McNicoll, Sylvia
	Wennick, Elizabeth
Cobourg	Scrimger, Richard
Dundas	Chan, Gillian
Eden Mills	Wilson, Janet
Georgetown	Fitzgerald, Joanne
Guelph	Badoe, Adwoa
	Bogart, Jo Ellen
	Lewis, Robin Baird
	Little, Jean
	Munsch, Robert
Hamilton	Dale, Mitzi
	King, Thomas
	Roberts, Ken
Havelock	Thornhill, Jan
Kanata	MacGregor, Roy
Kenora	Anderson, Lil
King	Love, Ann
Kingston	Edwards, Frank
Kitchener	Daniel, Alan
Lion's Head	Zimmermann, H. Werner
London	Haworth-Attard, Barbara
	Katz, Welwyn Wilton
Manitoulin Island	Griggs, Terry
Millbrook	Slavin, Bill
Minaki	MacDonald, Jake
Mississauga	Orenstein, Ronald
	Walters, Eric
Mountain Grove	Rainey, Kaitlin
Newton	Hofer, Ernst and Nelly
Oakville	Newfeld, Frank
Orillia	Bell, William
	Ye, Ting-xing
Ottawa	Andrews, Jan
	Carrier, Roch
	Cumyn, Alan

Ottawa (*cont'd*)	De Lint, Charles
	Gilmore, Rachna
	Lunn, Janet
	Yerxa, Leo
Owen Sound	Bradford, Karleen
Palgrave	McGugan, Jim
Perth	Wynne-Jones, Tim
Peterborough	Fernandes, Eugenie
	Harrison, Troon
	Johnston, Julie
Port Hope	Staunton, Ted
Port Perry	Clark, Brenda
	Fernandes, Kim
Ridgeway	Merritt, Susan E.
Rockwood	Carver, Peter
	Hendry, Linda
	Morin, Paul
	Stinson, Kathy
Sarnia	Broda, Ron
Stratford	Beddows, Eric
	Burdett, Lois
	Jocelyn, Marthe
Thunder Bay	Slipperjack, Ruby
Toronto	Ageda, Belinda
	Aldana, Patricia
	Allinson, Beverley
	Archbold, Rick
	Armstrong, Shelagh
	Baillie, Marilyn
	Barton, Bob
	Batten, Jack
	Bedard, Michael
	Book, Rick
	Booth, David
	Bourgeois, Paulette
	Cameron, Scott
	Carpenter-Davis, Sandra
	Chan, Harvey
	Clement, Gary
	Collins, Heather

Toronto (*cont'd*)

Crysler, Ian
Daigneault, Sylvie
Davis, Aubrey
Deines, Brian
Drawson, Blair
Ellis, Deborah
Fagan, Cary
Farris, Katherine
Fernandez, Laura
Fitzgerald, Joanne
Gal, Laszlo
Galloway, Patricia
Garay, Luis
Gillmor, Don
Godkin, Celia
Gorrell, Gena
Granfield, Linda
Grassby, Donna
Grater, Lindsay
Greenwood, Barbara
Harris, Pamela
Hartry, Nancy
Holdcroft, Tina
Jacobson, Rick
Jennings, Sharon
Kacer, Kathy
Keens-Douglas, Richardo
Khan, Rukhsana
Kilby, Don
Kogawa, Joy
Konzak, Burt
Kovalski, Maryann
Krykorka, Vladyana Langer
Lee, Dennis
Lesynski, Loris
Levine, Karen
Lottridge, Celia Barker
Mackay, Claire
MacLeod, Elizabeth
Martchenko, Michael

Toronto (*cont'd*)

Martin, Eva
Marton, Jirina
Maybarduk, Linda
McLean, Dirk
McLeod, Chum
Milich, Zoran
Miller, Ruth
Moak, Allan
Monkman, William Kent
Moore, Christopher
Morgan, Allen
Muller, Robin
Ng, Simon
Nichol, Barbara
Ohi, Ruth
Oppel, Kenneth
Pearson, Debora
Petričić, Dušan
Priest, Robert
Priestley, Alice
Reid, Barbara
Ricci, Regolo
Roddie, Shen
Ruhl, Greg
Sadu, Itah
Setterington, Ken
Sheppard, Mary
Singh, Rina
Springett, Martin
Stewart, Sharon
Stone, Ras
Tennant, Veronica
Toten, Teresa
Toye, William
Tregebov, Rhea
Von Königslow, Andrea Wayne
Waboose, Jan Bourdeau
Wallace, Ian
Wishinsky, Frieda

Saskatchewan

Clavet	Eyvindson, Peter
Moose Jaw	Moore, Yvette
Regina	Brynjolson, Rhian
Saskatoon	Goobie, Beth
	Savage, Candace
	Slade, Arthur
Weyburn	Bannatyne-Cugnet, Jo